Frontier and Overseas Expeditions from India

Frontier and Overseas Expeditions from India

(in 7 Volumes)

Compiled in the
Intelligence Branch,
Army Headquarters, India

Vol. 7
Official Account of the Abor Expeditions

Low Price Publications
Delhi-110052

Distributed by
D.K. Publishers Distributors (P) Ltd.
4834/24, Ansari Road, Darya Ganj,
New Delhi-110002
Phones: 23278584, 23278368, 23261465
e-mail: dkpd@del3.vsnl.net.in
url: www.dkpd.com

First Published 1907-11

Reprinted in LPP 2004

ISBN 81-7536-323-1 (Set)
ISBN 81-7536-330-4 (Vol.7)

Published by
Low Price Publications
A-6, Nimri Commercial Centre,
Near Ashok Vihar Phase-IV,
Delhi-110052
Phones: 27401672, 27452453
e-mail: lpp@nde.vsnl.net.in
url: www.lppindia.com

Printed at
D K Fine Art Press P Ltd.
Delhi-110052

PRINTED IN INDIA

CONTENTS.

CHAPTER I.

POLITICAL EVENTS LEADING UP TO THE EXPEDITION.

PAGES

Necessity for fixing a definite frontier—Mr. Williamson's frontier tours—Murder of Mr. Williamson and Dr. Gregorson—Decision to despatch an expedition against the Abors—Friendly mission to the Mishmis—Policy—Miri Mission ... ... 1—4

CHAPTER II.

GEOGRAPHY, TRIBES, CLIMATE, AND SEASON FOR OPERATIONS.

Boundaries—Mountains—Difficulties of road making—System of cultivation—Rivers—Tribes—Tribal system—Tribes on left bank of the Dihang—Tribes on the right bank of the Dihang—Climate—Best season for operations—Health ... ... 5—11

CHAPTER III.

NARRATIVE OF THE MURDER OF MR. WILLIAMSON AND DR. GREGORSON AND EVENTS PREVIOUS TO THE EXPEDITION.

Constitution of the party—Objects of the journey—Abors discuss the advisability of murdering the party—Alarm of the Abors—Messengers murdered—Dr. Gregorson murdered—Mr. Williamson murdered—Flight of survivors—Receipt of the news in Dibrugarh—Villages implicated in the crime—Despatch of Military Police—Attitude of the tribes—Captain Hutchins reconnoitres the Kebang road ... ... 13—16

CHAPTER IV.

OBJECTS OF THE EXPEDITION AND PLAN OF CAMPAIGN.

Objects of the expedition—Plan of operations—A single main column to be employed—Line of advance—Kebang the primary objective—Routes to Kebang—Dihang route adopted ... ... 17—21

CHAPTER V.

CHOICE OF BASE AND PREPARATIONS.

PAGES.

Brahmaputra as a line of supply—Considerations in choosing a base—Saikhowa Ghat—Pobamukh—Selection of Kobo—Supply and Transport arrangements—Weight of cooly loads—Water-proof bags—Ammunition boxes—Constitution of Force—Arrival of troops—Method adopted for protection of baggage ... ... 23—27

CHAPTER VI.

FIRST PHASE OF THE OPERATIONS.

Military.

Reconnaissance to locate Oyang—March of the Ledum column—March of main column—Method of conducting march—Procedure on arrival at camp—Advanced base—First contact with the enemy—Janakmukh—Furthest point to which mule transport used—Sirpo river—Destruction of New Renging—Difficulty of reconnaissance—Effect of slowness of advance—Advance to Igar stream—Attack on stockade—Advance to Rotung—Enemy located at Kekar Monying—Plan of attack—Destruction of Kalek—Ledum column not used to co-operate—Establishment of ferry over the Dihang—Night march—Column attacked by Abors—Party arrives in position—Fire opened prematurely—Flight of Abors—Operations on right banks—Pursuit—Effect of the action—Use of Telephone—Fall of Kebang—Destruction of Yemsing—Ledum column—Reconnaissance to Mishing—Plan of action—Reconnaissance to Sireng river—Reconnaissances to Kaking and Sireng river—Capture of a stockade—Combined movement against Korang and Kaking—Co-operation with the main column—Break up of the column—Effect of the operations—Events after the fall of Kebang—Organised resistance at an end—Envoys sent to call in *Gams* of neutral villages—Hostile villages come in—Dihang exploration sets out—Head quarters established at Yembung ... 29—47

CHAPTER VII.

REVIEW OF MILITARY OPERATIONS.

Effect of military operations—Slowness of the advance—Road-making difficulties—Supply and Transport difficulties—Supply depôts—Boat transport—Forms of transport employed—Systems of working transport—Artillery—Bomb-throwing mortars—Maxim guns—Rifle grenades ... ... 49—52

CHAPTER VIII.

SECOND PHASE OF THE OPERATIONS.

Political, Survey and Exploration.

PAGES.

Panggi Mission—Mission to Damro—Connection and trade with Tibet—Milang—Return of Mission—Dihang exploration—Start of the exploration—Attitude of Yekshing—Trade with the plains—Tyranny of Kebang—Leisurely advance—Orders for acceleration—Arrangements for the exploration—Advanced base at Simong—Attitude of Simong—Supply and Transport difficulties—Singging—Return to Simong—Difficulties of line of communication and supply—Exploration abandoned—Meeting of *Gams*—Withdrawal of troops from the left bank—Shimang and Siyom explorations—Withdrawal of Force—Trial of murderers—Rotung abandoned—Demobilisation ... ... 53—67

CHAPTER IX.

RESULTS OF THE EXPEDITION.

Political results—Future policy—Relations with the tribes—Effect of the mule-road—Geographical results—Question of the Dihang and Tsang-po—Northern frontier ... 69—71

APPENDICES.

		Pages.
I	Orders for the organization of the force	75
I(a)	Composition of the force	79
I(b)	Staff of the force	80
I(c)	Allotment of field staff offices	81
I(d)	Approximate strength of the force	82
I(e)	Special equipment	84
I(f)	Scale of issue of books and maps	85
II	Details of troops and units	87
III	Information regarding navigability of the Brahmaputra river and facilities for transport of troops	89
III(a)	Time-table showing movements of troops, etc., by steamer on mobilisation and demobilisation	91
IV	Press correspondents and press arrangements ...	98
V	Scientific specialists who accompanied the force ...	100
VI	Extracts from standing orders of the force	103
VII	Report on the Supply and Transport	107
VII (a)	Supplies	113
VII (b)	List of Local Supplies purchased	121

		Pages.
VII(c)	Statement showing percentage of losses on supplies ...	124
VII(d)	Equipment	127
VII(e)	Special method of marking bags and boxes	130
VII(f)	Transport	132
VII(g)	Carrier Corps—Nagas and Gurkhalis	133
VII(h)	Boat Transport	142
VII(k)	Elephant Transport	149
VII(l)	Mule Transport	150
VII(m)	Menial Establishment employed	156
VII(n)	Approximate distances between Posts on the Line of Communication	157
VIII	Report on the working of all arms	159
IX	Report on the working of the Base and Lines of Communication	163
X	Report on the medical history of the expedition	171
X(a)	Report on the Ashanti Hammock	191
X(b)	Report on the "carriers, canvas, man" ...	192
X(c)	Proposals for improving the medical service in future expeditions on the North-East Frontier	194
XI	Report on engineering operations ...	197
XI(a)	Notes on engineering equipment	205
XI(b)	List of stores expended from Engineer Field Park ...	207
XII	Report on Signalling and Telephonic communication ...	209
XIII	General Bower's despatches describing the operations ...	211

ILLUSTRATIONS.

Panorama of Abor Country, from Signal Hill (near Yembung) ...	Frontispiece.
Abor types	8
Naga Scouts	30
View up Dihang from near Janakmukh	32
Sketch plan of action at Igar stockade	35
Stone chute near Igar Stockade	36
Sappers and Miners' raft-ferry	38
Sketch plan of action at Kekar Monying	40
Sketch showing signalling communication during attack on Kekar Monying	40
View of Kekar Monying position	4[illegible]
Komsing Village	47
Naga carriers	133
" Carrier, canvas, man"	192
Method of carrying sick and wounded by means of "carrier, canvas, man"	193

MAPS.

Map of Abor Country 1911-12	In pocket at end.

PREFACE.

The Abor Expeditionary Force of 1911-12 having been the first military expedition of any importance to undertake operations in the hill regions north of Assam, it has been considered desirable to attach to the history, as appendices, somewhat full extracts from departmental and other reports referring to details of organisation, etc., peculiar to the country.

CHAPTER I.

POLITICAL EVENTS LEADING UP TO THE EXPEDITION.

Before proceeding to give an account of the Abor expedition it is necessary to discuss the various problems connected with the Indo-Chinese and Indo-Tibetan frontier, for it was due to these problems that the expedition assumed so much importance.

Necessity for fixing a definite frontier.

The action of the Chinese in Tibet since 1910; their intrigues among the states and tribes bordering that country; their adoption of an agressive policy throughout the extent of the debateable border land and their evident intention of pushing their administration up to, if not beyond, their political frontier, forced to the front the necessity for the discovery and definition of a suitable frontier line *vis à vis* China and Chinese possessions, in order that a check should be put on Chinese pretensions.

The most easterly limit of the demarcated Indo-Tibetan frontier is at a point some ten miles north of Odulgiri (approx. lat. 26° 40′ long 92° 10′). The administration of the Assam Government extended only as far as the foot of the hills, *i.e.*, to the "outer line". Beyond that only loose political control was exercised, which amounted, in practice, merely to the exaction of reparation for outrages on British subjects and for raids into British territory, with the payment of *posa* or allowances to certain of the tribes. The whole of the territory between the "outer line" and the uplands of Tibet was practically a *terra incognita*. Previous expeditions had merely penetrated its fringe. The southern confines of Tibet and the ethnographical and geographical limits between that country and the Assam border tribes were unknown.

Mr. Williamson's frontier tours.

To get into closer touch with the border tribes, Mr. Noel Williamson, Assistant Political Officer at Sadiya, had made a practice of touring a short distance into the hills. In 1908 he toured along the foothills between Pasighat and the Dijmur river, visiting all the Pasi villages, the Minyong foothill villages of which Ledum is the most important, and various settlements of the Galong group. In 1909, accompanied by

Colonel D. M. Lumsden and the Revd. W. L. B. Jackson of the American mission at Sadiya, he made a journey up the Dihang, with the object of unveiling the mystery still surrounding the falls of the Tsang-po, and of establishing friendly relations with the tribes. The party reached Kebang but were prevented from going further owing to an intertribal war between the Minyongs and the Panggis. Mr. Williamson was, however, well received by the tribesmen and they even invited him to make another visit in the future. In the following cold weather he made a journey up the Lohit river to Walong in the Mishmi country and obtained information of the action of the Chinese in this direction which clearly showed the desirability of taking steps to counteract their activity.

Having obtained this information, he at once realised the necessity of finding out how far the influence of the Tibetans extended into the tribal country up the Dihang. With this object in view, and relying on the invitation he had received on his previous visit, in March 1911 he made a second journey up that river accompanied by Dr. Gregorson. While on this expedition he and his companion with nearly all their followers were treacherously murdered under circumstances which will be detailed in a later chapter. The murder of this excellent frontier officer was a great loss to Government, for by his tact and knowledge of the people he had already established good relations with the local tribes, while his personal influence brought them, to a greatly increased extent, under the control of Government.

Murder of Mr. Williamson and Dr. Gregorson.

These two later journeys of Mr. Williamson were made without the knowledge or sanction of the local Government and were contrary to well known standing orders which prohibited the crossing of the outer line without permission. But although Mr. Williamson's action was contrary to orders there is no doubt that his conduct was that of a brave and zealous officer who was willing to risk his life and the possible displeasure of Government in order to obtain information which he knew to be of the highest value.

Decision to despatch an expedition against the Abors.

It was impossible in the interests of the general security and peace of the frontier to overlook the treacherous behaviour of the Abors and, in framing proposals for a punitive expedition, it was decided that advantage should be taken of the opportunity to survey and explore the tribal territory with a view to obtaining as much information as possible which might assist in the future determination of a suitable boundary between India and Chinese possessions; and it was at the same time decided to send a friendly mission into the Mishmi country with the double object of preventing the Mishmis from making common cause with the Abors and of obtaining information of the nature and limits of that country. This mission was to have an escort of military police.

Friendly mission to the Mishmis.

As regards future policy it was not intended that the Mishmis should be given a definite guarantee of protection, but it was proposed to leave them, as well as the Abors, in no manner of doubt as to their being under us, or as to their having to look to us for future punishment or reward according to their behaviour and it was at the same time suggested that cairns and boundary stones might be erected on what was considered to be a suitable frontier line.

Policy.

Later there arose further developments in the Chinese policy of aggression which emphasised the importance of the boundary question. In April 1911, a party of Chinese appeared in the Akha country close to the administrative frontier of Assam; the Chinese officials at Rima sent a summons to the Mishmi tribal headmen in the Lohit valley to appear before them with a view to the annexation of their country; and it was reported, in connection with the recent disturbances in the Pomed country, that the Chinese Government had approved of the despatch of a force down the Dihang river towards the Abor country, a measure which, if carried out, might have led to claims on tribal territory and even to more serious complications.

Circumstances, therefore, rendered it necessary that endeavours should be made immediately to secure geographical information regarding the border regions from Bhutan up to and including the Mishmi country. So long as the tribal territory lay between us and a peacefully dormant Tibet, an undefined frontier presented neither inconvenience nor danger. With the recent changes in that country, however, the question of a boundary, well defined and at a safe distance from our administrative border, became one of imperative importance and admitted of no delay, for we have within the administrative border of Assam one of the wealthiest districts of British

India, a district where large sums of private European capital have been invested and where the European population outnumbers that of almost any other district in India.

Miri mission.

It was decided, therefore, that, in addition to the two above mentioned expeditions, a third should be despatched into the so-called Miri hills, in the neighbourhood of the Subansiri river, with a view to obtaining information in this district also which might assist in a future settlement of the whole frontier.

CHAPTER II.

GEOGRAPHY, TRIBES, CLIMATE AND SEASON FOR OPERATIONS.

Boundaries.

The Abor country extends from the Yamne-Sesseri watershed on the east to the Subansiri river on the west, and is bounded on the south by the territory between the foothills and the Brahmaputra, in the subdivisions of North Lakhimpur, Dibrugarh and Sadiya.

On the west our knowledge is vague, as little is known of the tribes on the upper waters of the Subansiri. Abors inhabit the left bank of this river, but whether they extend to the right bank is not known. It is, therefore, impossible to determine with accuracy the boundary between the Abors and the Subansiri Daphlas.

On the east are the Chulikatta Mishmis, and on the south the poor and weakly tribe of Miris, who live in British territory, chiefly along the banks of the Brahmaputra and its larger tributaries.

The northern boundary has yet to be accurately determined, but it may be said to be the line of the great snow range known to the Abors as *Killing*, which lies roughly in Lat. 29° 30′ and through which the Dihang breaks about Long. 95°. On each side of this range there appears to be a tract of uninhabitable country in which may prove to lie the ethnological and geographical boundary between Tibet to the north, and the Assam border tribes to the south.

Mountains.

The great snow range runs in a north-easterly and south-westerly direction, and the main area of the Abor country on the right bank of the Dihang consists of a series of spurs jutting out more or less at right angles to it, forming the watersheds between the Subansiri, the Siyom, the Shimang and the Sigon (Sira Pateng) rivers.

Southwards from the point where the Dihang breaks through the great snow range, there is no large tributary joining the river from the east. There appears to be, therefore, a continuous range of mountains leaving the great snow range to the north of the sources of the Yamne, probably forming the watershed between the Dihang and Dibang systems and throwing off minor spurs which divide these rivers from the Yamne and the Sesseri.

To the south of the Abor country is a wall-like ridge known as the "outer range," the peaks of which vary in height from 5,000 to 7,000 feet. This is penetrable only in a few places, and shuts off all view of the interior. This fact was formerly largely responsible for the lack of knowledge of the country behind it. From this range a spur branches off to the north near Misshing, and leads to Kebang, and, forming the backbone of the area occupied by the southern section of the Minyong tribe, is of considerable strategical importance. From all these spurs a tangle of underfeatures is thrown off apparently without system. These underfeatures, from their complexity and steepness, form a serious obstacle to a force advancing into the country and it was to this fact that the slowness of the main advance was chiefly due.

The Abor hills vary in height from 6,000 to 13,000 feet and it is not till the great snow range is reached that there are any peaks of importance. The highest peak which has been fixed in this range is roughly 26,000, while several others of from 17,000 to 18,000 have been observed. All the hills of Aborland proper are densely covered with forest, except where they have been cleared for cultivation. Above 9,000 feet and up to 10,000 feet, where conifers are met with, the jungles are not so thick and rhododendrons are common. In addition to being covered with thick jungle, these hills are for the most part composed, in the neighbourhood of the rivers, of shaly soil which is continually slipping, thus considerably increasing the difficulties of road making.

Difficulties of road-making.

The system of cultivation is that known as *jhuming*. A patch of jungle is cut down, allowed to dry, and then burnt. The surface of the ground is then lightly scratched and the seed sown. After three years, owing partly to the impoverishment of the soil and partly to the growth of weeds, the patch is abandoned and allowed to recover, while a fresh patch is treated in the same way. The original piece of ground may not again come under cultivation for 10 or 15 years, but, near the larger villages, the rotation is much quicker, as the available

System of cultivation.

land can only just support the population. The jungle grows up rapidly on the abandoned patch in an impenetrable tangle forming an even greater obstacle to the movement of troops than the original forest itself.

Rivers.

The chief rivers of the Abor country are :—

1. *The Dihang.*—This breaks through the great snow range close to Lat. 29° 39′, Long. 95°, and is the same river as the Tsang-po of Tibet From here to Jido it is said to flow through a precipitous and impassable gorge. At Jido the valley is said to become wide and open. From below this point to Puging it is narrow and precipitous. From Puging to Dosing it opens out and is more thickly populated, all the lower slopes of the hills being covered with old and new cultivation. From Dosing to Kebang it is more contracted though still cultivated on the spurs, but from here to Pasighat where the river debouches into the plains, the valley is contracted and covered almost everywhere with primary forest to the water's edge.

2. *The Sigon* (or *Sira Pateng*).—This joins the Dihang from the west below Singging. Little is known of it except that, at its mouth, it flows through a narrow and apparently uninhabited valley.

3. *The Shimang.*—This rises near Moling peak and flows entirely through Minyong country ; for the first ten miles of its course it drains a narrow valley, which, however, widens out,. is much cultivated and traversed by good paths. The easiest route to the Bori country is through this valley. At Dosing village, near its mouth, the Shimang is 60 to 70 yards wide in the cold season and unfordable. At Yibuk village the river is 30 to 40 yards wide, very rapid and fordable in a few places.

4. *The Siyom.*—This is the largest of the known tributaries and rises about Lat. 29° 15′ Long. 94°, joining the Dihang near Yekshing village. The valley is inhabited by Bori, Minyong and various Galong tribes. At the confluence of the Puitgong stream, the river is about 100 yards wide and from 15 to 20 feet deep with a three mile current and is said to be easily navigable from this point down to the Dihang by Abor rafts.

5. *The Yamne.*—This joins the Dihang from the north. It is rapid and unfordable. At its confluence with the Dihang it is about 80 yards wide. It flows from north to south through a valley inhabited by the Panggi on the west and the Padam on the east and north. The valley is, with the exception of the narrow gorge between Dukku village and the Siyat stream, wide and open, more especially round Damro and to the north. The easiest route into the Yamne valley is probably over the outer range from the direction of Membu, and this valley affords the shortest route into the Dihang valley north of Geku.

Tribes.

The term *Abor* is a purely Assamese word, meaning *savage*, and could be applied, therefore, with equal truth to all the tribes inhabiting the remoter hills of the north-east frontier. It came to be applied, however, in a special sense to the inhabitants of the Dihang valley, who were formerly supposed to belong to a single tribe divided up into various subsections such as the Pasi, Minyong, etc.

Tribal system.

Although this conception of a single tribe was no doubt ethnologically correct, practically it conveyed quite a wrong impression and led in the past to a considerable amount of confusion. In the case of an outrage, for instance, it was never properly known whether the whole group or merely a certain section were involved. Dealings with the tribes would have been facilitated had the Abors been regarded as a group of separate tribes and had the fact been realised that, although they are doubtless closely related, connection between them is very loose, and they are, therefore, seldom capable of combination and often deeply suspicious of each other. Even this subdivision into tribes is hardly appropriate, for in many cases the tie of the village to the tribe is very slight, and villages act independently of each other in accordance with the rulings of their village councils. This is largely accounted for by the remoteness of the villages from each other, which is again due to the *jhum* system of cultivation, which necessitates the allocation of a very large area for the support of any one village.

The lack of knowledge of these facts previous to the expedition greatly increased the difficulties and militated against the collection of information.

Photo.-Engraved & printed at the Offices of the Survey of India, Calcutta, 1914

Abor Types.

[To face page 8.

Tribes on the left bank of the Dihang.

The chief tribes are as follows. (Limits are marked on the map.)

Padam—a large tribe having their headquarters at Damro in the Yamne valley. They inhabit the left bank of the Yamne and extend thence eastwards along the foothills to the Dibang. They are probably the most warlike of the tribes, and are, as a rule, the tallest and strongest men. It was against them that the expedition of 1894 was undertaken. Their chief villages are Damro, Sibbuk and Dukku in the Yamne valley and Membu, Silluk, Dambuk, Bomjur and Yebuk south of the outer range. Their fighting strength is about 3,500 men, including the Milang, Pasi and Aieng group, but not the Pasi villages round Pasighat.

Aieng—inhabit the foothills and the plains where the Dihang leaves the hills. They are a subsection of, and dependent on, the Padam. Their group of villages consists of Kumku, Kuglek and Padu.

Milang—a small tribe north of the Padam (on whom they are dependent) and east of Simong. Their villages are Milang and Modi.

Panggi—are a small tribe inhabiting the right bank of the Yamne and extending into the Dihang valley at Geku. They are shut in on all sides by stronger tribes and have little chance of trading. They are consequently miserably poor and have a bad reputation as cattle thieves. Some of the Minyong villages have a large Panggi element in them. Their chief villages are Geku (their capital), Pongging, Shumsing (or Kemsing), Jaru and Sibbum. They can muster some 1,500 fighting men.

Komkar—a small tribe north of Panggi and west of Milang. They are an off-shoot of the Padam. They appear to keep aloof from intertribal quarrels and have a great reputation for sorcery. They have only one village, after which they are called, and could muster 200 fighting men.

Simong—a tribe closely related to the Panggi and only separated from it by their geographical situation. All the villages on the left bank of the Dihang north of Simong village belong to this section. The chief villages are Simong, Gette, Puging and Rikor. They could probably muster 2,000 fighting men.

Tribes on the right bank of the Dihang.

Pasi—originally inhabited the Yamne valley, from which they migrated, and are now established in the foothills and at the edge of the plains on the right bank of the Dihang where it enters the plains. Their villages are Gina, Tigra, Balek, Roying, Romkang and Mongku. They could probably muster some 300 fighting men.

Minyong—the most powerful tribe of the eastern section of the Abors. They live on both sides of the Dihang, the Siyom and the Shimang valleys. They have 55 villages and it is estimated that they could, if they combined, put 5,000 fighting men into the field. They appear to be at enmity with all or nearly all their neighbours. Their chief villages are Riga, Riu and Komsing to the north, and Kebang to the south, but the latter has now lost a great many of its fighting men and nearly all its reputation.

Galong—are apparently a collection of tribes inhabiting the country between the western limits of the Minyong and the Subansiri river. Certain of these tribes, whose names were unknown before the expedition, have been visited, but our knowledge of them is still very incomplete.

Bomo-Janbo—inhabit the valley of the Dihang in the neighbourhood of the mouth of the Sigon river. They are said to be peaceful and more given to trading than fighting, but they have never been visited and very little is known of them.

Bori—north of the Minyong and west of Bomo-Janbo. Little is known of them.

Mimat—only vague information is available of this tribe. They are said to inhabit the mountainous and snowy country near the sources of the Siyom and Sigon rivers. The Abors say that they are cannibals and trade salt in return for dead bodies.

Menba—a tribe living in the Dihang valley to the far north and apparently emigrants from the Tibetan side of the main range, but they do not appear to be true Tibetans nor under Tibetan rule.

Climate.

The climate is remarkable for its heavy rainfall which is, perhaps, the greatest of any country in the British Empire.

The year may be divided into two seasons, the rains, from May to October, and the cold weather from November to April. The driest season is during November and December and these two months are the most suitable for survey operations, but even at this time rain falls every few days. After the end of December the weather gets steadily worse and, as the spring advances, interferes more and more with survey and military operations. The haze becomes especially bad from March onwards, and in 1911-12 it was no uncommon experience for a survey party to remain three weeks on the top of a hill before observations could be taken.

Best season for Military operations.

Health.

Considering the amount of rainfall, however, the Dihang valley is extraordinarily healthy, and during the expedition the health of the troops remained wonderfully good in spite of continuous soaking. On the other hand the lower part of the foothills and the flat country on the north bank of the Brahmaputra are unhealthy at all seasons of the year.

The year may be divided into two seasons, the rains, from May to October, and the cold weather from November to April. The driest season is during November and December and these two months are the most suitable for survey operations, but even at this time rain falls every few days. After the end of December the weather gets steadily worse and, as the spring advances, interferes more and more with survey and military operations. The haze becomes especially bad from March onwards, and in 1911-12 it was no uncommon experience for a survey party to remain three weeks on the top of a hill before observations could be taken.

Best season for military operations.

Health.

Considering the amount of rainfall, however, the Dihang valley is extraordinarily healthy, and during the expedition the health of the troops remained wonderfully good in spite of continuous soaking. On the other hand the lower part of the foothills and the flat country on the north bank of the Brahmaputra are unhealthy at all seasons of the year.

CHAPTER III.

NARRATIVE OF THE MURDER OF MR. WILLIAMSON AND DR. GREGORSON, AND EVENTS PREVIOUS TO THE EXPEDITION.

During the expedition fresh light was cast on the proceedings of Mr. Williamson's party prior to the massacre and it will not be out of place to give a short account of this affair here.

Constitution of the party.

The party consisted of Mr. Noel Williamson, Assistant Political Officer at Sadiya, Dr. J. D. Gregorson, a doctor with a large practice on the tea gardens round Tinsukia in the Lakhimpur district and much interested in the frontier tribes, their three servants, two orderlies, ten Miris, and 34 Gurkhali coolies. Assembling at Pasighat, they started thence on March the 18th and reached Rotung on the 20th. The object of the journey was to ascertain, if possible, the extent of Tibetan influence in the Abor country, and was to extend over a period of about six weeks. At Rotung some rations and a case of liquor were found to have been stolen by the Abor coolies who supplemented the Gurkhalis, and Mr. Williamson told the villagers that he would require satisfaction on his return journey. This seems to have been the cause of some anxiety in Rotung, and the advisibility of murdering Mr. Williamson was discussed in the village council that night. The matter was reported to Mr. Williamson, but he, knowing that the Abor is stronger in council than in action, considered that nothing serious was intended and next day continued his journey.

Objects of the journey.

Abors discuss advisability of murdering the party.

Carefully avoiding the territory and village of Kebang, which was not only of doubtful friendliness, but infected with small pox, the party crossed the river and marched up the left bank to a point below Pang-i village, where a camp was made and the return of the coolies, who had been sent back to bring up the remaining stores, was awaited. On the 28th one of the Miris, by name Manpur, was sent back with three sick coolies and some letters. In Rotung, Manpur boasted that the letters contained orders to send up sepoys to punish Rotung and Kebang; this, of course, was quite untrue, but, coming as it did on the top of their previous alarm, so excited the Rotung

Alarm of the Abors.

men that, on the following day, they followed the four men, and, while they were halting for their evening meal fell upon and killed them all.

Messengers murdered.

The murderers at once returned and, strengthened in numbers, hurried on to Kebang, picking up on the way the men of the small village of Babuk. By this time they numbered close on a hundred men. They crossed the Dihang, and, finding in the Pang-i camp only Dr. Gregorson, the Miri interpreter and three or four sick coolies, killed them all on the spot. Dr. Gregorson, who was resting in his tent, was instantly cut down. This occurred at about 1 P.M. on 30th March. That same morning Mr. Williamson and the rest of the party had marched on to a camp on a large stream, the Ribung, which flows past the foot of the hill on which Komsing stands. There were still a few Abor coolies in his camp and news reached these of what had happened down stream. This news was deliberately withheld from Mr. Williamson. The following morning the party moved up and encamped in the village. At about 10 A.M., while the coolies were cooking their food, Mr. Williamson started for the village to visit the *gam*,* Lomben, who had come up with him on the previous day. Three men went with him on the pretext of showing him the house. Taking him into a side street they suddenly set upon him and cut him down.

Dr. Gregorson murdered.

Mr. Williamson murdered.

The rest of the Abors who had crossed from Rotung and Kebang attacked the coolies at the same time. Only five or six were killed in the village, the remainder reaching the river bank in small parties. There, after exhausting the little ammunition in the possession of the few men with guns, they were all killed, with the exception of five coolies who managed, after great hardships, to make their way to the plains. A servant of Mr. Williamson, who reached the Panggi village of Pongging, was well received and afterwards was allowed to join the expedition at Renging. The principal Miri interpreter who swam the river was taken by Babuk men to their village and killed.

Flight of survivors.

Three of the survivors reached the Pasi-Abor villages where the Dihang enters the plains and were there well received. The Pasis sent in news of the massacre to Sadiya, whence it was forwarded to Dibrugarh and was received by the Deputy Commissioner and Political Officer at 9 A.M. on April the 5th.

Receipt of the news in Dibrugarh.

* Headman.

There are certain points in connection with the murder which are worth noting, as they have a certain bearing on the military and political action during the subsequent expedition. In the first place, there is little doubt that the villages of Kebang and Rotung held the prime instigators of the murder, while the inhabitants of Babuk, Sissin and Pang-i had accounted for some of the fugitives. It seems unlikely that the people of Komsing were privy to it, for their women and children were in the village when the murder took place. When an affair of this kind is contemplated, the Abors always remove these, and from other evidence it appears that the villagers of Komsing were taken quite by surprise. A village must, however, be held to a certain extent responsible for events which take place within its precincts.

Villages implicated in the crime.

It is certain, or almost so, that men of Yebuk village incited those of Rotung to the murder, pointing out that if they did not kill the *sahibs*, their village would be burnt, as Yebuk had been on a previous occasion. Again, two of the men who took prominent parts in the actual murder hailed from the villages of Yagrung and Bosing. Yebuk, Yagrung and Bosing are all within British territory.

When the news of the murder was received at Dibrugarh, a party of military police at once set out for Pasighat which, by dint of working night and day, was reached within 100 hours after leaving Dibrugarh. Owing to the proximity of the rainy season Government did not consider it advisable for an advance to be made at once and a post was therefore established at Balek, while it was decided to send up an expedition at the beginning of the cold weather.

Despatch of Military Police.

In the meantime satisfactory relations were established with the Pasi villages in the neighbourhood; and communication was established with the Aieng, a small section of the Padam who inhabit the foothills on the opposite bank of the Dihang. No communication could be entered into with the hostile tribes as no one could be found who would venture into their country; messages were, however, received from them, showing that, not only had they no wish to make any reparation for their act, but indicating the assumption on their part of the most defiant attitude.

Attitude of the tribes.

Captain Hutchins reconnoitres the Kebang road.

During April the paths towards Renging and over Bapu hill were reconnoitred and, during May, Captain Hutchins performed a remarkable reconnaissance up the path from Ledum towards Kebang, getting within a day's march of Kebang itself. The effect of this reconnaissance was excellent from the political point of view, more especially as the history of our previous enterprises in these hills had been practically one long record of ignominious failures. It showed an enterprise and a mobility on our part for which the Abors were quite unprepared, and had the effect of keeping quiet the whole country side through a period of great anxiety; for the hills overlooking the plains are full of Minyong colonies who might be expected at any moment to raid the British villages on the north bank of the Brahmaputra.

CHAPTER IV.

OBJECTS OF THE EXPEDITION AND PLAN OF CAMPAIGN.

From the chapter dealing with our frontier policy it will be seen that the Abor expedition, far from being an isolated expedition against a frontier tribe and possessing merely a local significance, was, in reality, an act of Imperial policy owing its importance to the necessity for fixing a definite and sound strategical boundary between ourselves and China.

The objects of the expedition as officially laid down, were as follows :—

Objects of expedition.

(1) To exact severe punishment and reparation for the murder of Mr. Williamson and Dr. Gregorson and their party, and, by establishing our military superiority in the estimation of the tribes, to endeavour to compel the Minyongs to surrender the chief instigators and perpetrators of the massacre.

(2) To visit as many as possible of the Minyong villages and to make the tribe clearly understand that, for the future, they would be under our control, which, subject to good behaviour on their part, would, for the present, be of a loose political nature.

(3) To visit the Padam village of Damro, which the expedition of 1893-94 had failed to reach. Provided that the Padam behaved themselves, it was decided that the visit to their country would not be of a punitive nature.

(4) If, during the expedition, Chinese officials should be met, endeavour should be made to maintain amicable relations. If, however, such officials or troops be met within territory on this side of the recognised Tibetan-Chinese limits they should be invited to withdraw and, if necessary, compelled to do so.

(5) To explore and survey as much of the country as possible, visiting, if practicable, the Pemakoi falls and incidentally settling the question of the identity of the Tsang-po and Brahmaputra rivers.

(6) To submit proposals for a suitable frontier line between India and Tibet. * * * * It was laid

down, however, that no proposal should be settled on the ground without the orders of the Government of India except in cases where the recognised limits of Tibetan-Chinese territory were found to conform approximately to the line indicated in the instructions and to follow such prominently marked physical features as are essential for a satisfactory strategic and well-defined boundary line.

Plan of operations.

In considering the strategy of the campaign it must be remembered that nearly all the previously mentioned geographical facts were unknown; that our only knowledge of the country was obtained through the Yamne expedition in 1894, Mr. Williamson's first journey to Kebang, and the reconnaissances of the military police, including that of Captain Hutchins up the Ledum—Misshing—Kebang road after the former officer's murder. All the rest of our information was based purely on the unreliable evidence of the Abors themselves.

It was known for certain, however, that the nature of the country and climate combined in making the conduct of military operations a matter of the greatest difficulty and it appeared probable that any sort of combination by widely separated forces would be impossible.

Two plans suggested themselves—

(1) a simultaneous advance on several lines,

(2) the advance of a single main column operating successively in different directions.

The adoption of the first method appeared to offer the following advantages:—

(*a*) the resistance of the tribes along any one line would be lessened, for they would have to hold several positions instead of being at liberty to combine at one point or on one line,

(*b*) a larger area would be traversed by our troops in a shorter time,

(*c*) more information of the country would be obtained,

(*d*) the moral effect of traversing the whole region at one time would be considerable.

On the other hand this method had the following disadvantages :—

(*a*) the very fact that it would lessen the resistance on any one line would militate against the attainment of the primary object of the campaign, *i.e.*, to inflict as heavy a loss as possible on the enemy in actual combat,

(*b*) it was more likely to drive the enemy into adopting guerilla tactics where the advantage would lie with him,

(*c*) the supply arrangements on several lines would be more difficult,

(*d*) the expense of the expedition would rise out of all proportion to its importance, for the nature of the country, precluding all possibility of mutual support between columns, would necessitate a strength for each individual column not greatly inferior to that required for a single one,

(*e*) accurate co-operation between the columns would be impossible, as the country does not lend itself to visual signalling, owing to the thick forests and the prevalence of fogs.

The second method, that of an advance by a single main column, offered the following advantages :—

(*a*) there would be more chance of bringing the tribesmen to battle,

(*b*) it would be less expensive and more in keeping with the small importance of the tribe,

(*c*) supply and transport difficulties would be minimised,

(*d*) once the main opposition had been broken it would be possible to divide up the column into smaller units and thoroughly scour the country,

(*e*) one main line of communication would be more easily guarded, for the reserves at the base could easily move up to meet any attempt against it.*

---

* It is quite in accordance with Abor tactics to break back and attack points on the lines of communication.

It was decided, therefore, to adopt the method of a single main column during the first advance.

A single main column to be employed.

It now became necessary to choose the best line of advance for this column. The primary objective of the expedition was the village of Kebang. This village was not only chiefly responsible for Mr. Williamson's murder, but, on account of its reputation for truculence and fighting power, appeared to dominate the whole of the Minyong tribe.

Line of advance.

Kebang the primary objective.

Routes to Kebang.

To Kebang there were two routes :—

(1) up the valley of the Dihang,

(2) *viâ* Ledum and Misshing by the route which Captain Hutchins had followed in his reconnaissance in the previous May.

The advantages of the Dihang route were that :—

(*a*) it was better known and had always been considered to be the main route to Kebang,

(*b*) its use would have a good effect in keeping quiet the tribes on the far bank of the river,.

(*c*) boat transport would be made available as far as Pasighat, but this would probably have been more than compensated for by the greater directness of the other route.

It had the disadvantages that :—

(*a*) it led through a very involved and difficult country. This was well known to the Abors who left it unblocked and doubtless trusted for our defeat to the difficulties of the road and the strength of the positions commanding it, which they were able to choose,

(*b*) following the long sweep of the Dihang, it was considerably longer,

(*c*) owing to the deep, shut-in nature of the valley, reconnaissance would be rendered very difficult.

The advantages of the second route were that :—

(*a*) by avoiding the long sweep of the Dihang and the very difficult and involved country between Pasighat and Rotung, it was more direct, (*b*) the force would have been on interior lines and able to strike at a greater number of Minyong villages,

(*c*) a force moving in this direction would have been able to advance against Rotung and Kalek from a more favourable direction. It might, moreover, have been possible to utilise one column to operate directly against them while another cut their communications with Kebang and the north,

(*d*) reconnaissance would have been much easier, as the force would have been on higher ground and less shut in,

(*e*) the road would have been easier to align, for the underfeatures, which are such an obstacle to any advance near the river, would have been avoided,

(*f*) the police post at Balek, being quite sufficient to guard the passes leading out of the hills at that place and at Pasighat, the necessity for a second column at the beginning of the operations would have been obviated,

(*g*) it was altogether an easier route This is conclusively shown by the fact that the Abors blocked it carefully, while they left the Dihang route open, hoping to induce us to follow the latter.

It possessed the disadvantages that:—

(*a*) the Abors might find themselves outflanked by the force and take to the jungle without making organised resistance,

(*b*) it would have made the organisation of the Damro column more difficult,

(*c*) it had not been actually followed as far as Kebang, though Captain Hutchins had reached a point within a long march of that place.

Dihang route adopted.

The advantages of the Dihang route however, appeared to outweigh the disadvantages and this route was accordingly adopted, while, in order to prevent raids into the plains and overawe the villages in that direction, arrangements were made to send a subsidiary column to Ledum and Misshing.

CHAPTER V.

CHOICE OF BASE AND PREPARATIONS.

The base for operations in the Abor country must, of necessity, be on the Brahmaputra river. This river affords the most direct and most economical line of supply from the large centres of India and the stations whence the majority of troops had to be despatched. It is navigable throughout the year by the largest class of river steamers as far as Dibrugarh. In the flood season these can also ply to Saikhowa Ghat. The smaller class of steamers can surmount the rapids at the pebble bed just above Poba in the dry season only. The Dihang is navigable, by country boats only, as far as Pasighat during the dry season, but when the river is full, these can be taken, not without difficulty, over the Pakpuit rapids to Janakmukh. The points to be taken into consideration, therefore, in choosing a base were that :—

Brahamputra as a line of supply.

Considerations in choosing a base.

(1) it should be situated on the right bank of the Brahmaputra at a convenient point for the two routes leading into the Abor country, by Ledum and Pasighat, and for the boat convoy to Janakmukh,
(2) steamers should be able to ply to it throughout the year,
(3) the anchorage should be good,
(4) landing facilities should exist,
(5) in order that the camp might be out of reach of floods, the bank should be elevated and dry,
(6) there should be level and ample space for troops and stores.

Saikhowa Ghat.

Saikhowa Ghat, the northern terminus of the Dibrugarh-Sadiya section of the Assam railway was not suitable. It was on the wrong bank of the river, a mile short of which the railway terminated. It is true that country boats could have plied from there to Pasighat, but there would have been a largely increased handling of stores, and moreover the line of railway, although more rapid, was not so direct nor so economical a line of supply as the Brahmaputra river.

Pobamukh, at the mouth of the Poba river, offered certain advantages. Large steamers could reach it throughout the year, there was a good landing place, it avoided the difficult rapid below Kobo and there was a suitable site for a base camp. The distance to Pasighat was, however, unduly long and would have required one more day's march; the boat convoy also would have taken an extra day's journey and would have had to negotiate the very difficult rapid over the pebble reach; while, to reach Ledum, a long detour would have had to be made at the beginning of the year to avoid the flooded tributaries of the Poba river. Thus, although the actual distance from Poba was shorter than from Kobo, the route which would have to be traversed by a force was longer.

Pobamukh.

Kobo, a point some six miles above the junction of the Poba river with the Brahmaputra, was well situated for both lines of advance; large steamers could reach it during the early part of the season, and smaller ones throughout the year; while it afforded a convenient starting point for the boat convoy and a suitable site for a base camp. For these reasons it was decided to locate the base there and landing stages, godowns and a small defensive post were constructed, while a rough road was made to Pasighat. This was greatly improved by the force on its first advance. Owing to the rapids at the pebble beach between Poba and Kobo, the larger steamers were unable to reach the latter place during the dry season, but had to unload at Poba and the men and stores were brought up by a road constructed by the force previous to its advance.

Selection of Kobo.

On the 21st August the scheme of operations was received by the Assistant Director, Supply and Transport, and the collection and purchase of stores and the other necessary details of supply were at once put in hand. Calcutta, with its large markets and wholesale firms, is eminently suitable for meeting the requirements of expeditions, and thence the bulk of supplies, not available locally, was obtained. All supplies and equipment from there were conveyed to the base by the steamers carrying troops and no extra expense accrued on this account.

Supply and Transport arrangements.

For operations in an unknown country like Aborland, consisting of dense tropical forests, where no roads exist and where the rainfall is continuous, special precautions must be taken with supplies, and particular arrangements have to be made for their transport. The chief means of conveyance being by carrier, rations and other loads had been fixed at an all round weight of 60 lbs. gross. Our mobilisation equipment is generally constructed on the assumption that mule, camel, or cart transport will be used in the field, and is packed, as a rule, in loads of one maund (80 lbs.). These had, therefore, to be altered and fresh ones made up for the expedition. The usual gunny bags of India are designed to hold one or two maunds, hence stores in these had to be repacked, while a special water-proof bag was adopted after careful experiment and proved admirably suited to the needs of the expedition. Kegs of rum, limejuice and vinegar had, in a like manner, to be constructed of special sizes. Much delay and inconvenience was caused in this respect by the fact that the official weight of a cooly load was altered several times previous to the expedition. The contracts had to be altered accordingly, but, fortunately, in spite of this delay, everything was ready in time.

Weight of cooly loads.

Water-proof bags.

Ammunition was put up into special boxes containing 480 rounds, but some mistake seems to have occurred in this case, for these boxes only weighed $43\frac{1}{2}$ instead of 60 lbs. and hence, to avoid waste in carriage, to each load of ammunition, a man's kit had to be added which was an additional cause of delay and inconvenience.

Ammunition boxes.

Owing to the tardy appointment of the Assistant Director of Supply and Transport and the consequent delay in the placing of contracts, prices rose considerably in the local supply markets, and it was only with great difficulty that reasonable rates were obtained. A great saving was, however, effected by arranging for the carrier corps marching down from the Naga hills to bring as much rice as possible with them, and thus the fictitious prices put upon this commodity by the local contractors was avoided.

Unluckily, the flat in which the stores were being carried to Kobo buckled. Fortunately another was available at Dibrugarh and, by dint of hard labour, the stores were transhipped to it within 24 hours. The stores began to arrive at the base on the 16th September and, by the 10th October, the force was assembled at Kobo ready to move.

The force consisted of 32nd Pioneers, 1-8th Gurkha Rifles, a wing, 1-2nd Gurkha Rifles, No. 1 Company, 1st Sappers and Miners and 400 rifles Military Police, a total strength of about 2,500 rifles; in addition to this, a wing of the 1-2nd Gurkhas was mobilised as a reserve at Dehra Dun, and, when the lines of communication became long and caused a severe drain on the striking force, was sent to Kobo. At the beginning of the expedition the transport of the force consisted of 5 Corps of Naga carriers, in all 3,000 men.

Constitution of the force.

The troops, with the exception of the 8th Gurkhas, who came from Shillong *viâ* Gauhatti, were brought all the way from Calcutta by boat. They suffered somewhat from overcrowding and in many cases only a limited number of the men were able to lie down at one time.

Arrival of troops.

On the 8th, October, the weather broke and very heavy rain came on. The river began to rise steadily and it was obvious that no advance could be made until the weather improved, for the country inland was impassable and the camping ground at Pasighat, where it was proposed to establish the advanced base, was reported to be under water. On the 13th the Brahmaputra had risen 17 feet and its width at Kobo exceeded 1½ miles. Eventually the river began to drop on the 14th October and the outlook became more hopeful.

During this period, however, the force had not been idle. A road was constructed to Pobamukh, another as far as the Kemi river in the direction of Ledum, while the men not employed on these were kept busy strengthening the defences of the base camp, and in parades for the instruction of the Naga coolies. These were very necessary, for the difficulties inherent to the advance of a long column in single file through dense jungle, when sudden attack is to be expected, are very great. The system adopted and adhered to, as far as possible, throughout this expedition was as follows. The carriers were divided up into groups of six. In front of and behind each of these groups was interposed a rifleman, so that each group of six carriers had two riflemen to protect it. After six of these groups followed a formed party of six riflemen under a non-commissioned officer.

Method adopted for protection of baggage.

The great defect of this system was that it broke up tactical units, the numbers being adhered to irrespective of whether the men belonged to one section or not. It would have been better to have modified it so that two men per section would have been dropped until about six men remained, and then to have put in the residue under the section commander This would have maintained the tactical unit of the section intact, and men would have been always under their own non-commissioned officer, which would have more than compensated for the few extra men made necessary by odd numbers.

CHAPTER VI.

FIRST PHASE OF THE OPERATIONS.

Military.

As we have already seen, the general plan of operations was for the main body to move up the Dihang *viâ* Pasighat, while a second and smaller column operated in the direction of Ledum and Misshing. Before the latter could move it was necessary to cut at least a part of the road and to locate Oyang, the first village on the way to Ledum. The fact that the position of Oyang was marked some four miles out of once on the map gives a good idea of the lack of knowledge [illegible] country which prevailed at this time; it is only a few miles from the river and is well within British territory.

Reconnaissance to locate Oyang.

On the 16th October a reconnaissance was pushed out to locate this village. A bridge over the Kemi river had been constructed on the 10th, but, in the meantime, had been washed away by the heavy rains which caused this river to rise nine feet. The party, under Major Lindsay, 2nd Gurkhas, camped on the river and succeeded in locating the village on the 17th, a matter of some difficulty owing to the thickness of the jungle, which limited the view to a few yards, and the flooded state of the country which was in places waist deep.

March of Ledum Column.

Oyang having been located, it was now possible for the Ledum column to advance, and a move was made on the 20th. The column consisted of headquarters, 2nd Gurkhas, two companies, Lakhimpur Military Police, and two 7 pr. guns, under Colonel Fisher, 1-2nd Gurkha Rifles.

MAIN COLUMN.

March of Main Column.

The main body, under General Bower, was then free to advance, and the march towards Pasighat commenced on the 22nd. The allowance of baggage for both these columns was 10 lbs. per man and 60 lbs. per British officer.

Method of conducting march.

Owing to transport difficulties the advance of the main body was made in two columns, one following the other at a distance of a day's march. On the 26th the force concentrated at Pasighat without incident. The march was in file and, being conducted on principles which were successfully followed throughout, it may be of interest to describe the method adopted.

The advanced guard left camp very slowly and, as soon as it had given room for the whole force to clear camp, halted for a quarter of an hour to allow the rear guard to close up. When the latter arrived in position it gave a whistle signal which was repeated until it reached the advanced guard, which again moved forward. After every hour a similar halt was made to counteract, as far as possible, the tendency of the long column to open out unduly, and to make the pace easier for the long line of carriers.

Procedure on arrival at camp.

On arrival at the end of a day's march it was impossible, owing to the density of the jungle, to demarcate the camp or align the perimeter, so the following procedure was adopted. To enable the various units to recognise the location of their camp, a standard plan was drawn up and adhered to whenever possible. On arrival at the camping ground the centre of the camp was marked by the flag of the General Officer Commanding and the directions of the cross roads were aligned either by flags or on trees. As the carriers arrived in camp their loads were dumped as nearly as possible on the site of the camp of their respective units and they and the men were at once set to clear from the centre outwards. As the ground was cleared it became possible to select the line for the perimeter. This was generally formed of the jungle which had been cleared off the site.

At Pasighat it was found that the river was still high and that a stretch of gravel, on which it had been proposed to camp, was cut off from the mainland by an unfordable channel. A camping ground had, therefore, to be cut out of the heavy jungle on the river bank.

Advanced Base.

Pasighat, being the limit of navigation by country boats, was selected as the advanced base. The first boat convoy arrived the day after the force. It was afterwards found convenient to shift the advanced base to Janakmukh, although the boat convoy could only reach that place during a short period, and, for the greater part of the expedition, had to be unloaded at Pasighat, whence the stores were brought up by mules or carriers.

At Pasighat the Pasi Abors came in and swore and oath of loyalty on a *mithun**, which they brought with them for

* The *mithun* is a domesticated form of the wild gaveal (*Bos gavealis*) which is kept by the majority of the hill tribes in this region. No use is made of it for milking purposes, but the flesh is highly esteemed and is devoured in large quantities at feasts and on occasions of general rejoicing. It appears also to be regarded with semi-religious veneration.

Photo Engraved & printed at the Offices of the S. I., Calcutta, 1911.

Naga Scouts.

[*To face page 30.*

that purpose. They pointed out that, far from being unfriendly to us, they had not joined the Padam in 1894 nor the Kebang men this year, but that they had assisted and fed the fugitives of Mr. Williamson's party. They reported that the Panggi Abors would make common cause with Kebang, but that Riu and Komsing were likely to be friendly to us. They were told that, as long as they remained actively friendly, they had nothing to fear, and from our friendship alone had they everything to gain.

First contact with enemy.

While the force was encamped here, news was received that the Ledum column had got into touch with hostile Abors near Missing. Ledum was deserted, but the *Gams* or head men had subsequently come in. This was obviously part of their policy of not committing themselves to either side until they saw which was the stronger.

Janakmukh.

On the 27th October, a reconnaissance was made towards Janakmukh and a start was made with road-making in that direction. Two days later the force advanced, having been reinforced by 5 companies of Pioneers. It was hoped that it would be possible to bring mules with the force as far as Janakmukh, but the last part of this march was found to be so precipitous that they had to be returned to Pasighat, while their loads were afterwards brought in by carriers. This camp had to be approached down very precipitous ground and the jungle on the camping ground was so thick that it was only with difficulty that the advanced guard could cut their way into it, but, by dint of hard work, they had it more or less clear by the time the main body arrived. A curious feature of this camp was a narrow, precipitous ridge about 30 feet high forming a natural rampart protecting the south face of the camp. This had room for a small picket on top and, when *panjied** on the outer side, offered complete security from an attack on that side, while the northern face of the camp was protected by the river.

About three miles further on could be seen the gently sloping ridge on which was situated the cultivation of the village of Renging. This was open and covered with fine crops. The ground between it and the camp, however, was exceedingly difficult, being a series of knife-edge ridges, covered

---

* *Panjis* are spikes of bamboo or other hard wood, sharpened to a needle-like point and hardened by fire. They are inserted firmly in the ground, inclined towards the front, and form an obstacle in the nature of *chevaux de frise*. They are quickly and easily made and are much used by the tribes on this frontier, their presence being often skillfully concealed.

with almost impenetrable jungle, and dropping sheer to the river. The Abor path apparently led along the rocks by the water's edge, but was at present covered by the river, and a new path had to be aligned by the Sappers and Miners. By the 2nd November, this had been carried past the worst of the ground, and the force was able to advance and camp on the Renging *jhums*. This camp was known as Ramidumbang.

On the 4th November a reconnaissance was made to the Sirpo river, a distance of about six miles. The path leads up a high ridge and thence down a steep descent, so precipitous that in one place the Abor path had been carried down by a ladder. The top of the pass on this section of the route was the furthest point to which mule transport was afterwards regularly used. At the Sirpo river a couple of the enemy's scouts were seen and a new bridge had been constructed over the river. The latter circumstances pointed to the fact that the enemy's chief defences were on this route, for the Abor, while he blocks all other tracks, is in the habit of leaving open the path up to what he considers his impregnable defences.

Furthest point to which mule transport used.

Two days later the force moved to the Sirpo river and occupied a camp on the high bank overlooking the stream. During this advance a village was sighted on a spur above the stream. A party was sent out on the 8th November to visit and, if it proved hostile, to burn it. The party climbed the ridge between the Sirpo and Ramidumbang, thence, striking south-west along the ridge, crossed the stream and, ascending some 800 feet, reached the village. The few inhabitants having fled at the approach of the party, the village was burnt and a large quantity of husked rice and maize was destroyed.

Sirpo River.

Destruction of new Renging.

On the 9th, the force marched to the old site of Renging village, which was burnt to avoid the chance of infection. There was not room for the whole force in one site so a second camp had to be cleared for the carriers. In the course of this, the remains of four men, who had been hacked almost to pieces, and some remnants of Mr. Williamson's property were discovered. This afterwards turned out to be the scene of the murder by Rotung men of the Miri, Manpur, and the sick men sent back by Mr. Williamson on the 28th March.

Heavy rain now began to fall continuously. This, turning the camping grounds into morasses, caused severe hardship to the troops and followers, more particularly to the Naga carriers, who, in addition to being inadequately clothed, were exhausted by the difficulty of keeping their footing under their heavy loads on the slippery tracks.

In spite of the weather every effort was made, by continuous reconnaissances, to find a suitable line of advance, for which reason a considerable delay occurred at this camp. Line after line was tried, but each had in turn to be abandoned owing to the difficulty of the ground. The Abor paths were found to be quite useless as guides to finding a suitable alignment for a road, as they went up and down the hill at an angle which was far too steep for loaded transport. Finally, a suitable line was found in the neighbourhood of the ridge, right away from the Abor path. On the way back from one of these reconnaissances, Captain Hutchinson, Assam Valley Light Horse, was wounded severely by an arrow fired by Abors in ambush, who unfortunately escaped.

The delay was probably caused in some part by the employment of too large a force to carry out the reconnaissances. Had smaller bodies been used they could have scoured the country more thoroughly in a much shorter time and the best line would undoubtedly have been more quickly found. The question of reconnaissance in such country is a very difficult one, for strong columns are immobile and cover very little ground, while if small columns are used they are liable to be cut up. On the other hand the success of the Ledum column shows to what a distance small columns of one or two companies can work with safety, and what success they will attain. They can beat up small scouting parties of the enemy and, while generally clearing up the situation, discover the best line for road-making. The Ledum column carried out this work over a front of 40 miles with inappreciable loss to themselves, quickly obtaining a knowledge of the nature of the country and the attitude of the enemy, while the main body had to grope its way blindly and slowly forward. It must not be forgotten, in this connection, that the greater part of the striking force consisted of Gurkhas. The latter is to a great extent a savage himself and remarkably well able to look after himself in the jungle if he is encouraged to use his own initiative, and this instinct, coupled with the

Difficulty of reconnaissance.

fact that he has been trained to think, makes him quite able to cope with almost any jungle man.

Effect of slowness of advance.

The results of a slow advance were two-fold and not altogether to our advantage. In the first place the Abors were obliged to leave their positions to get rations, so that when we finally attacked them, their stockades, instead of being strongly held and offering a stout resistance, were very weakly defended by a handful of men, and the loss inflicted on the enemy was, in consequence, slight. Secondly, when active opposition had finally broken down, the season was so far advanced that very little time was left for carrying out the very important explorations to the north.

While the force was encamped at Renging, the headmen of Damro arrived and solemnly protested their innocence of any connection with Mr. Williamson's murder. These protestations were probably true and they were told that, so long as they remained friendly, they had nothing to fear; that a friendly mission was shortly going to proceed to Damro; and that they were to see that the roads were open for it. These instructions they promised to obey, and, on the despatch of the Yamne mission, it was found that they had loyally carried out their promises.

On the 19th November, the main column again advanced and followed the newly constructed path until the Yernu ridge was reached. From here the Abor track was followed. On reaching the Lelek stream two companies were detached to climb the hill in order to outflank the pass on which it was expected that a stockade had been constructed. None was found, however, and the descent to the Igar stream was commenced. This was very precipitous and in several places rock chutes were found, showing that the enemy were active in the neighbourhood.

Advance to the Igar stream.

At the bottom of the valley near the stream there was a limited space for a camping ground and the force started clearing this, in spite of the fact that the ground was commanded by a precipitous hill on the far, or enemy's bank of the stream.

On his arrival, the General Officer Commanding decided to make a short reconnaissance up the hill on the opposite bank of the stream with a view to deciding on the action to be adopted next day. Escorted by half a company, therefore, he set off up the path. Soon the scouts reported a stockade ahead and suddenly a shot was fired, wounding one of the guides, a survivor of Mr. Williamson's party. This was followed by a shower of arrows, and several stone-chutes were started. Several of the leading men were brushed off the path by stones and it is wonderful that no one was hit by the flights of arrows which fell in all directions, one of them actually grazing the hand of the General.

Attack on stockade.

Fire was at once opened on the stockade, reinforcements were ordered up from camp by telephone and a party of 6 men under Lieutenants Buckland and Kennedy and Subadar Jaichand Thakur were sent to outflank the enemy's right. This party had a steep and perilous climb, in the course of which they had to pass below part of the stockade. They were in full view of the enemy and were treated to showers of arrows and the discharge of several stone-chutes, which fortunately caused no loss. Eventually the detached bastion on the right of the stockade was entered. Here there was some sharp hand to hand fighting before the enemy fled, its capture enabling the party to enfilade the main stockade. The Abors, finding themselves taken in flank, abandoned the position, which was then occupied by our troops. In this action Subadar Jaichand Thakur, 2/8th Gurkha Rifles, greatly distinguished himself and was afterwards awarded the Indian Order of Merit, 3rd class.

It must be confessed that the discovery of this stockade was something of a surprise, although a warning had been given by one of the guides, a survivor of the massacre, that there would probably be a stockade in this position, which the Abors considered one of the gates into their country. The work was very skilfully sited, flanked as it was on one side by a precipice and on the other by a bastion and stone-chutes, while it was invisible from a few yards to the front. Some 8 Abors were killed but no doubt many got away wounded. A picket was left in the stockade and the force returned in the dark to camp.

On the following day the force marched to Rotung which was found to have been burnt by the retiring Abors. One company was detached to work up the Igar stream and succeeded in destroying many stone-chutes.

Advance to Rotung.

On the 21st, reconnaissances were made back towards Renging with a view to finding the best alignment for the road. The country was very difficult and it was only after repeated attempts that a practicable line was found. In the meantime, parties patrolled the country to beat up small, scattered bands of the enemy which were known to be lurking in the vicinity. One of these parties surprised and killed four of the enemy in a house, while on their return two more were encountered on the road and met the same fate.

Enemy located at Kekar Monying.

Two days later, a reconnaissance sighted a large number of Abors, near Kekar Monying and the existence of a stockade in the vicinity appeared probable. On the 24th and 25th November, further reconnaissances were made and a large stockade was located just above the Kekar Monying or Black Rock. This is a great cliff standing some 150 feet sheer above the river and about 500 yards in length. Along its foot runs the narrow footpath commanded by jungle-covered cliffs on which great numbers of stone-chutes had been placed. The Abors considered this position to be impregnable and regarded it as the chief gate of their country.

Plan of attack.

It was obviously essential to turn the position, for, from the configuration of the ground, a frontal attack could hardly fail to be costly and must preclude the possibility of inflicting appreciable loss on the enemy.

Before the attack took place the force was strengthened by the arrival of part of the Ledum column which brought the available force up to nearly 1,300 rifles.

The plan of attack decided on was as follows. (*Vide* panorama and sketch plan). Three companies, 8th Gurkha Rifles, one company, 2nd Gurkha rifles, one maxim gun, Assam Valley Light Horse and one maxim gun, 2nd Gurkha rifles, were to cross the river under the command of Captain Coleridge and get into the position marked Q * * * S on the plan. From here the enemy's position could be enfiladed. The movement was to be executed at night, in order to surprise the enemy. This party received orders not to commence firing before 8-30 A.M. After this hour the question of opening fire was left to the discretion of the officer commanding the party, but, if he was not discovered, he was to wait, if possible, until the main body reached the green rock marked on the plan and the left flanking party reached the neighbourhood of the Side stream cutting off the Abors' retreat.

SKETCH PLAN OF ACTION AT IGAR STOCKADE
19-11-11. 3-20 P. M. TO 4-15 P. M.

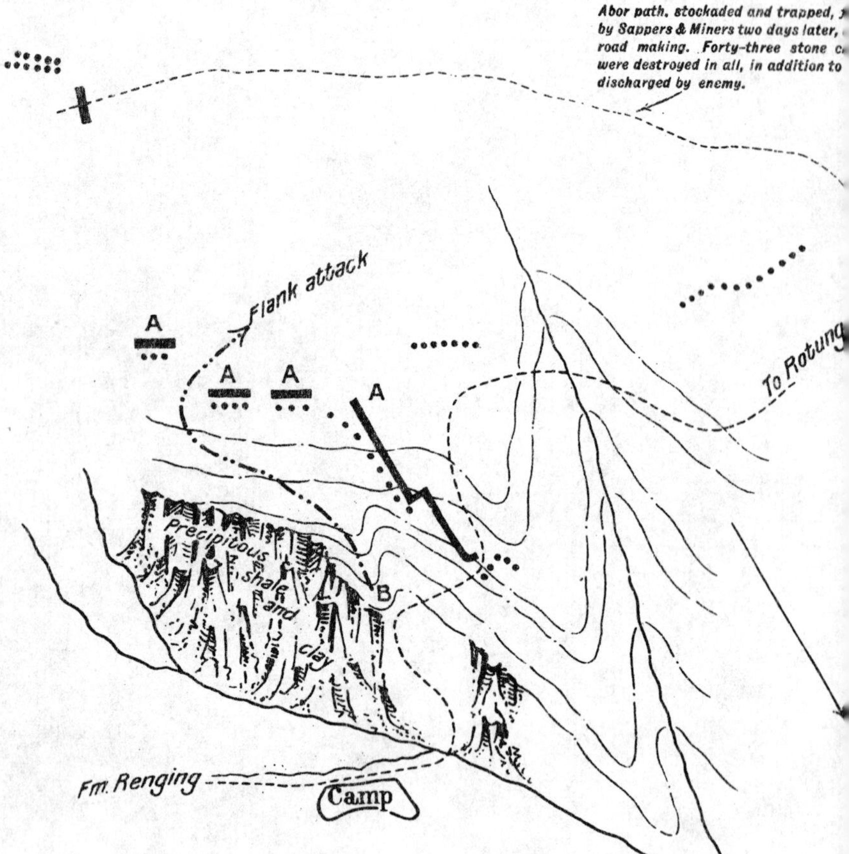

A. Stockade
B. Position of S. O. C. & Staff, and holding attack.
Stone chutes • • • •
Precipitous shale and clay
Hills covered with dense tree and bamboo jungle, cleared for 30 yds., in front of stockade.
Stockade, 8′ to 10′ high, bamboo & timber, backed with large stones.

(Sd.) W. R. HORE, Captain,
Int. Officer A. E

S. D. O. No. 854 January, 1914.

A left flanking party of three companies under Captain Giffard was to move round the enemy's right and get above the stockade in a position to intercept his retreat in the direction of the Side river (T * * * * *M). It was estimated that this party, after crossing the Sireng river, would take $4\frac{1}{2}$ hours to get into position.

The main body was to march up the bank of the river and, allowing time for the left flanking party to get into position, to attack the position in front, communication with the flanking parties being kept up by telephone.

Before Captain Coleridge's party could cross the Dihang it was necessary to find a suitable place to establish a ferry. While this was being done and materials being got ready for the rafting operations, a party of three companies, under Colonel Murray set off, on the 26th, to burn the village of Kalek which had been giving trouble on the lines of communication towards Misshing. The village was found to be deserted and was burnt. It was unfortunate that the Ledum column could not have been used to co-operate against this village while the main body was advancing to Rotung. Kalek was within easy striking distance of the depôt established by that column on the Sireng river. Had a force marched on it, timed so as to arrive there on the same day as the main body reached Rotung, it would have found Kalek occupied and would probably have been able to intercept and inflict severe loss on the enemy retiring from the Igar stockade and Rotung. Under the conditions imposed by the plan actually adopted, the enemy retired from these places completely unmolested and Kalek village, when visited by Colonel Murray s party, was found to be deserted.

Destruction of Kalek.

Ledum column not used to co-operate.

Meanwhile efforts were being made by the Sappers and Miners, under Captain Tylden-Pattenson, to effect a crossing of the Dihang. Soon after 5 P.M. a small party succeeded in reaching the far bank on a raft. Owing, however, to the strength of the current, it became necessary to cut the line attached, thus leaving the party isolated on the far bank. Several unsuccessful attempts were made during that night and the next day to complete the ferry and it was not till 5-30 P.M. on the 27th that this was finally established. Shortly afterwards Captain Coleridge's party commenced crossing and were all over by 10-35 P.M., the passage being completed in 19 trips, without hitch and without noise.

Establishment of a Ferry over Dihang.

While the detachment was crossing, the scouts under Lieutenant Buckland had fortunately discovered a path running towards Sissin and had followed this for 1½ miles without meeting the enemy. Night marching through an ordinary country after careful reconnaissance is always a difficult and trying matter. The difficulties in this case were very much multiplied for the jungle was dense, the route had not been reconnoitred, and the probability of meeting a cunning and savage enemy had to be reckoned with. Luckily the moon was bright and the sky clear. For 2,000 yards the path lay along the river bed and then turned up-hill into the jungle at a point from which the Abor watch fires across the river were distinctly visible.

Night march.

About 2-30 A.M., just as the moon was setting, firing broke out in the rear of the column. It lasted for about half a minute and then ceased. Some Abors had charged the column, killing two men of the 2nd Gurkhas with a discharge of their guns, and then breaking through the column with drawn swords. No one else was hurt in the rush but the butt of one man's rifle was severed. The Abors lost two killed and probably some more wounded. A rifleman of the 2nd Gurkhas behaved with great gallantry, jumping down the steep hillside to where his injured comrade lay some yards below the road, and remaining with him in a most exposed position until the affair was over. He was subsequently awarded the Order of Merit, 3rd class, for his plucky action. It was fortunate that the sound of the firing did not alarm the Abors at Kekar Monying, but it was drowned by the roar of the river. It was now pitch dark and the column halted till dawn, spending an anxious night, for a steep hill side overhung the force and the enemy could be heard from time to time moving in the jungle.

Column attacked by Abors.

At 6 A.M., the column moved off again and soon reached the pass south of Sissin. Here it wheeled to the right and formed up under cover. It was a misty morning, but, at about 8-30 A.M., the mist cleared and a remarkable view presented itself. Directly below was the stockade and in it were a few Abors. Behind it and near the river were more, some sitting about and others cooking. The presence of the party was obviously unknown to them and there was nothing be gained by opening fire. News being received of the advance of the main body the detachment accordingly took up a concealed position.

Party arrives in position.

STONE CHUTES NEAR IGAR STOCKADE

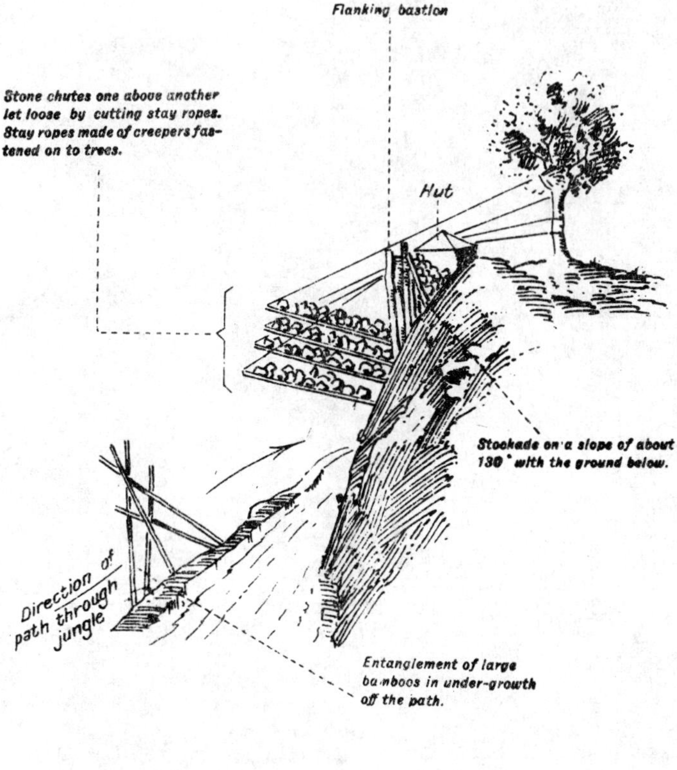

S. D. O. No. 855 January, 1914.

At 10-45 A.M. the left attack became visible, well above the stockade on the hills across the river. This news was sent to the main body with a suggestion of a further advance. This would have had the effect of bringing the rest of the Abors into the stockade thereby offering a better target and, at the same time, would have allowed the left attack to reach the neighbourhood of the Side river, where they would be in a position to cut off the Abors' retreat.

Fire opened prematurely.

Unfortunately, while this message was being sent, the main body prematurely opened fire and the Abors began to leave the stockade. It became imperative therefore for the right column to open fire immediately.

Flight of Abors.

The Abors at once fled from the stockade and, as they darted through the jungle, presented a difficult mark. Each company took up the fire in turn as the enemy passed them and, by the time the latter reached the Side river, they were hopelessly demoralised.

Operations on right bank.

Let us now turn to the operations on the right bank of the river. At 5-30 A.M. the left flanking party under Captain Giffard left camp and crossed the Sireng stream at 7-15 A.M., being followed by the main body a quarter of an hour later. The latter halted by the stream while a position for the 7-pounder and maxim guns was reconnoitred. An advance was then made, and, at 10-30 A.M., the main body reached a position some 1,300 yards from the enemy, whence fire was somewhat prematurely opened, as above described, on the Abor stockade. This resulted in the flight of the occupants before Captain Giffard's flanking party could operate with effect, and thus the success of these combined operations was considerably neutralised.

The Abors apparently trusted, not in a strong stockade, but in the natural difficulties of the position backed by over a hundred stone-chutes. Long before the attackers arrived in the effective zone of these, however, the enemy had been driven out by rifle fire and none were discharged. The force then marched through the position without hindrance. Four companies were despatched in pursuit to Babuk, which was destroyed that evening, and Captain Coleridge's party advanced and burnt Sissin.

Pursuit.

Effect of the action.

Altogether some 8 Abors were found dead in the stockade and in the neighbourhood, and it is certain that the number of wounded was still greater. Although the actual loss was small, the moral effect must have been very great, for the heavy fire to which the Abors were subjected for a few moments, would naturally prove very terrifying to savages unaccustomed to the report of fire arms. It is, moreover, a significant fact that, after this action, the active resistance of the Abors came to an end.

On the following day, the four companies returned from Babuk, which had been found deserted, and Captain Coleridge's party recrossed the Dihang. Half a company was employed in reeling up the telephone wire which had been laid out by Captain Giffard's party. This was an arduous task and is the chief objection to the use of the telephone in this sort of country. It is, however, the only possible means of communication on similar occasions owing to the thickness of the jungle, which makes visual signalling impossible unless there is time to clear stations; the view, moreover, is liable to interruption owing to the prevalence of thick mists.

Use of telephone.

After three days spent in reconnaissance and road making, the force advanced in two columns to Kebang which was found deserted and a site for a camp was selected in the direction of the river. Next day the force moved forward to the mouth of the Yembung river, where a large sandspit offered a fine site for a permanent camp.

Fall of Kebang.

On the 13th December, a column was sent out to Yemsing village which was reached and burnt on the following day. During the course of this operation four Abors were killed and seven wounded.

Destruction of Yemsing.

LEDUM COLUMN.

Let us now turn to the operations of the Ledum Column. The rôle of this column was to overawe the villages and keep the Abors busy in the direction of Ledum, thus protecting the flank of the main column and preventing the chance of an inroad into the plains. The column accordingly left Kobo on the 20th October and tried the experiment of marching in four short columns instead of one long one, thus avoiding the straggling inseparable from the march of a long column in single file through the jungle. This method proved a great success and effected a considerable saving of labour both to the men and carriers.

On reaching Oyang, the first camp, the column was met by the head men of that village and of Dorak and Mangang, who expressed their willingness to guide the party to their

Photo.-Engraved & printed at the Offices of the Survey of India, Calcutta, 1914.

Sappers and Miners' raft-ferry.

[*To face page 38.*

SKETCH
SHOWING SIGNALLING COMMUNICATION DURING ATTACK ON KEKAR MONYING
ON DECEMBER 4th 1911

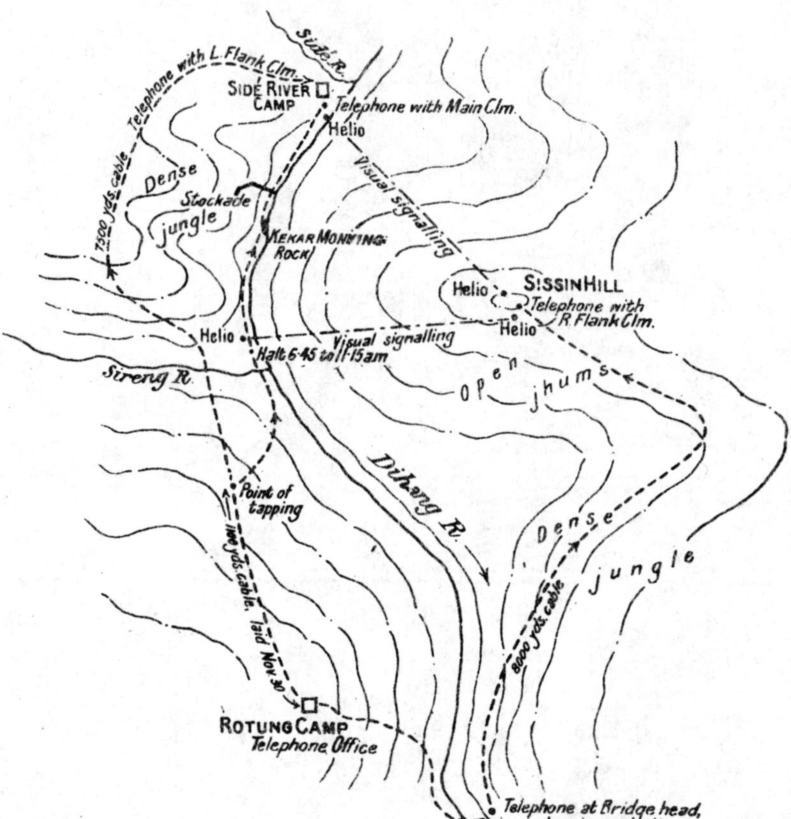

S. D. O. No. 850 January, 1914.

SKETCH PLAN OF ACTION AT KEKAR MONYING

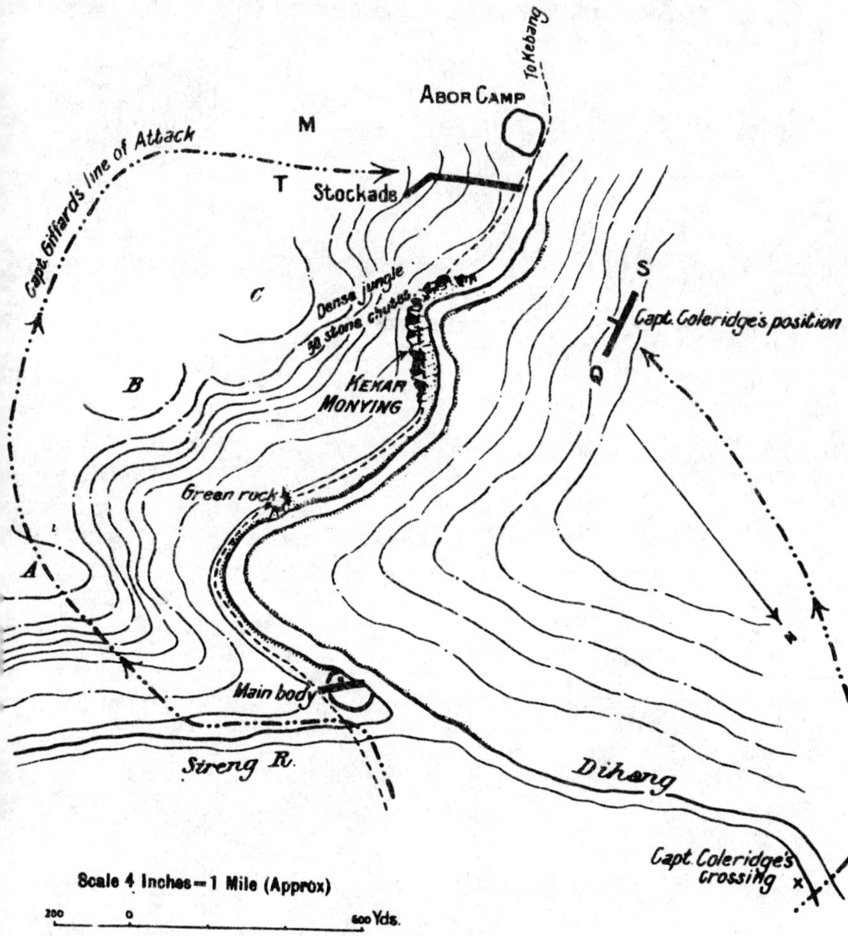

S. D. O. No. 861 January, 1914.

villages, while they gave information that the head men of Ledum had refused to come in, but that no Kebang men had visited the village, which was occupied by all its fighting men. During the advance to Mekong, two days later, this information was confirmed and it was further reported that the Ledum people had cut their crops before they were ripe which pointed to a hostile attitude on their part. On the 23rd, a reconnaissance was pushed out to Ledum village which was found to be deserted. The village was situated on the low foothills some 8 miles north-west of the position assigned to it on the map issued to the force. The column moved to this place on the 25th, where three of the village *gams* came in, while a certain number of the inhabitants also returned.

Reconnaissance to Missһing.

From Ledum, signalling communication with Kobo was impossible, so next day a reconnaissance was pushed out to Misshing to look for a suitable spot for the headquarters of the force in that neighbourhood. The advanced guard of this reconnaissance came into contact with an Abor picket, and, opening fire, killed a Kebang man. Later on in the day about 50 men were seen retiring across the cultivation on Misshing Hill and fire was opened on them from a maxim gun, causing them to disappear. A suitable site was found here for a camp and the party returned to Ledum. On the following day a party was sent to bivouac on this camping ground and to picket the hills in the vicinity. On reaching the site of the camp, the advanced guard of the party came under a heavy arrow fire and, by searching with fire the jungle round, succeeded in killing two Abors.

By the 28th, the village of Ledum having paid its fine, the head men were released, and on the 29th the column moved to Misshing. From here signalling communication was opened with Kobo.

Plan of action.

The only way to protect the flank of the main colum efficiently while it marched up the difficult and intricate gorge of the Dihang, was to adopt a vigorous offensive in all directions. Plans were therefore formulated for a systematic clearance of the enemy from the jungles round Misshing, followed by increasingly wider reconnaissances. "To march fast and move far, to harry the enemy in every direction of the compass, to show that he was never safe from surprise save when out of reach, such were the methods adopted by the Ledum Column."*

---

* Major Lindsay, in an article in "The Army Review," April 1913.

On the 30th, a reconnaissance was pushed over the high ascent north of Ledum and followed the Kebang road as far as the Sireng river.

Reconnaissance to Sireng river.

A few stone-chutes were found and the path was barricaded for some distance, but the advance was not opposed, although there were obvious signs of the enemy having been in recent occupation of the road. On the same day a convoy proceeding to Ledum was fired on but there were no casualties. On the following day this was repeated. It was obvious that there were many small parties of the enemy lurking in the vicinity. On the two succeeding days, therefore, the jungle round was scoured by small parties of from 6 to 10 men These surprised and rushed three small bodies of the enemy and inflicted loss on them. On the 31st, a reconnoitring party found the new village of Misshing (Captain Hutchins had destroyed the old village in May) and burnt it after killing one of the enemy. The next day was spent in destroying crops and supplies in the neighbourhood of this village while a party reconnoitred towards Kaking. Two days later a further reconnaissance of 50 rifles was pushed out towards the latter village and penetrated within 5 miles of it. A detached party of this column, reconnoitring up a side track, came on a party of 15 of the enemy and, taking them by surprise, inflicted heavy loss on them, capturing all their bows and arrows and most of their clothing. On the 2nd November, a party of 100 rifles reconnoitred to the Sireng river and improved the road. No signs of the enemy were seen, although numerous stone-chutes were visible on the far bank of the stream. Next day the garrisons which had been left behind at Mekong and Ledum rejoined, bringing the strength of the force up to 490 rifles.

Reconnaissances towards Kaking and Sireng River.

The Misshing—Bahming road was reconnoitred on the following day and a party marched along the Kebang road to the Sireng river, cutting a path 2 miles down it towards Kalek. While this work was in progress a reconnoitring party, stealing down the bed of the stream, surprised a party of the enemy and killed one man. The Kebang road, on the far side of the river, was found to be badly blocked. A further advance was made in this direction on the 5th, when a party crossed the Sireng river and, cutting round the barricade, reconnoitred the road for some distance in the direction of Kebang. The road was found to be excellent and no signs were seen of the enemy. Meanwhile the cutting of the path down the Sireng towards Kalek was continued.

ler
ch-
ch
be
ch-
his
se
be
he
rly

y.
no
e.
ed
he
y,
re
ed
he
ed
g
ur
in
he
d.
it
ed
nt

al
n
g,
k
of
d.
he
g

operating in the destruction of Korang and, having accomplished it, to unite and reconnoitre towards Kaking.

The second column, on reaching Ledum, found the village again deserted. This was probably due to threats from Kebang, who had warned the village, that, if they helped us in any way, they would be cut up. On leaving Ledum the column struck west along the path to Kaking, making a Ledum youth prisoner. This man was taken on as a guide and reported that Kaking was defended by a big stockade and the enemy were awaiting us there, while the road to Korang was good.

A few miles beyond Ledum the road was blocked by trees felled some months previously, and it was apparent that our advance had always been expected along this route and that the reconnaissance to Doshing on the 5th, coming from an unexpected quarter and avoiding all their carefully prepared paths, had completely surprised the Abors. It was clear, too, that the village of Ledum must have been cognisant of these obstacles all along and had carefully refrained from reporting them. At length, after much cutting through the jungle to avoid felled trees, the top of a ridge was reached from whence a long spur could be seen across the valley. Towards the south end of this was a village said to be Korang.

From this point two paths were reported leading to Kaking, one up the bed of the Sido river *via* Doshing, and the other up the opposite ridge and through Korang. The officer commanding decided to use the latter, in order to try to get into signalling communication with Misshing from the ridge, and to visit Korang village *en route*. There was a stiff climb up to the ridge and the road was badly blocked, so that the column was very late in reaching the top. As there was no water it was decided to return to the valley and camp, while a party was sent on to reconnoitre the village. The retirement to the valley was rather unfortunate as, next morning, the village was found to be deserted, although it had been occupied when reconnoitred in the evening. Had an immediate attack been possible, the enemy must have suffered severely.

In the morning the force retired to Misshing, having previously detached a party to surround Korang and, having accomplished the destruction of that village, to get in touch with the other column. The latter, instead of marching through Doshing, had moved down a spur to the Silli river and thence over to the bed of the Sido river, where they camped for the night. Next morning the march was continued to Doshing up the river bed, and the village was reached without opposition. Several stone-chutes and an unoccupied stockade were, however, found on the road below it.

On the 10th, 100 military police, sent out to support this column, reached Doshing at about 3 P.M. They found on the way that the stockade, destroyed on the 5th, had been rebuilt, but was unoccupied, probably because it had been turned by the column moving down the Sido river on the 8th.

A reconaissance was now pushed out towards Kaking. There was a good road all the way and Kaking, which was visible from the spurs opposite, did not appear to be stockaded. This reconnaissance was fired on, and, returning the fire, killed an Abor armed with a muzzle loading gun. The column then retired to Misshing having lost 1 kahar killed.

These energetic operations now began to bear fruit, for in the next few days the *gams* of nearly all the villages in the neighbourhood, and even at some distance, came in, and it became evident that active opposition in this direction was almost at an end.

Till the end of November parties daily scoured the country over a wide front extending from near Kalek and the Side river on the north, to Kaking on the west. To allow of these reconnaissances being as extended as possible, a party of 100 rifles was detached to Kaking, while, in order to facilitate the expected co-operation with the main column towards Kebang, a similar party was posted on the Sireng river, where a store depôt was formed. From here the routes to the Dihang *viâ* the Side river and *viâ* Kalek were reconnoitred, the party penetrating within 2 miles of the latter place.

Co-operation with main column.

In order to render this work possible, the troops had to be called on to do the work of carriers, for the latter were insufficient for requirements. The weather had broken on the 8th November and for 10 days it rained steadily. This, coupled with the hard work, the light scale of kit and the lack of meat, began seriously to affect the health of the column and, by the 21st of November, 30 per cent of the men and 50 per cent of the British officers were incapacitated by malaria and dysentery. The medical question now became one of the greatest difficulty as there was only one medical officer and two assistant surgeons with the force and both the latter were sick. There was thus only one officer left to attend to the multifarious duties connected with the medical charge of the column.

On the 28th November, orders were received for the break up of the Ledum column and, on the 30th, a double company of the 2nd Gurkhas marched to Rotung *viâ* Kalek to join the main column on

Break up of the column.

the Dihang; 150 military police were left at Misshing, while the remainder proceeded to Balek.

Effect of operations.

The vigorous and untiring work of this column had been of the greatest service. From their central position they had completely overawed and kept quiet the Minyongs in the neighbourhood, and the whole of the Galong tribe. They had inflicted severe loss on the enemy and, while they had actively protected the flank of the main body from attack during the slow advance through the difficult gorge of the Dihang, they had rendered any incursion by the Abors into the plains quite out of the question. They had proved the advantages, in this sort of warfare, of the swiftness and mobility of small parties when compared with the slow and deliberate movements to which larger columns are restricted.

EVENTS AFTER THE FALL OF KEBANG.

Let us now return to the operations of the united columns after the fall of Kebang. The force now took up permanent quarters at Yembung while small parties were employed in reconnoitring in all directions and in destroying grain and supplies which might have been made use of by the enemy hiding in the jungle. A permanent crossing was also constructed over the river by means of a flying raft-bridge so as to open up communication with the villages on the further bank.

Organised resistance at an end.

The reconnaissances carried out after the fall of Kebang proved that organised resistance had come to an end although a few armed parties of the enemy still lurked in the jungle. When Yemsing had been destroyed, therefore, it appeared desirable to get into communication with the villages whose inhabitants were known to be innocent of complicity in the murder, to establish friendly relations with them, and to open up a path for further explorations to the north.

Envoys sent to call in gams of neutral villages.

On the 15th December, the Pasi *gams*, who had accompained the force, were sent to the villages of Pang-in on the right and to Komsing and Riu on the left bank, to advise the head men to come in.

It will be remembered that, while the actual murder was committed in Komsing, the inhabitants of that village took no part in it and were probably as much taken by surprise as the victims themselves. It was believed that the people of Riu

Photo. Engraved & printed at the Offices of the Survey of India, Calcutta, 1914

Komsing Village.

[*To face page 47.*

had disapproved of the murder and would readily come in if opportunity offered, while Madu, the head man of the village, was known to be a man of considerable influence with whom it was desirable to get into touch.

The envoys were prevented by Kebang men from reaching the village of Pang-in, but they crossed the river and reached Komsing in safety, delivering their messages to the headmen concerned. The latter came in on the 18th and succeeded in exculpating themselves from complicity in the murder. It was, however, necessary to hold the village responsible to a certain extent for events which took place within it. The head men of the Panggi tribe also arrived the same evening and cleared themselves of all cognisance of the actual murder, though it was realised that some of the men of this tribe had taken part in the pursuit of the fugitives. All these headmen were told that they must henceforth look to the Government of India as their supreme power, that they would not be interfered with as regards matters which were usually settled by the village council, and that they were free to trade with the plains whenever they wished to do so. It had been a long standing grievance of the tribes to the north, that Kebang maintained a monopoly of this trade and that they were only allowed to obtain articles from the plains at exorbitant rates, and, indeed, were often altogether cut off from them.

Hostile villages come in.

Messages were now sent to the guilty villages of Kebang and Sissin that it would be to their advantage to come in. This advice they followed after a certain amount of delay, and fines were imposed on them in accordance with the degree of their guilt. These fines were all slowly paid up.

Dihang exploration sets out.

On the 29th December, the Dihang exploration party set out, and, on the 7th January, a column under Colonel Murray left for Komsing to keep up communication with it, and to place a suitably inscribed tabl[illegible] on the spot where Mr. Williamson was murdered. This was accomplished with befitting ceremony and the headmen of the village were informed that they would be held responsible for its protection.

Headquarters established at Yembung.

Headquarters were now established in permanent camp at Yembung and from here the movements of the various exploration parties were directed. An account of these will be found in a subsequent chapter.

CHAPTER VII.

REVIEW OF MILITARY OPERATIONS.

Effect of Military Operations.

With the fall of Kebang the active opposition of the tribes came to an end. The operations had been uniformly successful and had avoided the regrettable incidents of former campaigns, and, although the actual loss inflicted on the tribesmen was small, the moral effect of the campaign must have been very great. The Abors had been driven out of their selected and carefully prepared positions without difficulty; they had been shown that an armed force could visit with ease any part of their country; their crops and villages had been destroyed wherever resistance had been offered; and a road had been made through the heart of their country. The force employed by us must have seemed very large to them, for the Naga carriers, of whom there were several thousand, from their numbers, their bearing and their fierce aspect, no doubt appeared very formidable. Again, the rapid fire to which they were subjected for a brief period at Kekar Monying, although its actual effect was small, must have been very terrifying to savages unaccustomed to the report of fire arms. Had it been possible to intercept their retreat and harass their scattered parties in the depths of the jungle, the effect of the campaign must have been greatly increased.

Previous to the expedition, the power of the Abors was greatly overated owing to the reverses suffered by former expeditions. It was not realised that the tribe were quite incapable of combination, and that the failure of these enterprises was due, not so much to the strength of the enemy, as to lack of organisation on our part. For this reason, the strength of our force on this occasion was unnecessarily great, and whenever the enemy made a stand, they found themselves so greatly outnumbered that they realised that resistance would be useless and they fled before heavy loss could be inflicted on them.

Slowness of the advance.

The somewhat deliberate advance also militated against inflicting a heavy loss on the enemy. The Abor stockade is not usually situated in close proximity to his village, as is the case with many jungle tribes, but often at some distance from it. The Abor brave carries, as a rule, some 7 days' rations on his person. This is his only means of supply, and when it is exhausted he must return to his village for more. Consequently, if a stockade is threatened for long, the defenders, after occupying it for some time, begin to melt away, and, when the attack is finally delivered, but few will be found in position. At Kekar Monying stockade the enemy had dwindled to less than one-third of their original strength when the attack was finally made.

The slow progress of the expedition was due to several causes. In the first place the country presented the greatest difficulties. These were greatly increased by the fact that the force was advancing by the longest and most difficult route to Kebang, while the obstacles encountered were rendered still greater by the difficulty of reconnaissance. Further delay was caused by the necessity of establishing supply depôts at Pasighat, Rotung and Renging. It was decided that no advance could be made from each of these depôts until 15 days' rations had been collected there. These had to be brought up entirely by carrier. Each carrier could carry on an average, 20 rations, so, to carry food alone for 1,000 men for this period, 750 carriers had to be employed. In addition, the carrier's own rations, men's kits, ammunition, hospital stores and all the different necessaries of a campaign had to be brought up.

Road-making difficulties.

The operations of the force were greatly retarded by keeping it tied to the head of the road. Road making in a country of this nature must, of necessity, be slow, for the hills are precipitous, the soil continually slipping, and the jungle so thick that alignment is difficult. The latter difficulty was much increased by the lack of reconnaissance which compelled the pushing of the road blindly forward without the possibility of a previous survey. The shortage of transport, also, precluded the possibility of carrying tools for the whole force, with the result that a large number of men, who might have been employed in road-making, were compelled to stand idle for lack of picks and shovels.

Supply and Transport difficulties.

The supply and transport question was one of the greatest difficulty throughout the expedition. There were practically no supplies available in the country and everything had to be brought up to the front through a mountainous and difficult country, generally in pouring rain, which made the roads slippery and the loads heavier.

Supply depôts were established at Pasighat (this depôt was moved to Janakmukh early in November), Renging and Rotung. From the base at Kobo to the first of these depôts at Pasighat two routes were used:—

Supply depôts.

(1) Up the Dihang by country boat, a distance of about 35 miles. For a short time boat convoys ran as far as Janakmukh, but this had to be discontinued as soon as the river got low. The boat convoy, under the able management of Lieutenant Webb, 5th Gurkha Rifles, was of the greatest assistance throughout the expedition, but, more particularly, previous to the arrival of the mule corps, when the only other available method of transport was by carrier.

Boat Transport.

(2) From Kobo to Pasighat by road. This route was level and good and was suitable to the employment of carts, had they been available.

At the beginning of the expedition only carriers were available, but, when the mules arrived, they were employed as far as Janakmukh. When the mule road had been completed to Renging, they were used as far as that place, but it was soon found that the road cut up badly and it was found better to employ them only as far as 'Cooly Col', half way between Janakmukh and Renging. From here forward the transport was entirely by carrier.

Forms of Transport employed.

One carrier corps was kept with the striking force, and, at the beginning of the expedition, supplies were brought up to it by through convoys. This wasteful and trying system was soon discontinued and for a short time the staging system was adopted. This was finally abandoned in favour of the staging-meeting system which was found to be the most satisfactory in every way. The Ledum Column was rationed by through convoys of carriers, occasionally assisted by elephants.

Systems of working Transport.

The 7-pr. guns taken with the force proved to be a useless encumbrance. At the short ranges, at which alone action is possible in this country, these have a flat trajectory and are deficient in searching power, while they are unable to pierce a a well built stockade by direct fire. They are extremely

Artillery.

heavy and require a large number of overloaded carriers to transport them. These take up a great deal of road space, every extra yard of which causes delay to the column and adds to the danger in the case of an attack. In fact, the amount of delay and inconvenience which they cause is altogether out of proportion to their utility.

Bomb-throwing Mortars.

More effective weapons for this sort of warfare are the wire-wound wooden mortars constructed by the Sappers and Miners. These consist of wooden tubes wound with wire, firing a projectile in the nature of a large jam tin with a bursting charge of 4 lbs. of dynamite propelled by a light charge of powder. They are light and easily transported, and, from the steep angle of descent and consequent searching power of their projectile, should be very effective against a stubbornly held stockade. The explosion of their charge is terrific and must have a very great moral effect, even though their killing power may not be very great. Unfortunately, the Abors never held their stockades long enough to make their use necessary and were always turned out by rifle fire.

Maxim guns.

The maxim guns suffered from the same disadvantages with regard to transport as the 7-prs. They were actually used effectively at the Kekar Monying stockade, but this one occasion was not sufficient to make up for the difficulty and delay involved in their transport on the narrow and precipitous jungle paths, where every carrier was of the greatest importance. On the other hand, they might be very useful in the case of an attack by the enemy on one of our posts, particularly at night, but they proved unsuitable for use with the striking force in the jungle. Should their use, however, be desirable in the future with a force operating in a similar country, it would be well to design some method of carriage by which the gun and mounting would be carried each by a single man. The present system of carrying each of these between two men on a long pole is a most cumbersome and inconvenient arrangement in the jungle, for, in addition to the amount of road space they take up, they cause trouble at sharp corners on the paths.

Rifle Grenades.

Hale's rifle grenades might have been useful in the case of a stubbornly held stockade, but, though ordered, they failed to arrive in time for the expedition.

CHAPTER VIII.

SECOND PHASE OF THE OPERATIONS.

Political, Survey and Exploration.

To turn now to the second phase of the operations. The active operations of the tribes having been overcome, it became possible to utilise the strength of the expedition in survey and exploration in order to acquire the geographical knowledge necessary for fixing a definite frontier to the north. The strength available was quite insufficient to allow of the explorations being pushed forward by force, and for the maintenance, in a hostile country, of the long lines of communication which the explorations rendered necessary.

In order, therefore, that these could be pushed far afield, it was necessary that friendly relations should first be cultivated with the tribes nearer at hand, through or close to whose villages an advance would have to be made. Of these, the Panggi tribe, by its geographical situation, became the most important. The line of an advance to the north, whether by the left bank of the Dihang, or by the Yamne valley, led either through, or was closely flanked by, the territory occupied by this tribe, and the first step, therefore, in the explorations was the assurance of a friendly attitude on its part.

Panggi Mission.

On the 26th December, therefore, a friendly mission under the command of Colonel D. C. F. Macintyre, crossing the Dihang below Rotung, started towards the Panggi country. Eight days' rations for the mission were carried by friendly Abors, who, both men and women, in spite of the delay caused by their objection to early rising, proved to be excellent carriers.

In Political charge	Colonel D. C. F. Macintyre.	
Intelligence officer and Commanding escort.	Major A. B. Lindsay ...	1-2nd Gurkhas.
Survey officer ...	Lieutenant Oakes, R.E.	
Medical officer ...	Lieutenant Macdonald, I.M.S.	
Escort	1 Gurkha officer	1-2nd Gurkhas.
	1 Bugler	1-2nd Gurkhas.
	48 Rifles	1-2nd Gurkhas.
	10 Rifles	32nd Pioneers.
Survey ...	1 Jemadar, 9 Khalassis.	
Followers ...	1 Miri Interpreter.	
	1 Nepalese servant.	
	3 Public followers.	
	4 Private followers.	
	60 Naga carriers.	

Passing through Pongging, the party reached the Yamne valley at Jaru on the 28th, and Sibbum on the 29th. Here a halt of two days was made. On the 31st the party moved on Shomshing and arrived at Peram (Geku) on the following day.

Though at first the villagers were suspicious, they were soon put at their ease and proved most friendly, offering every assistance in their power, by bringing supplies and clearing camping grounds. The services of the medical officer were in great request and proved a strong factor in establishing confidence.

At Peram, although the reception was most cordial, enquiries as to the road forward received evasive answers. The villagers no doubt feared that the party might push on to the Minyong-Padam village of Komkar. On an assurance being given, however, that the party had no intention of doing so, the villagers became much more communicative and volunteered a great deal of information, although they still appeared somewhat suspicious.

The country in this neighbourhood is jungle-covered, but to a much lesser degree than in the neighbourhood of Rotung, and the spurs run down to the river less steeply and are more cultivated.

On the afternoon of the 2nd January, Colonel Macintyre held a durbar which was attended by all the influential men of the tribe. It had been a long standing grievance of this tribe that they had always been prevented, by the tyranny of the Padam and Minyong, from trading with the plains. They were informed that, in future, trade with the plains would be free to all, at which they showed themselves most delighted. The intentions of Government with regard to the future control of the tribes were also explained to them and the meeting broke up in the most friendly spirit.

In the meantime the survey also had had a most successful trip and had been able to fix the course of the Dihang for a considerable distance to the north, as well as the positions of many of the higher villages.

On the 3rd of January, the party started on its return journey, and reached Rotung on the 7th. During an absence of 12 days friendly relations had been cultivated with the whole of the Panggi tribe, while a large tract of previously unknown country had been surveyed.

Mission to Damro.

It will be remembered that the expedition of 1894 had been directed against Damro and had been obliged to turn back when in sight of that village. Both for the maintenance of our prestige, and for the purpose of acquiring information, it was very necessary that this village should be visited, and it was hoped that the mission would be received in a friendly spirit and not be compelled to make its way by force. While the force was at Renging, the Damro headmen had come in and promised that they would render every assistance, and would welcome a party visiting their village. On the 20th January, a column, strength as below, concentrated at Janakmukh and formed a camp on the left bank of the Dihang, opposite the post, with a view to carrying out this important mission.

The column was met, on the 21st, by the headmen of the villages to be visited, and made a start on the 22nd. The men of these parts seemed to be a particularly fine lot, superior in health and physique to the rest of the Abors. The party reached Bordak, the scene of the massacre in 1894, the same evening, and camped on the left bank of the stream From Abor accounts the road ahead was very bad, but this, as usual, proved to be an exaggeration.

Officer Commanding	Colonel D. C. F. Macintyre.
Intelligence Officer	Major A. B. Lindsay, 1-2nd Gurkha Rifles.
O. C. Escort	Major Sweet, 1-2nd Gurkha Rifles.
Survey Officer	Lieutenant Oakes, Royal Engineers.
Medical Officer	Lieutenant Macdonald, Indian Medical Service.
Escort	50 Rifles, 1-2nd Gurkhas.
	10 Rifles, 32nd Pioneers.
	10 Rifles, Lakhimpur Military Police.
Carriers	80 Nagas.
	80 Nepalese.
Followers	10
Survey Party	11 Men.

The whole carried rations for 10 days, two of which were carried on the person.

Passing through Silli, Dukku was reached on the 25th, all the villages visited *en route* proving exceedingly friendly and richer than is the rule in this country. They also showed a preference for money rather than for barter, the result of the freedom of their trade with the plains.

Beyond Dukku the precipitous gorge of the Yamne was entered and, the route by this gorge being extremely difficult, often consisting merely of footholds cut out of the face of the precipice, it was decided to leave it and follow another path leading to the Pasi group of villages. This group includes Sibbuk, Bina and Sitkor. The route followed proved to be easy, but would have been difficult to force in the face of opposition.

From the village of Sibbuk a magnificent view of the Yamne valley presented itself, the country being quite different to what had been expected. It consisted of a wide amphitheatre entirely *jhumed*, the tops of the hills only being covered with jungle, with the villages of the Pasi group on one side and those of Damro or Padam on the other. The route into this settled valley might be rendered very difficult in the event of hostilities, but it afterwards transpired that a much easier one probably led into it from the direction of Membu. The Abors were most reticent on the subject from fear of giving away information in case of future trouble.

On the 26th, a halt was made at Sibbuk to rest the coolies and allow of survey work, and, next day, the party marched by an easy road to Damro. The reception met with at these villages was most friendly, though the people of Damro were inclined to be suspicious until our intentions were fully explained. The inhabitants of Damro appear to be the ruling element in this district and are apparently treated with the greatest deference by the other villages.

Here the party halted until the 3rd February, while a survey party was sent to the top of the highest hill in the neighbourhood which is known as Kallang. Bad weather interfered with the work but the valley was mapped as far as the snow-covered range to the north. A party under Major Lindsay also reconnoitred a fairly good track leading into the Mishmi country, by which the Abors trade freely with the Mishmis, from whom a great many of their commodities are purchased. The Padam Abors appear to have no direct communications with Tibet, although they have a good many articles of Tibetan manufacture, including a few guns,

Connection and trade with Tibet

for which, however, they have no ammunition. It appears that the hills to the north are, in their opinion, uninhabitable wastes of snow and ice, and that they have no knowledge of any people living beyond them. All their Tibetan articles appear to be purchased from the Mishmis.

Milang.

The people of Damro maintained a great deal of mystery with regard to the Milang group of villages further north in the Yamne valley. The headmen of these villages were sent for, but the party were informed that they had gone to the plains to trade. It was protested, also, that the road to Milang was very bad, and every possible obstacle was thrown in the way of an advance to that place. The party, however, moved there on the 3rd February, met one of the headmen who was said to be in the plains, and found the road easy. It is difficult to imagine why so much secrecy was observed as to this village. Possibly it may be a slave colony of Damro, and the Damro people, having already denied the possession of slaves, feared discovery. A curious point about the Milang group of villages is that the language there spoken is different to that of the other tribes. It is hard to account for this, as they could give no information pointing to a separate origin.

On the other side of the river is the Simong village of Dalbuing. An attempt was made to reach this, but the road was bad, the distance greater than was expected, and the trip had to be abandoned.

By this time the objects of the expedition had been fulfilled, so, the valley having been surveyed, the position of the snowy range to the north determined, and friendly relations with the tribes established, it was decided to return.

Return of mission.

On the 5th February, the party left Milang and reached Damro in the evening. Next day the party took leave of the Damro people, who seemed really sorry at their departure, and, marching *viâ* Pongging, reached Rotung on the 10th. News was received on the march which corroborated the hostile intentions of the Simong people towards the Dihang exploration and it was reported that envoys had been received by the Panggi tribe asking them to co-operate with Simong in hostile measures. This was refused, doubtless owing to the exposed position of the Panggi villages in the event of hostilities.

The Damro mission was well and thoroughly carried out and had the result of establishing excellent relations with the whole of the Padam tribe. Unfortunately, bad weather prevented the extent of survey work which might have been expected, considering the distance covered and the trouble taken.

Dihang exploration.

Of the objects of the expedition, perhaps the most important was the exploration of the northern frontier between Indian and Tibetan territory. The intention was to take advantage of this exploration to settle once and for all the identity of the Tsang-po and the Dihang, while the falls of Pemakoi were, if possible, to be visited.

The General Officer Commanding considered that the political situation rendered these explorations undesirable, for he feared that an advance north of Riga would have to make its way by force; that this would lead to unfriendliness; and would be liable to drive the tribes into the arms of Tibet. It must be remembered, too, that the northern tribes were quite innocent of any collusion in Mr. Williamson's murder, and it was not, at present, necessary to inflict any punishment on them, while, if they showed themselves openly hostile to the advance of exploration parties, it might become necessary to undertake punitive measures against them. He, therefore, explained these objections to Government, and contented himself, until an answer should be received, with despatching a friendly mission up the Dihang as far as Riga.

From the military point of view, there was little reason why the exploration should not have been pushed forward as soon as Kebang had fallen and the resistance of the tribes had been finally crushed. If, owing to the uncertainty of the attitude of the tribes, it was still considered impolitic to send out an exploration party far to the north, an advanced depôt might have been established towards Geku, and preparations could have been made for an advance as soon as the situation became clearer. This would have been a great gain, for a large part of the delay in carrying out the exploration was due to the necessity of forming this depôt as the exploration party advanced. Every day, as the spring progressed, the weather grew more uncertain and less suited for exploration and survey alike. Had a start been made as soon as Kebang fell, not even the slow rate at which an advance was finally made, could have prevented the exploration party from reaching the confines of Tibet.

Start of the exploration.

On the 27th December, the party finally set out on its friendly mission towards Riga and the intermediate villages. Pang-in was reached and the party halted there in the hopes that the headmen of Yekshing would come in.

Attitude of Yekshing.

The latter, however, were distrustful of our motives, and refused to have any dealings with the party. The political officer, therefore, fearing a collision, decided to cross over to Komsing, on the left bank of the river, where a friendly reception was certain. News of this decision, fortunately, was sent to the General Officer Commanding, who decided that it would be very impolitic and involve a great loss of prestige to allow our force to be turned aside by a small village such as Yekshing; such lack of decision on our part would only be attributed by the Abors to fear. He, therefore, instructed Mr. Bentinck to visit the village. The wisdom of this movement was soon apparent, for, when the party arrived in the vicinity of the village, the headmen came in and the people proved themselves to be quite friendly. The party then returned to Pang-in, and, crossing the Dihang on the following day, reached Komsing on the 1st of January, and camped near the village.

Trade with plains.

Here again the inhabitants proved friendly and brought in various presents. All these villages expressed their pleasure when they were informed that they were free to trade with the plains, for, in the past, they had only been allowed to do so with the grudging permission of Kebang.

Tyranny of Kebang.

It was very curious to observe how Kebang, neither a large nor particularly powerful village, seemed to have tyrannised over its neighbours, even debarring Riga, a much larger village, from access to the plains.

On the following day the party, with the assistance of various Abors who carried the extra loads, reached Riu. Here they remained three days and then moved on to Geku, camping in the vicinity of the village. This had been visited by the Panggi mission some days previously and friendly relations had already been established.

Leisurely advance.

On the 10th of January, these leisurely movements were continued, the party marching off to cross the river towards Riga. The crossing was not hurried in any way, and operations were abandoned whenever it rained, with the result that the crossing was not completed until the 15th. It will be noticed that, in 21 days, the party had moved some 30 odd miles and this through a region where the inhabitants were friendly and which for the Abor country was distinctly easy. This slowness of movement naturally greatly accentuated the ration difficulty. Next day, Mr. Bentinck visited Riga, which consisted of some 250 or 300 houses. The villagers complained that they were very much overcrowded and begged to be allowed to send a colony to the unoccupied ground in the neighbourhood of Rotung which, having been conquered by us, they considered to be at our disposal. This would have made their free access to the plains a certainty, and finally liberated them from the tyranny of Kebang.

Orders for acceleration.

While these movements were in progress, the General Officer Commanding received orders from headquarters to push on the exploration of the Dihang in accordance with the instructions issued at the beginning of the campaign. Mr. Bentinck was accordingly advised of this and directed to push on up the river, while supplies were sent up to him with that object. It was necessary for his party to cross the river, for it was obviously unsound to make a long advance to the north with the difficult crossing of the Dihang athwart the lines of communication.

Arrangements for the exploration.

The plan to be adopted was as follows. Mr. Bentinck was to be in supreme charge of the exploration, while the senior military officer, Captain Coleridge, assumed the responsibility on all military matters. It was arranged that this officer, with the escort and rations, should join Mr. Bentinck on the left bank and form an advanced base at Simong. Mr. Bentinck's party, therefore, crossed the river.

Advanced base at Simong.

Arrangements were now made that Captain Coleridge and Mr. Bentinck should march to Komkar with 150 carriers and 100 rifles, and a party of 50 rifles and 200 carriers should return to Komsing for more rations, while Captain Giffard's party, who were still on the right bank with carriers and escort, should cross to the left bank.

The advanced party marched on the 11th, and, passing through Komkar, reached a spot 2½ miles south of Simong on the following day. Here they were met by the headmen of

Simong, who appeared to be well disposed. On the 20th the village was visited and the officers of the party were well received, although it was obvious that the villagers were eager to dissuade them from a further advance. The remainder of the rations were brought up on the 22nd, and it was arranged that a party consisting of Mr. Bentinck, 4 British officers, 75 riflemen and 130 carriers should leave, on the next day, for the north, rationed up to the 31st. The remainder were to stay at Simong on ½ rations, ready to push up further supplies as they arrived

The salt, which had been brought up as an article of barter, was not acceptable to the inhabitants, who could not be induced to accept it in exchange for rice. This resulted in a shortage of rations.

Attitude of Simong.

A start was made at 8 A M., on the following day. On arrival in the village, the inhabitants proved to be in a state of great excitement and insisted that the party should stop and accept their hospitality. The crowd was great, and, when the column attempted to push their way forward, there was a good deal of jostling and a square had to be formed. Mr. Bentinck, afraid of a collision, decided to return. He refused the proferred hospitality and gave the headmen till the next day to decide whether they would make way, or whether it would be necessary to appeal to force.

In the evening, the headmen came to camp, very repentant, and promised that there would be no difficulty about a passage through the village on the following day. The inhabitants do not seem to have been actively hostile, and their action, apparently, was merely an attempt to keep up the appearance that we were being allowed to pass through the village only on sufferance. Nevertheless, the situation was trying and a conflict was only averted by the forbearance and good temper of officers and men under very difficult circumstances. Had a collision occurred, exploration to the north would have been very much delayed, if not altogether prevented, for the force at our disposal was quite insufficient to make its way by force through a hostile country at such a distance from its supports.

Next day, the party passed through the village without any difficulty and halted on the Shimar stream, halfway to Gette. The following morning, that village was reached, and, as it was apparent that a passage through it might be accompanied by a repetition of the incidents in Simong, it was decided to circumvent the village and camp beyond it. In the evening, the headmen came in and agreed to accompany the party as far as Puging. Two Tibetans were met in the village. The party marched again on the following day and, camping for the night on the Sin river, reached Puging on the 26th, where the inhabitants proved quite friendly.

On the 27th, a convoy, with three more days rations, arrived at Puging. The exploration party marched over the difficult Kitkor Pass on the following day and reached the Sissi river after a very steep and difficult descent. The Naga carriers were, by this time, very weary, and extreme measures had to be taken to induce them to advance.

Supply and Transport Difficulties.

On the 29th, the party marched up the right bank to Rikor. The Dihang here flows through a narrow gorge, not more than 80 yards wide, above which are miles of rapids. The path crosses two feeders *en route*, one of which, the Siring, is a large stream, over which there is an old cane bridge, too unstable for use. On reaching Paling, next day, it was discovered that the river, instead of turning to the west, as was expected, made a sudden turn to the north east. Information was also received that a large tributary, the Sigon (Sira Pateng) joins the Dihang from the west near Singging.

Singging.

The latter village was reached, on the 31st, after severe ascents and descents, and proved to be a small and miserably poor collection of some 30 houses, the inhabitants of which were well disposed.

Return to Simong.

On the 3rd February, the party started on their return journey and reached Rikor on the following day. Here, news was received of rations left by Captain Coleridge's party near Paling, and the carriers had to be sent back for them. Three days later, the party passed through Gette, and, on reaching the Shimar camp, Captain Coleridge was met bringing up another 12 days' rations. On the following day the united parties marched back to Simong and the next few days were spent in survey work round that village.

Difficulties of Line of Communication and Supply.

While the exploration was in progress up the Dihang, considerable anxiety had been caused by the attitude of the villages of Geku and Simong, and these villages were obviously only prevented from becoming openly hostile by a strong show of force. The garrisons left there had, therefore, to be increased and, on the 2nd February, the disposition of the forces north of Yembung was as follows:—

Exploration party ...	5 British officers. 70 rifles, 8th Gurkhas. 131 carriers. 22 followers.
Convoy between Simong and Exploration party	1 British officer. 60 rifles, 8th Gurkhas. 90 carriers.
Simong, support to above... convoy	70 Rifles, 8th Gurkhas.
Geku to Simong ...	1 British officer. 40 rifles, 8th Gurkhas. 130 carriers.

(The above subsisted on the direct convoy system)

Geku, support to Simong...	100 rifles. 68 carriers.
Riu	50 rifles. 143 carriers.
Komsing	50 rifles. 160 carriers.
Yembung	80 carriers.

(Up to Geku supplies were forwarded by the staging system.)

The organisation, therefore, of a line of communication to carry rations and give the necessary support to an exploration party of 70 rifles, demanded a force of no less than 370 rifles and some 800 carriers. It was quite impossible to live on the country and, at the same time, maintain friendly relations with the inhabitants, and, had these been hostile, it is hard to see how the exploration could have been attempted at all with the force then available in the country. It had been expected that the country north of Komkar would be sparsely populated, and it was hoped that only small escorts would be required, but it afterwards transpired that this was the most densely populated part of the whole country traversed, and, hence, the escorts had to be largely increased in order to overawe the large villages on the lines of communication. On the 23rd, it was decided to abandon any further exploration to the north on account of possible resentment by the inhabitants to a further advance, moreover, the season was late, the weather bad, and the Naga carriers were growing more and more discontented and worn out.

Exploration abandoned.

The interval was in no way wasted, however, for the time was spent in survey work, and every opportunity was taken to improve our relations with the tribesmen.

Meeting of Gams.

On the 25th, a large gathering, consisting of the headmen of Riu, Simong, Damro, Komkar and several Panggi villages, was called together and the intentions of the Government were fully explained. It was made clear that all would be free to trade at Rotung, and that no tribe or village must stand in the way of another; that when tribes or villages had a dispute amongst themselves they were not to fight it out, but to bring it to the British for settlement; that we did not want to interfere with matters which were usually settled at their village councils; and that we did not want their land nor their villages, but that they could continue to hold the territory that they now occupied.

Apparently, the headmen were well satisfied and departed on friendly terms with us and each other. They were obviously pleased with the idea of a general peace maker among them, for, although the fighting was seldom severe nor were the losses heavy, their wars dragged on, sometimes for years, without a settlement, and interfered greatly both with trade and agriculture.

Withdrawal of troops from the left bank.

By the 25th February, the Government had decided that further exploration up the Dihang was not feasible that year, so all troops on the left bank were withdrawn as soon as the survey in the neighbourhood of Simong was completed. The troops in the latter place were withdrawn to Geku, whence 100 rifles and 200 carriers were crossed over the river to Arte hill, some five miles west of Riga, for survey work in that direction. In order to ease the strain on the carrying power of the force, the 2nd Gurkhas were concentrated at Kobo with a view to their withdrawal to their peace station. They left Kobo on the 14th March.

The Naga carriers had become very discontented as they had already been retained beyond the limits of the period for which they had been originally enlisted. They were, therefore, replaced by newly raised corps of Gurkhalis and sent to their homes. Unfortunately, the strength of the Gurkhalis was much reduced by an attack of mumps.

By the 6th of March, all the troops of the left bank had been withdrawn and lines of communications established up the right bank.

Shimang and Siyom Explorations.

On the 23rd February, a party had been sent out, under the command of Captain Molesworth, to explore the Shimang and Siyom rivers, but, when it appeared desirable to concentrate all the strength of the expedition on a further advance up the Dihang, this party had to be withdrawn before useful results could be obtained.

Strength, including convoys afterwards received.—
3 British officers.
1 Political officer.
3 Gurkha officers.
71 rifles.
2 hospital staff.
11 survey followers.
8 followers.
170 carriers.

When, however, the Dihang exploration had finally been abandoned, this party, considerably strengthened, was again sent out and reached Dosing on the 28th. Considerable delay was caused on the way by the fact that the villagers had destroyed the road which the party had made on its previous visit. There was also a certain amount of passive resistance in the villages which was only overcome by the display of considerable firmness on the part of the officer in command of the party.

On the 26th of March, Pareng was reached and the party was well received. From here, an advance was made up the left bank of the Shimang to near Yingku. The latter village gave no assistance whatever and adopted a policy of passive resistance. When an advance was made, next day, the party, after having marched several miles, discovered that they were being led up a wrong road. On their return from this abortive march, they found that the bridge, which they had erected over the river, had been destroyed, and the old Abor bridge so weakened that, when the first man attempted to cross it, he was precipitated into the river below, but, fortunately, was rescued without having sustained any damage. On account of this, twelve men were taken as hostages from the village and a fine was imposed. The village was informed that the prisoners would not be set free until the fine was paid in full.

Next day, the correct path was found and the force advanced, passing through Yibuk village *en route*. The people of this village proved to be very friendly and afforded great assistance throughout. The column camped in the evening near the river on the road to the Ngurrung pass.

The ration problem was now, as usual, making itself felt, as several bags had been spoilt by getting soaked during the crossing of the river. The men were, therefore, put on $\frac{3}{4}$ rations.

While the party was encamped here the fine imposed upon Yingku was brought in and the hostages were released.

From here, it was intended to climb a high hill, known as Moling, from which it was hoped that good survey work could be done. This ascent was accomplished after the greatest difficulty, the country traversed being of the most difficult description. The summit was finally reached on the 15th March but, although the survey party remained in position for three days, but poor results were achieved owing to the thick mists. The top of the hill was, moreover, under some 10 feet of snow, making the work of clearing very hard for the carriers. The party returned to Yembung on the 24th March. The only results obtained by this exploration was the mapping of the Shimang river and its immediate vicinity.

In the meantime, Mr. Bentinck's party, having returned from their abortive exploration of the Dihang, crossed from Riga over the Arte hill, from which good survey work was done, and then proceeded into and across the Shimang valley to Yibuk. From here they crossed the divide between the Shimang and Siyom and entered the Siyom valley at Rangku. It was hoped to get in touch with the Bori tribe in this direction but this was not possible as the Boris were too far to the north. The party, however, got into communication with some of the Galongs living on the right bank of the Siyom.

Withdrawal of the force.

On the 26th March, orders were received for the force to retire to Rotung and concentrate as many men as possible at Kobo with a view to the break up of the force. Mr. Bentinck's force, accordingly, returned from Arte hill on the 28th, and, on the following day, the troops began to move down to the base, headquarters reaching Pasighat on the 1st April.

During a halt here six prisoners were tried who were accused of taking a leading part in Mr. Williamson's murder. Five were found guilty and one was acquitted.

Trial of the murderers.

Government had not yet decided on the question of the establishment of a post at Rotung. In the meantime, therefore, 201 military police were left at Rotung and 100 at Balek, each of these posts being supplied with 9 months' rations. In order to keep up communication with Rotung, and also to bring away these supplies if the posts were abandoned, 325 rifles of the 1-8th Gurkhas, 2 sections Field Ambulance, 1 Carrier Corps and 1 Mule Corps were retained, while the remaining units of the force were despatched to their peace stations.

On the 6th May, orders were received to abandon Rotung, while retaining the posts at Pasighat and Kobo. The lines of communication to the former place were accordingly withdrawn, and the demobilisation of the force was completed by the 21st May.

Rotung abandoned.

Demobilisation.

CHAPTER IX.

RESULTS OF THE EXPEDITION.

Political results.

The expedition resulted in the punishment of all the hostile villages and the exaction of punishment for Mr. Williamson's murder. All the men who had taken a leading part in this were tried and punished and practically all the looted property was restored. The Minyong tribe was crushed and its villages brought to submission, while the power of Kebang, which for years had terrorised its neighbours, was finally broken. This village lost a large number of its fighting men, and its reputation was so shattered that it will probably take years to recover.

There is little doubt that, at the beginning of the expedition, many of the tribes were waiting to see which side was the stronger, and, had we suffered a serious check early in the operations, we should have had to encounter much more general hostility, and would have found ourselves actively opposed by tribes who, after the fall of Kebang, were most profuse in their protestations of friendship.

The disgrace and memory of our former defeat was wiped out and the tribes were shown that, while resistance to the British was useless, we could with ease visit any part of their country. The tribes who had not proved themselves openly hostile, were visited by friendly missions, which behaved with great judgment and tact, proving to the people that, while the hand of the British was heavy in dealing with aggression or avenging insult, nothing was to be feared by the well-behaved.

Many of the weaker tribes had been quite debarred from visiting the plains in order to trade, and had, in general, been tyrannised over by their more powerful neighbours. The advent of the British and the messages they conveyed made clear to all that weak and strong alike would be allowed to visit the plains and that no tribe was in future to be prevented from doing so by another, while our ability to enforce this could no longer be questioned.

Future policy.

It was announced to all the tribes that, while we had no intention of taking over their country, they must look to us in future as the supreme power. Disputes, which had formerly been settled by long drawn out wars, would, in future, be decided by us, but, on the other hand, we had no intention of interfering in matters of custom and the like which were usually settled by the village councils.

Excellent relations had been established with all the tribes visited by us, with the possible exception of Simong whose attitude will have to be closely watched in the future. This was due, not only to fear of our armed forces, but to the tact and friendliness displayed by the officers in charge of our various missions and to the good behaviour and excellent discipline of the men who escorted them.

Relations with the tribes.

A very great factor in the establishing of a healthy respect for the British was the mule-road which traversed the country from Kobo to Yembung. Apart from the military value of this engineering work, the speed and skill with which it was constructed appeared almost superhuman to the savage tribesmen and created a deep impression on them.

Effect of mule-road.

The geographical results of the expedition, although not as full as had been expected, owing to the climate and physical difficulties of the country, were still of great value. Practically the whole of the country was surveyed accurately as far as Lat. 28° 40′ N. The whole of the valley of the Yamne was surveyed up to the snow ranges; the Shimang river was mapped throughout its entire length; the course of the Siyom was roughly traced; and the valley of the Dihang was followed as far north as Singging, Lat. 28° 52′ (approx.), a point within 25 or 30 miles of the most northern Abor village. The identity of the Dihang with the Tsang-po, though not absolutely proved, was at any rate practically established, and there is little doubt that part of the district traversed by Kinthup in his famous exploration from the north, was visited.

Geographical results.

Question of Dihang and Tsang-po.

Although it was not possible to determine accurately the natural frontier between the Abor country and Tibet, a rough idea of its nature and position was obtained. Points on the great snow range to the north were definitely fixed and a way was paved for an accurate determination of the boundary in the future while the chances of Chinese aggression in this region were greatly reduced.

Northern Frontier.

Although there was little actual fighting, the successful conclusion of the military operations was no small achievement. The popular imagination likes to be fed with accounts of battles and daring, but it is not in these that the whole test of an army lies. The continual struggle with natural difficulties and with hardship and privation without the loss of a cheerful discipline, and the self-control required when dealing with ignorant and arrogant savages, represent a very high standard of military efficiency.

APPENDICES.

APPENDIX I.

Orders for the organization of the Abor Expeditionary Force, by the Chief of the General Staff.

1. The object of this scheme is to provide a force for operations against the Abors. **Object.**

2. The Force will be composed of the units detailed in these orders and will be mobilized and concentrated in accordance with the instructions contained herein. **Order to mobilize and concentrate.**

3. Except where otherwise provided for hereinafter, all arrangements mentioned in these orders will be made under the direction of the General Officer Commanding, 8th (Lucknow) Division, in direct communication with all concerned. **Responsibility for execution of the orders.**

4. The Commander of the Force will have full political control, assisted by such political officers as may be necessary, who will be appointed by the Foreign Department. **Political.**

5. (*a*) The composition of the Force is given in Appendix I (*a*). **Composition of the Force.**

(*b*) The Assam Government will place 4 companies of Military Police at the disposal of the Commander of the Force, for subsidiary operations.

6. The details of the commands and staffs are given in Appendix I (*b*). With reference to F. S. Regulations, Part II, Section 5 (1), the officers required will be appointed by the Military Secretary to His Excellency the Commander-in-Chief. **Headquarters.**

7. The allotment of field staff offices for the Force is given in Apppendix I (*c*). These will be despatched by the officers in charge of them to the places of assembly detailed in Appendix I (*b*). **Field Staff offices.**

8. The base of operations will be at Kobo, at which place the Force will concentrate. An advanced base will be formed at Pasighat. **Base.**

9. (*a*) Units of the Force will move on field service scale of establishments and equipment. The approximate strength of the Force is given in Appendix I (*d*). **Strengths, establishments and Depôts.**

(*b*) The complement of British officers of all units will be made up under the orders of Divisional Commanders from units stationed within their commands, or from linked battalions in communication with the General Officers Commanding Divisions concerned. Officers on privilege leave out of India will not be recalled.

(*c*) Deficiencies in medical personnel will be completed under the orders of the Principal Medical Officer in India.

(*d*) Depôts of Indian Infantry will be on scale B.

Departmental establishment. 10. Any conservancy establishment required in excess of those authorized by regulations will be arranged for under the orders of the Inspector of Communications.

Intelligence. 11. The Commander of the Force will engage locally such men as are required for intelligence duties.

Clothing and equipment. 12. (*a*) Clothing will be on summer scale, except for transport coolies. Additional articles of clothing to complete to winter scale will be sent in bulk to the base, but will not be distributed to units until the necessity for it arises. Followers will be equipped with boots instead of shoes.

(*b*) Tents will be taken by units to the base.

*(*c*) Deficiencies in maxim guns will be made up from units in the division.

Changes in establishment and equipment. 13. The Commander of the Force will make such changes or reduction in the authorized field service scale of equipment, stores, baggage, followers, &c., as may be considered necessary for the effective operations of the Force and for its economical working.

Special equipment. 14. (*a*) The special equipment given in Appendix I(*e*) will be provided by the departments of supply concerned.

(*b*) Any further special equipment required will be ordered by the Commander of the Force.

Ordnance. 15. (*a*) The Director-General of Ordnance will arrange to supply the two 7-pr. (150 lbs.) R. M. L. guns to the Officer Commanding, 1st Battalion, 8th Gurkha Rifles, together with 200 rounds of ammunition per gun and the necessary stores.

(*b*) The full scale of Small Arms Ammunition per rifle laid down in F. S. Regulations, India, Appendix XII, will be taken for the Force.

(*c*) All ammunition will be packed in special boxes, the gross weight of each of which is not to exceed 50 lbs.

(*d*) The Director-General of Ordnance will arrange for the formation of a small ordnance base depôt.

(*e*) The Director-General of Ordnance will arrange for a reserve of Engineer stores which will be placed in charge of the Officer Commanding, Field Company, Sappers and Miners.

Books, maps and stationery. 16. (*a*) The books and maps detailed in Appendix I (*f*), packed separately for each unit, and the necessary ciphers, will be despatched by the General Staff at Army Headquarters to the Inspector of Communications, who will distribute them to units.

(*b*) Such stationery and accessories as may be required will be provided by the Controller of Printing, Stamps and Stationery, on requisition by the Inspector of Communications.

---

* Two maxim guns were supplied from 7th Division.

17. (*a*) The Section Indian Field Ambulance will be equipped with 10 dandies and 15 slung hammocks instead of tongas. **Medical.**

(*b*) The Sections Indian Stationary Hospital required for the base and advanced base will not take their tongas with them, and will have only 1 dandy and 6 bearers each.

(*c*) In addition to those taken into the field by units, a reserve of 50 field stretchers, and 25 riding saddles will be prepared and stocked at the base under the orders of the Quartermaster-General in India, and a reserve of 35 slung hammocks under the orders of the Director-General of Ordnance.

(*d*) Such additional medical equipment or establishment as may be required will be supplied under the orders of the Principal Medical Officer in India.

(*e*) The Regimental Hospital at Dibrugarh will be utilized as a General Hospital.

(*f*) All medical stores, whether with fighting units or hospitals, must be repacked so as to form loads of not more than 50 lbs.*

18. The special signalling unit will be detailed by the Chief of the General Staff at Army Headquarters, from one of the Northern Army Signalling Companies. **Signalling.**

19. The Surveyor-General will arrange for such survey detachments as may be necessary. **Survey.**

20. (*a*) In addition to the supplies which accompany troops on regimental transport and in supply column, one month's supplies for the whole force will be placed and maintained at Kobo, and one month's supplies at Pasighat for the troops there and beyond it under the orders of the Quartermaster-General in India. **Supply.**

(*b*) The Quartermaster-General in India will arrange for the formation of the Supply units.

(*c*) All supplies must be packed in water-proof bags, and the weight of each package must not exceed 50 lbs.*

(*d*) The special scale of rations for transport coolies is given in an Appendix.

21. (*a*) The Force will be equipped with all cooly transport, the coolies being either Nagas, Manipuris, Gurkhas or Khasias. All loads for coolies will be made up into packages not exceeding 50 lbs.* But the equipment mules of the Pioneer Battalion, and of the Field Company, Sappers and Miners, will be completed at their mobilization station, and will accompany their respective units to the base. **Transport.**

* * * * * *

* **Afterwards altered to 60 lbs.**

(*d*) All transport required for the equipment and maintenance of the force, whether cooly, animal or river transport, will be arranged for by the Quartermaster-General in India in communication with all concerned.

(*e*) When the roads beyond Pasighat have been made fit for mules, such pack mules as may be required to supplement or replace cooly transport will be arranged for by the Quartermaster-General in India.

(*f*) The 40 coolies for carrying the 7-pr. guns, will be entertained by the Officer Commanding, 1st Battalion, 8th Gurkha Rifles.

Camps, etc. 22. The General Officers Commanding concerned will be responsible for such camps, detraining facilities and communications in their commands as may be required.

Telegraphs. 23. (*a*) Staff and Departmental officers of the Force, and other officers concerned with its maintenance and equipment in the field, who are authorized by the Commanders of the Force or Divisions, will send telegrams on O. H. M. S. telegram forms from all telegraph offices.

(*b*) General Officer Commanding will inform the Director-General of Telegraphs of the officers who are empowered to use the O. H. M. S. telegram forms and of their headquarters.

(*c*) The Director-General of Telegraphs will arrange for the extension of the telegraph line to Pasighat, for strengthening such existing telegraph offices, and for the further extension of such existing lines as may be required by the Commander of the Force.

Post offices 24. The Director-General of the Post Office will arrange for a 2nd class field post office for the force, and will take such steps as he may consider necessary to strengthen existing, or to establish additional post offices.

Concentrations. 25. The Force will concentrate in accordance with orders which will be issued to all concerned by the Quartermaster-General in India.

Concessions and privileges. 26. (*a*) Troops and followers will be considered to be on field service for all concessions and privileges from the date of arrival at Kobo. But such concessions as are only admissible from or between certain dates will have effect from those dates.

(*b*) Supply and Transport establishments will receive universal rates of pay, and 50 per cent *batta*.

Accounts. 27. (*a*) All accounts, which will be audited on the Field Service system, will be rendered to the Controller of Military Accounts, Eastern Circle, Lucknow, who will arrange for financing the Force.

(*b*) All vouchers, railway warrants, telegrams, etc., in connection with the operations will be enfaced "Abor Expeditionary Force 19—." All such telegrams, unless written on O. H. M. S. forms by officers duly authorized to use them, must be stamped.

APPENDIX I (*a*).

Composition of Force.

Station.	Units allotted.	REMARKS.
To be formed ...	Force headquarters	
Lahore Cantonment ...	32nd Sikh Pioneers .. ... *	
Shillong	1st Battalion, 8th Gurkha Rifles	To supply gun detachments for two 7-pr. (150 lbs.) R. M. L. guns.
Roorkee	No. 1 Field Company, 1st Sappers and Miners.	
To be detailed ...	One (Indian) Special Signalling unit.	
Calcutta	Section A, No. 168, Indian Field Ambulance.	
To be formed ...	Supply Column.	
	Reserve.	
Dehra Dun ...	1st Battalion, 2nd Gurkha Rifles	* Not to move from Dehra Dun unless ordered later.
	BASE AND LINE OF COMMUNICATIONS.	
	I.—*Defence.*	
To be formed ...	Headquarters.	
	Line of Communications Defence troops to be detailed by the Commander of the Force.	
	II.—*Administration.*	
To be formed ...	Headquarters.	
To be formed ...	Ordnance Base Depôt.	
Calcutta	Sections B, and C, No. 168, Indian Stationary Hospital.	
To be formed ...	Advanced and Base Supply Depôts.	

* This Battalion was eventually moved up to Kobo, half in October, to replace Military Police proceeding on the Miri and Mishmi Missions, and half later as reserve.

APPENDIX I (*b*).

Staff of the Force.

Appointment.	Allotment.
FORCE HEADQUARTERS. (*To assemble at Kobo.*)	
Commander ...	... General Officer Commanding, Assam Brigade, (Major-General H. Bower C.B.).
Orderly Officer ...	... From the Force (Captain L. S. H. Smithers, 17th Infantry).
Staff—General Staff Officer, 2nd grade.	(Major C. A. R. Hutchinson, 41st Dogras, Brigade Major, Assam Brigade).
Field Intelligence Officer ...	(Captain W. B. Hore, 120th Infantry.)
Signalling Officer ...	From the Special Signalling unit (Lieutenant T. H. Knight, R. A., Commmanding Brigade Section, 31st Divisional Signal Company).
Assistant Director of Medical Services.	Senior Medical Officer with the Force (Major J. Davidson, I. M. S.)
Assistant Director of Supplies and Transport.	(Major E. G. Vaughan, Supply and Transport Corps.)
BASE AND LINE OF COMMUNICATIONS. (*To assemble at Kobo.*)	
I.—DEFENCE.	
Commandant, Line of Communication Defences.	The Senior Combatant Officer on the Line of Communications.
II.—ADMINISTRATION.	
Administrative Commandant Base, and Inspector of Communications.	(Colonel D. C. F. Macintyre, Indian Army.)
Deputy Assistant Director of Medical Services.	From the Line of Communication Hospitals.
Assistant Director of Works...	From the Field Company, Sappers and Miners (Captain E. C. Tylden-Patterson, R.E.).
Base Supply and Transport Officer.	(Major H. M. M. Brooke, Supply and Transport Corps.)

APPENDIX I (*c*).

Allotment of Field Staff Offices.

Unit.	Office allotted.
Force Headquarters	Office of the 23rd Infantry Brigade at Fyzabad.
Administrative Headquarters of Base and Line of Communications.	Office of a Staff Officer of Communications, Northern Line at Fort William, Calcutta.

APPEN

Approximate Strength of Force

Unit.	COMBATANTS.									NON-COMBATANTS.	
	BRITISH.					INDIAN.				FOLLOWERS.	
	Officers.	Warrant officers.	Assistant surgeons.	Non-commissioned officers and men.	Total.	Officers.	Sub-assistant surgeons.	Non-commissioned officers and men.	Total.	Public.	Private.
1	2	3	4	5	6	7	8	9	10	11	12
Force Headquarters ...	3	...	...	1	4	...	...	...	...	...	8
Battalion, Indian Infantry (including carriage of 7-pr. guns).	13	...	...	...	13	17	1	73	753	40	32
Battalion Pioneers ...	13	...	...	...	13	17	1	735	753	59	32
Field Company, Sappers and Miners.	4	...	5	2	6	3	1	(a) 189	193	11	14
Signalling units	1	...	...	...	1	...	...	14	14	...	2
1 Section, Indian Field Ambulance.	1	...	...	1	2	...	2	4	6	7	7
Supply Column	...	1	...	...	1	...	...	1	1	6	4
5 Carrier Corps	5	...	...	...	5	...	...	...	...	...	10
Total ...	40	1	...	4	45	37	5	1,678	1,720	116	109
Reserve.											
Battalion, Indian Infantry ...	13	...	...	...	13	17	1	735	753	40	32
BASE AND LINE OF COMMUNICATIONS.											
I.—Defence—											
To be detailed by the Commander of the Force.	...	...	...	...	...	...	...	...	...	...	...
II.—Administration—											
Headquarters	2	...	...	2	4	...	...	3	3	2	3
Ordnance Base Depôts ...	...	2	...	2	4	...	...	1	1	17	5
2 Sections, Indian Stationary Hospital.	2 (b)	...	...	1	3	...	4	7	11	14	13
Advanced and Base Supply Depôts.	4	4	...	4	12	...	...	...	...	...	16
Total ...	8	6	...	9	23	...	4	11	15	33	38
RECAPITULATION.											
Field Force	40	1	...	4	45	37	5	1,678	1,720	116	109
Reserve	13	...	...	...	13	17	1	735	753	40	32
Base and Line of Communications.	8	6	...	9	23	...	4	11	15	33	38
Total ...	61	7	...	13	81	54	10	2,424	2,488	189	179

DIX I (*d*).

(*excluding Military Police*).

Animals. Horses.	Ponies.	Ordnance and rest line equipment mules.	Pack mules.	Transport coolies.	Supply and Transport personnel.	Ambulance Transport. Dandies.	Slung hammocks.	Bearers, A. B. Corps.	Guns.	Machine guns.	Remarks.
13	14	15	16	17	18	19	20	21	22	23	24
7	...	...	...	...	...	...	...	...	...	...	
14	1	...	...	40	...	2	...	12	2	2	
14	2	42	20	...	7	2	...	12	...	2	
5	3	18	32	...	15	1	...	6	...	...	(*a*) Includes 20 drivers of equipment mules.
2	...	...	...	...	...	...	...	...	...	...	
2	4	...	...	...	...	10	15	120	...	...	
1	1	...	...	...	...	...	...	...	...	...	
5	...	...	...	3,150	20	...	...	...	...	...	
48	10	60	52	3,190	42	15	15	150	2	4	
14	1	12	...	...	...	2	...	12	...	2	
...	...	...	...	...	...	...	...	...	...	...	
4	...	...	...	...	...	...	...	...	...	...	
...	1	...	...	...	...	...	...	...	...	...	
2	6	...	...	...	...	2	...	12	...	...	
2	10	...	...	...	24	...	...	...	...	...	(*b*) Includes 2 departmental officers with honorary rank.
8	17	...	...	...	24	2	...	12	...	...	
48	10	60	52	3,190	42	15	15	150	2	4	
14	1	12	...	...	...	2	...	12	...	2	
8	17	...	...	...	24	2	...	12	...	...	
70	28	72	52	3,190	66	19	15	174	2	6	

APPENDIX I (*e*).

Special Equipment.

Detail.	No.	Remarks.
Hale's Rifle grenades	500*	
Hand grenades (S. and M. supply) ...	500†	
Dahs, or Kukris	...	One per fighting man, follower and transport cooly.
Air bags	...	(Sufficient for forming a raft for ½ company, infantry.)
Light steel cable (with pulleys, etc.) ...	...	(Sufficient for making 300 yards of flying bridge.)
Berthon boats (without superstructure for bridge).	1	
Barbed wire ... ... Yards.	5,000	
Slung hammocks (without poles) ...	50	
Special carriers for sick	20	To be made up regimentally by the 1st Battalion, 8th Gurkha Rifles.
For Special Signalling Unit.		
Cable (18 lbs. per mile) ... Miles.	20	To be left at Pasighat until required.
Visual signalling equipment } Camp equipment ... } ...	...	As for 2 special signalling units (*vide* F. S. Regulations, India, Appendix I).

* These were too late in their arrival and were not used.

† Withdrawn as they proved dangerous.

APPENDIX I (*f*).

Scale of issue of Books and Maps.

Unit.	Handbook (1) of the Abor country.	Handkerchief Map of the Abor country.	REMARKS.
Force, Headquarters ...	10 (2)	10 (2)	(1) Contains a general map of the Abor and Mishmi countries.
Headquarters of Cooly Transport (5 Corps).	5	5	(2) 7 officers, 1 each: office 3.
Battalion, Indian Infantry ...	10	25	
Battalion, Pioneers ...	10	25	
Field Company, Sappers and Miners.	4	8	
Signalling unit	1	4	
1 Section, Indian Field Ambulance.	1	1	
Supply Column	1	1	
RESERVE.			
Battalion, Indian Infantry ...	10	25	
BASE AND LINE OF COMMUNICATIONS.			
Administration—			
Headquarters	10 (3)	10 (3)	(3) 5 officers, 1 each: office 5.
2 Sections, Indian Stationary Hospital.	2	2	
Spare at Base	11	30	
4 Companies, Military Police	5	12	
Total ...	80	150	

APPENDIX II.

Detail of Corps and Units employed with the Abor Expeditionary Force, 1911-12.

Corps or unit.	Date of arrival at Kobo.	STRENGTH.						
		British.	INDIANS.		Nagas.	ANIMALS.		
			Fighting men.	Followers.		Mules.	Ponies.	Elephants.
Headquarters Staff	7th October 1911 ...	9	...	11	...	...	...	...
1-8th Gurkha Rifles ... ... / Detachment, 2-8th Gurkha Rifles	7th October 1911 ...	13	758	136	...	...	12	...
32nd Sikh Pioneers	28th September 1911	14	753	90	...	63	...	...
1-2nd Gurkha Rifles ...	8th October 1911 / 12th November 1911 ...	13	757	69	...	...	...	...
No. 1 Company, 1st Sappers and Miners.	28th September 1911	6	93	46	...	50	...	...
Assam Valley Light Horse ...	10th October 1911 ...	13	...	15	...	...	...	...
Signalling Unit	8th October 1911 ...	1	14	2	...	...	...	...
Survey party	8th October 1911 ...	3	61	3	...	...	...	...
Lakhimpore Military Police ...	28th September 1911	6	450	50	...	...	...	...
A Section 168 Indian Field Ambulance.	28th September 1911	2	6	128	...	...	...	...
B Section 168 Indian Carrier Hospital.	8th October 1911 ...	2	6	16	...	...	...	...
C Section 168 Indian Stationary Hospital.	12th November 1911	2	8	16	...	...	...	...
D Section 169 Indian Stationary Hospital.	5th December 1911 ...	2	6	90	...	...	...	...
A Section 169 Indian Stationary Hospital.	12th January 1912 ...	2	8	25	...	...	...	...
Assistant Director of Medical Services.	28th September 1911	1	1	1	...	...	...	...
Naga Scouts	11th October 1911 ...	...	...	...	12	...	...	...
No. 1 Naga Carrier Corps ...	11th October 1911 ...	1	4	...	630	...	...	...
No. 2 " " " ...	11th October 1911 ...	2	4	...	630	...	...	...
No. 3 " " " ...	11th October 1911 ...	1	4	...	630	...	...	...
Carried over ...	......	93	3,028	698	1,902	113	12	...

APPENDIX II—*concld.*

Detail of Corps and Units employed with the Abor Expeditionary Force, 1911-12—concld.

Corps or unit.	Date of arrival at Kobo.	STRENGTH. British.	Indians. Fighting men.	Indians. Followers.	Nagas.	Animals. Mules.	Animals. Ponies.	Animals. Elephants.
Brought forward ...	......	93	3,028	698	1,902	112	12	...
No. 4 Naga Carrier Corps ...	10th October 1911 ...	1	4	...	630	...	...	...
No. 5 ,, ,, ,, ...	4th October 1911 ...	2	2	...	630	...	...	...
No. 1 Gurkhali Carrier Corps ...	7th January 1912 ...	1	4	624	...	...	...	...
No. 9 ,, ,, ,, ...	7th March 1912 ...	1	4	624	...	...	...	...
26th Mule Corps	28th October 1911 ... / 27th November 1911 ...	5	1	248	...	738	14	...
Boat Transport	7th October 1911 ...	3	1	229	...	...	...	...
Base staff	26th September 1911...	6	...	6	...	...	...	...
Conservancy establishment ...	4th October 1911 ...	...	...	...	60	...	...	...
Supply Corps at and beyond base	26th September 1911...	25	6	226*	...	...	...	24
Ordnance Field Park ...	28th September 1911 ...	3	...	15	...	...	...	...
Engineer Field Park	6th October 1911 ...	1	...	3	...	...	...	...
Field Treasure Chest Officer ...	28th September 1911...	2	...	1	...	...	...	...
Telegraph Department ...	30th September 1911...	22	...	152	53	...	...	...
Postal Department	25th September 1911...	1	5	33	...	...	...	...
Total ...	......	166	3,055	2,939	3,273	845	26	24
GRAND TOTAL MEN ...	9,453	...	...	...	...	...	...	...
ANIMALS ...	885	...	...	...	...	...	...	...

* Includes Public Works Department coolies employed at the Base and Advanced Supply Depôt, Pasighat.

APPENDIX III.

Information regarding navigability of the Brahmaputra river and available facilities for transport of troops.

Extracts from a letter from the Agents, Rivers Steam Navigation Company, Limited, Calcutta.

1. The combined fleets of the Rivers Steam and India General Navigation and Railway companies comprise some 240 steamers and 250 flats with a carrying capacity of about 5,000,000 maunds.

2. The most suitable type of steamer for transhipment of troops is our "Sherani" type of which we have 20 in commission. These steamers have a deck area available for passengers of about 12,500 square feet and first class cabins for 10 or 12 officers which number can be added to, if needed, and also second class accommodation. Their full carrying capacity inclusive of coal is about 15—18,000 maunds or 11,000 maunds exclusive of coal at 5 feet draft.

3. We can arrange to charter steamers of this type at Rs. 750 per day from date of leaving Calcutta to date of return here, subject to a reduction to Rs. 600 when running empty or under detention, loading, discharging, etc. The estimated time for a trip from Calcutta to Kobo and back is 16—18 days, allowing for embarkation and landing of troops.

4. The actual running time from Amingaon to Kobo would be about 3 days up and 2 days down, or from Dibrugarh to Kobo about half a day each way.

We can prepare a time-table on your advising what actual time will be needed for embarkation and landing, and what daily stoppages you would require to enable troops to land and cook food, etc.

5. The charge for detention of a "Sherani" class steamer at Dibrugarh would be Rs. 600 per diem, a smaller despatch steamer with 6,000 square feet deck area and 4,000 maunds capacity would cost Rs. 500 per diem, or a shallow draft feeder steamer with about 1,500 square feet deck space and 700 maunds capacity, Rs. 200 to Rs. 250 per diem.

Residential or cargo flats from Rs. 50 to Rs. 100 per diem.

6. (*a*) The Brahmaputra up to Kobo is reported to be navigable in normal seasons for vessels of the "Sherani" class until December, though the draft may have to be restricted after October and there is some uncertainty as to the feasibility of passing the Poba rapids in the winter months.

(*b*) Troops and animals can be embarked at Amingaon across our receiving vessel situated a few hundred feet from the railway.

7. (*a*) The river between Saikhowa Ghat and Kobo is normally navigable for small stern wheel steamers throughout the cool season, but there is some uncertainty as to their crossing the Poba rapids.

(*b*) We maintain no vessels on this [section of the river, but one or more might be chartered and sent up on the terms quoted in No. 5 above.

* * * * * * *

(*e*) A few hours would suffice for a trip between Saikhowa Ghat and Kobo subject to unforeseen difficulties of navigation or obstructions.

APPENDIX III (a).

Time-table.

Showing movements of steamers and flats conveying troops and stores on Mobilization and Demobilization of the Abor Expeditionary Force, 1911-12.

MOBILIZATION.

Names of vessels and flats.	Carrying capacity in maunds.	Date of departure from—	Date of arrival at—	Troops conveyed.	Remarks.
S. S. "Mirani" ...	13,590	Calcutta, 16th September.	Goalundo, 19th September ...	No. 1 Company, Sappers and Miners.	Transhipped to "Battani" at Dibrugarh.
			Dhubri Ghat, 22nd September	"A" Section, 168th Field Ambulance.	
			Gauhati, 23rd September.		
			Dibrugarh, 26th September.		
S. S. "Battani" ...	135,90	Calcutta, 18th September.	Goalundo, 21st September ...	32nd Pioneers ...	Field Ambulance and Sappers and Miners embarked from "Mirani" at Dibrugarh.
			Dhubri Ghat, 23rd September...	168th Indian Field Ambulance.	
			Gauhati, 24th September ...	Ordnance Field Park.	
				1st Company, Sappers and Miners.	

APPENDIX III (*a*).

TIME-TABLE.

Showing movements of steamers and flats conveying troops and stores on Mobilization and Demobilization of the Abor Expeditionary Force, 1911-12—contd.

MOBILIZATION.

Names of vessels and flats.	Carrying capacity in maunds.	Date of departure from—	Date of arrival at—	Troops conveyed.	Remarks.
Connected Flat "Tapti"	...	......	Dibrugarh, 26th September.	......	
			Kobo, 27th September.	......	
		Kobo, 28th September	Gauhati, 1st October ...	Empty.	
		Gauhati, 2nd October...	Dibrugarh, 5th October ...	1-8th Gurkha Rifles ...	Embarked at Gauhati.
			Kobo, 6th October ...	Headquarters Staff ...	
		Kobo, 7th October ...	Dibrugarh, 7th October ...	Empty.	
			Kokilamukh, 7th October ...	......	
Connected Flat "Kolapur."	20,000	Kokilamukh, 8th October.	Kobo, 11th October ...	3 Naga Carrier Corps.	
Flat "Bhagiruttee" towed by S. S. "Kishnaghar."	20,000	Dibrugarh, 25th September.	Kobo, 26th September ..	Stores.	

S. S. "Scinde" ...	...	Kokilamukh, 2nd October.	Kobo, 5th October ...	No. 5 Naga Carrier Corps.
S. S. "Sherani" ...	13,590	Calcutta, 23rd September.	Goalundo, 26th September ...	1-2nd Gurkha Rifles.
Flat "Mahanadi" ...	19,000		Dhubri Ghat, 28th September	(Headquarters ½ Battalion).
			Gauhati, 30th September ...	2 Sections, Indian Stationary Hospital.
			Dibrugarh, September, October, 6th.	Survey Party.
			Kobo, 8th October ...	......
		Kobo, 8th October ...	Dibrugarh, 9th October ...	Empty.
		Dibrugarh, 10th October	Kobo, 10th October ...	1 Naga Carrier Corps.
				Maxim gun detachment, Assam Valley Light Horse.
		Calcutta, 16th October	Pobamukh, 28th October ...	
S. S. "Chitrali" ...	...	Ditto ...	Ditto ...	
S. S. "Dewari" ...	...	Ditto ...	Ditto ...	26th Mule Corps.
S. S. "Battani" ...	...	Calcutta, 14th November	Pobamukh, 25th November ...	
S. S. "Madaya" ...	...	Ditto ...	Ditto ...	
S. S. "Moulmein" ...	...	Ditto ...	Ditto ...	
S. S. "Sherani" ...	13,590	Calcutta, 1st November	Gauhati, 8th November ...	Wing, 1-2nd Gurkha Rifles.
			Dibrugarh, 11th November ...	
			Pobamukh, 12th November ...	

APPENDIX III (a).

TIME-TABLE.

Showing movements of steamers and flats conveying troops and stores on Mobilisation and Demobilisation of the Expeditionary Force, 1911-12.

DEMOBILIZATION.

Names of vessels and flats.	Carrying capacity in maunds.	Date of departure from—	Date of arrival at—	Troops conveyed.	Remarks.
S. S. "Battani" ...	13,590	Dibrugarh, 6th March...	Pobamukh, 7th March ...	Empty	Chartered from Dibrugarh on 6th March.
		Pobamukh, 8th March...	Kokilamukh, 9th March ...	3 Naga Carrier Corps.	
		Kokilamukh, 10th March.	Pobamukh, 11th March ...	Empty.	
		Pobamukh, 11th March.	Kokilamukh, 12th March ...	2 Naga Carrier Corps.	
		Kokilamukh, 12th March.	Pobamukh, 13th March ...	Empty.	
With flat "Brahmini."	26,000	Pobamukh, 14th March	Dibrugarh, 14th March ...	1-2nd Gurkha Rifles.	
			Gauhati, 16th March ...	Various details.	
			Dhubri, 17th March.		
			Goalundo, 18th March.		
			Calcutta, 23rd March ...	......	Charter expired on 24th March.

S. S. "Iris" * ...	1,000	Kobo, 9th April ...	Dibrugarh, 10th April ...	31st Signal Company.	These transferred to Daily Steamer at Dibrugarh and proceeded to Calcutta.
				Survey Detachment.	
				Supply Column.	
				"C" Section 168 Indian Stationary Hospital.	
S. S. "Mahlong" ...	......	Pobamukh, 14th April...	Dhubri Ghat, 16th April ...	No. 1 Gurkhali Carrier Corps	
				"A" Section 168 Indian Field Ambulance.	
S. S. "Dawari" ...	13,590	Pobamukh, 14th April	Dibrugarh, 14th April ...	32nd Pioneers	Charter commenced Dibrugarh on 13th April.
With Flat "Hulanga"	23,500	......	Gauhati, 16th April.	Detachment 2-8th Gurkha Rifles (27 of all ranks).	
			Dhubri Ghat, 18th April.	Ordnance Field Park.	
			Goalundo, 19th April.	(Ammunition section) Supply and Transport Corps. (Details).	
			Calcutta, 23rd April.		
				1,290 maunds stores ...	Charter expired on 24th April.
S. S. "Shinawari" ...	......	Pobamukh, 15th April...	Gauhati, 18th April.	Wing 1-18th Gurkha Rifles...	To Gauhati for Shillong.
S. S. "Kabuli" ...	......	Pobamukh, 18th April...	Dibrugarh, 19th April.	No. 1 Company, Sappers and Miners.	Pobamukh to Calcutta.
			Gauhati, 21st April.		
			Dhubri Ghat, 23rd April.	Supply and Transport followers, Mules 50.	
			Goalundo, 24th April.	Ditto.	
			Calcutta, 28th April.		

* Not Chartered.

APPENDIX III (*a*).

TIME-TABLE.

Showing movements of steamers and flats conveying troops and stores on Mobilization and Demobilization of the Expeditionary Force, 1911-12.

DEMOBILIZATION.

Names of vessels and flats.	Carrying capacity in maunds.	Date of departure from—	Date of arrival at—	Troops conveyed.	REMARKS.
S. S. "Mahamuni" ...	13,500	Pobamukh, 22nd May...	Dibrugarh, 22nd May ...	Detachment 2-8th Gurkha Rifles.	
Flat "Bhagirati" ...	21,500	......	Gauhati, 24th May ...	Base Supply Depôt.	
			Dhubri Ghat, 25th May.	"D" Section, No. 168 Indian Field Hospital.	
			Goalundo, 27th May.		
			Calcutta, 31st May.	"A" Section, No. 169 Field Ambulance.	
				26th Mule Corps.	
S. S. "Rama" ...	5,800	Pobamukh, 22nd May...	Dibrugarh, 22nd May ...	200 Carriers, No. 2 Gurkhali Carrier Corps.	Disembarked at Dhubri Ghat.
Flat "Bishkali" ...	26,000		Gauhati, 24th May.	Supply and Transport details.	For Calcutta.
			Dhubri Ghat, 25th May.	Remainder 26th Mule Corps	For Calcutta.
			Goalundo, 27th May.		
			Calcutta, 31st May.		

S. S. "Bunerwali" ...	...	Pobamukh, 22nd May...	Gauhati, 24th May ...	Remainder 1-8th Gurkha Rifles.	Disembarked at Gauhati.
			Dhubri Ghat, 25th May ...	No. 2 Gurkhali Carrier Corps.	Disembarked at Dhubri Ghat.
S. S. "Mercury"* ...	100	Pobamukh, 22nd May...	Dibrugarh, 22nd May ...	Detachment, Lakhimpur Military Police.	

* Not Chartered.

NOTE.—In addition to the above vessels use was made throughout the expedition of the two small stern-wheel Feeder Steamers the "Iris" and the "Mercury" for the carriage of stores, details and sick between Kobo and Dibrugarh.

APPENDIX IV.

Press Correspondents.

Owing to transport difficulties it was decided that only one press correspondent should be allowed to accompany the force, and it was arranged that all papers, both English and Indian, should receive his telegrams on application, provided they undertook to share in the expense. This was done to avoid the unfairness which would be caused by making all the news a monopoly of one paper or group of papers.

A Military Officer, Captain F. G. Poole, D.S.O., East Yorkshire Regiment, was allowed to accompany the force in this capacity. He was to proceed in an entirely unofficial and non-combatant capacity and was on no account to be allowed to assume a command by reason of his military rank.

It would perhaps have been more satisfactory, both for the public and for everybody else concerned, if a regular correspondent instead of an amateur had been allowed with the expedition.

APPENDIX V.

Scientists.

The following scientists were allowed to accompany the force.

(1) Geologist.

(2) Botanist.

(3) Zoologist.

(4) Anthropologist.

(5) Forest Officer.

These experts, owing to the difficulties of transport, were not allowed to accompany the force during the first advance, but were permitted to proceed to the front when active opposition on the part of the Abors had broken down.

They were allowed the same amount of transport as British officers for themselves and their followers, and scientific equipment was kept down to its lowest possible limit. The expense in connection with scientific research was not borne by the expedition, but was debited to the Civil Budget.

APPENDIX VI.

Extracts from the standing orders of the Abor Expeditionary Force.

* * * * * *

TACTICAL NOTES.

(Notes on methods to be adopted in fighting Abors.)

Judging by previous experience, the favourite method adopted by Abors is to hold up the head of the column by a strong stockade impossible or difficult to turn, and, at the same time, to rush in on the flanks of the line of coolies. As the paths are so narrow that they only permit of moving in single file, and as the jungle is too thick to permit of the use of flankers, the guarding of the coolies is a matter of considerable difficulty. The first point that requires attention is preventing the line tailing out to an undue length. With a line of laden coolies it is obvious that, if straggling is to be avoided, the leading troops must move very slowly and halts must be frequent.

The guarding of a long line of coolies being liable to use up a great deal of the fighting strength of the column, it is desirable, when moving over ground where there is likely to be opposition, to reduce the number of coolies to a minimum. This can be done by advancing by very short marches and leaving the coolies with a suitable guard in a stockade. Men can be subsequently sent back to bring them up, gun porters and others who have advanced in the first instance being also sent back to bring up rations. So far as can be judged from former experience, Abors do not return to ground from which they have already been driven. This of course does not obviate the necessity of providing a suitable escort.

The Abor stockades, with which they hold up the head of the column, are often very formidable, defended by *panjis* and too strong to be breached by light artillery. The stockade on the north side of Kebang was reported by Mr. Williamson to be 14 feet high, with a ditch 12 feet broad. To attempt to rush such a work without due preparation would result in unnecessary loss. To approach the stockade the infantry will open out slightly, front rank men will sling arms and proceed with *dao* or *khukri* to cut their way through the jungle or *panjis*, rear rank men covering them with loaded rifles and fixed bayonets. Fixed bayonets will be the rule when in the jungle. As there is no chance of breaching the stockade, the guns will endeavour to clear the defenders from behind it by throwing double shell with a reduced charge and shortened fuse. Hand grenades will also be thrown over, scaling ladders brought up, and the assault delivered, In the meantime flanking parties will endeavour to turn the ends of the stockade. They should be provided with hand grenades.

In the meantime coolies will be closed up as much as possible. Coolies who cannot keep up will sit down by the side of the road and await the arrival of spare coolies. One spare coolie will march at the rear of every 30 laden coolies. One cooly with apparatus for carrying wounded will be allowed for every 10 fighting men. A proportion will be told off to accompany the rear guard.

When the path is in any way dominated by precipitous or very steep ground, a careful search should be made for stone-chutes and flanking parties should be detached for the purpose; if, when passing along the face of precipitous ground, stones should be thrown down, men must be instructed to press in close to the cliff.

The great thing is to remember that we must avoid hurry and it will often be advisable to ignore the Abor path and construct one for ourselves. The known path is sure to be prepared with pit falls, etc., and a common trick is to cut paths leading into positions for ambuscades dominating the known path. Great care must be taken to watch paths, either parallel or coming in from either side. It is a good plan to lay down a few *panjis* just in front of the men told off to watch the path.

* * * * * *

Marches.

* * * * * *

(3) There should be no interval between units, as gaps form vulnerable points.

* * * * * *

(4) Besides the authorised halts, it may be necessary to have intermediate halts in order to close up. A halt by the leading body of 15 minutes in every hour should not be excessive. Officers and non-commissioned officers in rear should signal to the head of the column in cases of straggling by means of short and long blasts on the whistle. Three blasts signifies that the column is closed up in rear. These to be repeated by all whistles. In the case of halts, ranks, front and rear, will turn outwards. At all halts, where possible, files should be pushed out a little way into the jungle to reconnoitre and lock for parallel roads or clearings and signs of the enemy.

* * * * * *

(9) * * * * The advanced guard should halt or slow down frequently to keep in touch with the column, while the rear guard should immediately signal ahead should it become detached or straggle * * * * * * * *. The advanced guard commander is responsible that all ground favourable for stone-chutes is searched before allowing the main body to pass

it. When side tracks are met with, the advanced guard commander should detach a file or more to proceed a short distance up it and watch it. * * * *

* * * * * *

(11) The baggage guard for the protection of the coolies will be distributed as follows :—

One sepoy at the head and one at the rear of each squad of six coolies. In addition there will be a squad of six sepoys between every group of six squads of coolies.

Should the enemy charge the baggage, each squad of coolies will close on their leading sepoy, clear the path, and, turning outwards, squat with their loads on their backs, holding their spears at the charge. The baggage guard, turning outwards, will stand with rifles at the charge, and, on seeing the enemy will fire only to the front so as to avoid hitting their own men should the path wind in the jungle.

If no enemy is seen the guard will remain at the charge.

* * * * * *

(12) Magazines will always be charged and bayonets fixed.

* * * * * *

APPENDIX VII.

EXTRACTS FROM REPORT OF ASSISTANT DIRECTOR, SUPPLY AND TRANSPORT.

General Remarks by Assistant Director, Supply and Transport.

* * * * * *

This report shows under what restricted conditions the Abor Expedition troops have advanced, lived and been equipped. It is rare, I believe, for a force to remain for so long a period without tents in the field, bivouacking for some 6 months in a country which has been lately described by a high authority as the " wettest corner of India."

* * * * * *

The transport has been limited to country boats, a few elephants, a pack mule corps and Naga and Gurkhali coolies.

Fuel and rice were the only supplies procurable in plenty.

* * * * * *

Temporary native store-keepers and followers have been replaced on the Abor Expedition by experienced British warrant and non-commissioned officers with great advantage to the State.

An excellent staff of British officers from the Corps has been provided, ensuring strict care and supervision over all matters of supply and transport.

The usual heavy losses and large surpluses of stores, which are almost invariably associated with the close of every campaign, are almost entirely absent in this case.

Except for the usual wastage and dryage on perishable articles, which cannot be avoided in the field, the percentage of loss on other supplies was so small as to be almost of no account.

* * * * * *

Mobilization Reserves.

Mobilization Reserves and Equipments in India are chiefly massed in the Punjab and North-West Frontier Province, and consequently there is much delay before they can reach Calcutta by rail.

In view of the rising importance of the north-east frontier it seems to be a matter for consideration whether a redistribution of these reserves and equipments would not be advisable.

Calcutta has of late years become an important centre for the concentration and accumulation of supplies for war and is likely to become still more so.

* * * * * *

For operations in an unknown country like Aborland, consisting of dense tropical forest and vegetation, where no roads exist, and where the climate is one of continuous rain, special precautions must be taken with supplies for troops and particular arrangements devised for their transport

* * * * * *

On my preliminary tour in Assam, I had personally interviewed firms and dealers, at Dibrugarh and elsewhere, likely to be of use to us in obtaining local supplies should an expedition be sanctioned, and had obtained guarantees from them to supply us at their ordinary peace rates, or as generally prevailed then in the markets, and had registered such offers.

Peace rates at Dibrugarh.

I now began to receive at Calcutta telegrams and letters from these firms at Dibrugarh inviting me to close with their original offers at once as the market was rising rapidly owing to the expedition having been sanctioned, and to circulars issued by the Divisional Supply Officer, Lucknow, throughout Assam, calling upon all and sundry to tender for supplies at Dibrugarh.

As there was some delay in my being appointed Assistant Director of Supplies and Transport for the expedition, I was, however, not in a position to accept these offers and confirm my personal agreements. The telegram from the Assistant Director of Supplies and Transport, 8th Division, notifying me of my appointment to the expedition, and directing me to report to the General Officer Commanding, Assam Brigade, was only received by me at Calcutta on the 26th August 1911.

Although I started at once, I found on my arrival at Dibrugarh that rates had considerably risen all round, nor could I induce firms to supply local products at the peace rates originally registered with me.

Rise of the market.

* * * * *

In order to avoid the heavy warehouse and other rents prevailing at Dibrugarh, to minimise expenditure and save unnecessary transfers of stores by cooly labour, and carriage, always very high charges at Dibrugarh, I considered it better policy to engage at once a flat from the Steamer Company at Dibrugarh Ghat on which the stores could be packed as fast as purchased, passed, and weighed over. I arranged with the Steamer Company's Agent, to charge no rent for this flat until she was finally chartered when full for conveyance direct to the Base at Kobo. In this way considerable economy was effected and unnecessary changes of stores avoided.

Hire of the "Kamrup."

This flat, known as the "Kamrup", was one of the largest belonging to the River Steam Navigation Company. In addition to serving as a warehouse and landing stage for steamers at Kobo she would have afforded excellent accommodation there for the sick, or as a floating hospital.

Shortly after leaving Dibrugarh Ghat on the 24th September, the 'Kamrup' being towed by the Kishengarh, a collision occurred between the two at a bend in the Brahmaputra in a strong current. The result was the

Start for Kobo.

'Kamrup' "buckled" and was so much damaged that the Captain of the "Kishengarh" decided to return at once Dibrugarh Ghat. Fortunately, owing to the water-tight compartments in the holds of the "Kamrup," the stores were not damaged.

The "buckling" of the "Kamrup."

* * * * * *

By using the patrol launch "Sissi", I was, however, able to return quickly to the Ghat and warn the Steamer Company's Agent. Another flat, the "Bhagiruttee" being fortunately available and quickly secured, the transfer of the stores to her from the "Kamrup" was at once commenced and continued most of the night by electric light.

Transfer to the "Bhagiruttee."

There is always a scarcity of cooly labour at Dibrugarh and throughout Assam generally. Our establishments of bakers, coopers, butchers, weighmen, etc., had all to turn to with the loads.

* * * * * *

The Assistant Director of Supplies and Transport, Lucknow, had fixed 15th September as the date for the arrival at Dibrugarh Ghat of the necessary equipments, packing materials, etc. This date might with advantage have been made earlier, as without scales and weights, bags, and packing material progress was much delayed. Some scales and weights, etc., were, however, with difficulty obtained on loan from the ship's agent and others, and work commenced. Supply establishments then began to arrive by rail, and work was pushed on with such rapidity that, by the 20th September, all local supplies ordered had been purchased, packed and shipped.

Delay in arrival of equipments.

The supply equipment, tents, etc., arrived by S.S. "Pagan" on the 15th September.

With the arrival of the steamer 'Kishengarh' on the 23rd September with Calcutta stores, a start for Kobo (the Base), was eventually made on the 24th September.

The Deputy Commissioner, Dibrugarh, had been able to obtain and place at my disposal on hire the launch "Sissi", a vessel of remarkable design, doubtful buoyancy, and inferior capacity, but which, in spite of these disadvantages, proved of great use in connecting up the markets at Dibrugarh with the base at Kobo, some 45 miles further upstream on the right bank of the Brahmaputra. It was also very useful in pushing up details, medical comforts, small equipments and stores in advance of the troops, while the jungle was being cut and the base prepared.

Hire of the "Sissi" launch.

* * * * * *

Afterwards the "Sissi" was of great use to the Base Supply Officer, for rapid transfer of the sick, for urgent requirements and demands, and for keeping in touch with firms at Dibrugarh.

* * * * * *

With the Inspector of Communications and stores and personnel for the base I proceeded to Kobo on the small S.S. "Mercury," the "Bhagirutee" in tow of the "Kishengarh" following us. Kobo was reached on the 26th September.

2nd start for Kobo.

* * * * * *

The "Kishengarh" returned the next day, the flat being left as a landing stage for other steamers and flats to discharge from. In this capacity she remained throughout the expedition, the rise and fall of the Brahmaputra with its vagaries and peculiarities rendering her retention necessary for this purpose. Being a covered flat, she also served the Base Supply Officer as a floating warehouse and store room for perishable supplies, and as a workplace for refilling the locally purchased stores from the one and two maund bags into our 60 lbs. carrier loads.

As the Brahmaputra rose as much as 18 feet shortly afterwards, within a few days overflowing the banks and delaying the start of our columns, while continuous heavy rain fell for days, a few more flats of the "Bhagirutee" type could have been employed with advantage for storage and protection of our supplies in preference to tents. The cost of their hire was, however, prohibitive.

Rise of the Brahmaputra River.

* * * * * *

Equipment for only one column had been sanctioned by the Assistant Director of Supplies and Transport, Lucknow, under the impression that our advance would be in one direction only.

Additional equipment.

* * * * * *

I may here mention that establishments and equipments for the expedition have been reduced to a minimum and to an extent quite remarkable when compared with the scales sanctioned in the Regulations.

Endeavours were made to obtain a maundage contract for stores landed at Kobo but without success, the difficulty of navigation beyond Dibrugarh and the paucity of boats and boatmen being given as reasons.

At this period, at Kobo. I was suddenly called upon to meet requirements of two other Missions, *viz.*, those for the Mishmi and Miri countries, regarding which I had received no instructions, nor had they been included in the Abor Scheme, the only one furnished me Two officers from the staff of these Missions arrived

The Mishmi and Miri Missions.

at Kobo asking for clothing and rations. With the approval of the General Officer Commanding the Abor Force, I was able to assist these Missions in making a start by drawing on our reserves, otherwise, they would have found themselves in very difficult positions.

* * * * * *

Sadiya, the Base for the Mishmi expedition, is some 25 miles to the east of Kobo up the Brahmaputra River and shallow draught steamers can proceed there direct from Dibrugarh most of the year, or supplies can be sent by rail from Dibrugarh to Saikhowa by the Dibru-Sadiya Railway, and thence by boats to Sadiya.

* * * * * *

Subsequently, these 2 Missions obtained their requirements in direct communication with Lucknow, or locally.

Their equipment and start threw a lot of extra work on the Supply and Transport at Kobo at a time when all ranks were particularly busy.

* * * * * *

Progress at the Base.

All this time, the Boat Transport Officer, Captain A. B. H. Webb, was busy collecting country boats and Miri boatmen. These were detailed to work between Kobo and Pasighat up and down the Dihang River. He had as his assistants two warrant officers of the Supply and Transport Corps.

* * * * * *

On the 4th October, the steamer "Scinde" arrived with the first Naga Carrier Corps under Captain O. E. Geoghegan.

* * * * * *

On the 6th October, the General Officer Commanding the Force with staff arrived, and, on the 8th, the steamer "Sherani" with our 70 days' Calcutta supplies and clothing, etc., which might with advantage have been despatched earlier, as the Force had by that date been practically complete for some time and we were drawing on our local Dibrugarh supplies to a large extent.

* * * * * *

On the 9th October, the remaining Naga Carrier Corps arrived and the Force was complete.

All tents were left at Kobo, the Force advancing on a bivouac scale (60 lbs. per officer, 10 lbs. per fighting man, and followers *nil*), establishment and equipment being reduced to a minimum, and this continued throughout the expedition.

Indian Troops carried three days' rations *plus* their emergency rations on their persons, the Naga Carrier Corps 1 day's ration in addition to their loads.

No. 2 Naga Carrier Corps was detailed for permanent duty with the 1-8th Gurkha Rifles, and No. 3 Corps with the 1-2nd Gurkhas.

* * * * * *

The small draught steamers "Mercury" and "Iris" brought up supplies to Kobo from Dibrugarh throughout the period of the expedition and even when the Brahmaputra was at its lowest.

An excellent road was made to Pobamukh along the river bank and some four miles from Kobo, and to this place big steamers and flats could come at all seasons.

* * * * * *

Camps and Exchanging Stations.

There is plenty of space for these on the vast *chapris* or grass prairies between Kobo and Pasighat; after that, space is more limited and restricted to clearings in the forest and on the steep sides of the hills.

The 6½ mile camp from Kobo, on the *chapri* close to the Kemi river, is an excellent exchanging place for mules. Pillung also has space and an excellent water-supply. Lokhpur is also good, but the water-supply is deficient in the dry season.

Rammidumbang, Pasighat and Rotung make excellent camps and exchanging stations.

* * * * * *

APPENDIX VII (*a*).

SUPPLIES.

Local Supplies.—These, when of good quality and suitable for the requirements of a mixed force in the field, have been drawn on to the fullest extent and mainly consist of rice, tea, dhan and potatoes with some ghee, gur and onions.

After obtaining the 70 days' requirements authorised in the Abor scheme, local markets were exhausted in some articles. and dealers commenced importing from Calcutta. It was then found more economical for such supplies to be obtained with the others being sent up from the Supply Depôt, Calcutta, direct to the base, especially as this avoided packing, weighing, marking and cost of transfer from Dibrugarh to Kobo.

Speaking generally, except for rice, tea, ghee, potatoes and onions, with of course a plentiful supply of firewood, Assam is a poor country to meet the demands of troops.

Rice.—The supply has been plentiful, good and varied. Altogether some half dozen descriptions were tried, the best being Manipur, Balam, Gojra, and Khasla.

Manipur rice was generally preferred, but stocks of this soon became exhausted.

I also wired to the Deputy Commissioner, Naga Hills, asking him to instruct all Commandants of the 5 Naga Carrier Corps to bring down with them to Kobo as much rice as possible.

Tea.—Plentiful and of excellent quality. Experiments were tried on the expedition with Lipton's compressed tea in tablets. The saving in transport by compressed tea is enormous and the idea should be followed up in other supplies where possible.

Ghi—Of Assam was very good on the whole, but facilities for boiling it under departmental supervision were not available and the packing of the tins into boxes gave trouble. The supply was also limited.

Gur—Was sweet enough to the taste, but, owing to the climate, was always in a liquid condition and not appreciated like the Indian gur. The transfer from the earthen pots called *kulsis* to tins, also gave trouble to the contractors and caused delay. The stock was chiefly issued to the Nagas, subsequent supplies being obtained with the other stores from Calcutta.

Potatoes—Were of excellent quality and much appreciated, keeping better than the onions. Some were actually grown at Kobo and despatched to the front.

Onions—Would not keep, sprouted lavishly and rapidly deteriorated, owing to the damp climate.

The chief losses in the expedition have been from deterioration of onions and potatoes. To reduce losses in the onion supply, that of potatoes, which keep better, was increased, a corresponding reduction being made in the onion ration.

* * * * * *

Dhan.—Large quantities are in the country but the Abors are too well off and independent at present to part with much. They appear also to grow only sufficient to meet their own requirements, although the soil is favourable for growing anything. Altogether some 7,000 maunds have been obtained and utilized on the expedition, thus effecting considerable economy in the grain supply for mules and ponies. Dhan was issued generally to mules and elephants in place of imported grain. Except for original despatches of grain with the mules from India for the steamer journeys from Calcutta, and with an occasional addition of gram to utilize any of the stock landed showing signs of deterioration, the mules have been fed and have thrived on dhan throughout the expedition. Some maize of excellent quality has also been issued from captured stocks at Rotung.

Grazing.—Local resources in this respect were satisfactory, rendering the employment of mule transport in the Abor country peculiarly economical.

A list of local supplies obtained by purchase is attached as Appendix VII (*b*).

Local Firms.—As regards Dibrugarh firms and contractors or *Khayahas*, as they are locally styled, my Base Supply Officer characterises them, with one or two exceptions, as a lot of sharks. But the exceptions are among those firms who had been recommended to me by the Commissioner, Assam Valley, and the Deputy Commissioner, Lakhimpur District, as reliable and trustworthy; and, had I been in a position to close with their original offers, without inviting competition throughout Assam, I have no reason to suppose they would have failed in their promises.

* * * * * *

The Planters' Stores and Agency, Limited, of Dibrugarh came forward and opened a Depôt at Kobo for the supply of various stores and miscellaneous stock which proved of much use and convenience, especially while troops were mobilizing there, as also for the supply of certain medical comforts for the hospitals and for meeting small unforeseen demands. Had the firm been more enterprising they could have considerably increased their business with the Base Supply Officer.

Fresh Meat.—This has been precarious. A regular meat supply on hoof in such a country not being possible, extra quantities of gur, for Indian troops and followers, must be seen to, and tinned beef and mutton in ½ lb. tins for British troops and details. With these latter should be issued a liberal supply of pickles and tin-openers. Slaughter cattle were scarce at Dibrugarh, and there was no local breed of sheep and goats, all being imported from Bhutan and India. The Supply and Transport Officer with the Mishmi Expedition of 1899-00 in his report, particularly mentioned the difficulty he had in obtaining goats ; and our experiences on the former Abor Expedition were similar.

* * * * * *

Goats and sheep.—With the help of the Deputy Commissioner, I was able to commence the collection of goats and a few sheep at the rate fixed, but the supply was uncertain throughout the expedition. It was rendered still more difficult from the preference shown by Indian troops for males and *khasis*, females being objected to. The average outturn of these goats for meat rations was 24 lbs. ; by the time they reached posts at the front and after long marches it was still less.

Sheep stood the marches and the climate worse than goats. In either case wethers were the hardiest. The goat-wether has very little of the typical goaty taste. Much mortality was saved by giving goats a platform in their pens as well as a covering over-head. Two weakly goats will travel comfortably on the march one on each side of a mule if placed in gunny bags with holes in them from which the animals heads can protrude.

Despatching goats on hoof would have necessitated heavy losses *en route.* When the troops at the Renging Post obtained their fresh meat ration, I arranged for a slaughter parade of goats for the next post at Rotung. The Officer Commanding placed at my disposal a couple of Sikhs, Punjabi Muhammadans and Gurkhas as butchers who each killed, cut up and dressed the number of goats allotted for their comrades at the next post, being assisted, where permitted, by some of the Naga coolies who have no caste prejudices. The meat was put into the empty onion baskets, covered over, and sewn up with gunny and sealed or marked by the respective butchers of the different castes. It was then sent off by the following morning's carrier convoy. The despatch of meat under such circumstances, however, gives a good deal of trouble and unless issued promptly it is liable to go bad.

The difficulties of driving goats and sheep in such country as Aborland, and the precautions necessary to prevent the heavy mortality that would otherwise occur among them while *en route* to posts, were great.

The Base Supply Officer tried importing goats and sheep from India for a time, which had a good effect in lowering prices to a certain extent, but establishments had to be sent with them on the steamer and there were other disadvantages, such as the supply of food *en route.* Even when landed at Kobo and in spite of casualties and contingencies, their cost compared favourably, with local prices.

* * * * * *

Mithan—Were met with in much larger numbers than had been anticipated, and, though of no use to most of the Indian troops on account of caste prejudices, were very welcome whenever issued to the Nagas. From Rotung onwards they were met with everywhere and I should like to have been able to issue a good many more to the Nagas and Muhammadans of the Force, but political reasons prevented this. The flesh is coarse and tough but that of a young mithan properly killed and dressed is better.

Tinned-beef and mutton—From our Mobilization Reserves were issued in large quantities for the march, forming as usual the principal meat supply.

Bacon—Was very much appreciated and should invariably form a portion of the meat supply for British troops. It was obtained from Calcutta in convenient small-sized slabs, covered in cloth. It kept well and, being in compressed form, took up little space, while furnishing a very welcome relief to the monotony of *bully*, the fat being also valuable for cooking purposes. For warm climates the cloth covered slabs should be sent up in tins.

Poultry.—In lands where fresh meat, which is so essential a factor for maintaining the health and fitness of troops in the field, is scarce, recourse must be had to other varieties and substitutes. These were provided by ducks and geese which in a water-logged country like Assam, are the only creatures, except mithan and fish, hat from a ration point of view, flourish and thrive.

The mortality of fowls on the march made them uneconomical. Ducks were much hardier and fatter and throve on the banks of the Dihang. It was, however, as a rule impracticable to carry them on mules, which were alarmed by their quacking. We were, therefore, dependent on boats and carriers for their carriage. When on carriers they travelled best in crates which had three partitions one above another, four ducks going into each portion. Geese, weight for weight, took up more transport than ducks, but in other respects were very satisfactory.

The scale fixed was one duck in lieu 1 lb. fresh mutton and one goose per 4 lbs. mutton.

* * * * * *

Base Supply Officer's Report.

The following remarks are made by the Base Supply Officer, regarding the excellent arrangements at the Base :—

Having only a limited number of British personnel, I arranged the following doubling up of sections :—

"A" and "B" Sections.

"C," "D" and "E" Sections.

Retail and "F" Sections.

Bakery and Butchery.

The division of labour was very fair; the Retail Section was fearfully rushed at the start, the whole force being at the base for three weeks, and as a move was expected forward any day, it was not possible for units to draw more than one or two days' rations at a time. Owing to the number of indents to be registered and written up, in future it would be only fair to allow to a clerk to each store-keeper, who has retail issues to make.

Once the main force moved forward, there was not much difficulty in keeping them supplied so long as transport was available. The Boat Convoy at the start could carry a good deal, but it was impossible to estimate accurately its carrying power, for at first large boats were used, and as the river dropped foot by foot, these larger boats had to be left behind and smaller ones used to get over the rapids. With bulky loads they could carry nothing like their full maundage; for these tended to make them top-heavy. As an example, early in the expedition, miscellaneous loads had to be carried and 500 maunds were considered the limit of the load; later, however, one boat convoy with the same boats had to take rice only, and 800 maunds in compact loads were comfortably taken.

Plenty of room had been chosen, in the plan of the Base, for the Base Depôt, and to this fact I attribute the ease, speed and regularity with which convoys were sent off. On one day convoys were handed over separately to 3 Carrier Corps, boat transport, and mule transport, without the slightest difficulty.

* * * * * *

For local labour at the Base, some 120 Nepalese coolies from the Public Works Department were taken on. There is no other labour to be had in these parts. These men proved simply invaluable. They are quick to learn and work very cheerfully. They soon learnt to read the markings on the bags, and after the first 3 weeks there was no difficulty in sorting the convoys. Moreover they are excellent jungle men and cut down trees, run up sheds and make platforms as well as any Gurkha.

* * * * * *

There is a general consensus of opinion that the rations provided for the Nagas were unsuitable. The Naga is essentially a meat-eater and yet this item was omitted in his ration. Mustard oil was allowed him, but he would not touch it. The whole stock had therefore to be sold. The Naga is, moreover, a very healthy eater and if given two days' rations, consumes the lot in a quarter of that time.

* * * * * *

Report on the working of the Supply Column, Abor Expeditionary Force, 1911-12.

* * * * * *

The advanced Supply Depôt was situated first at Pasighat, and then, as the force advanced, it was moved to Janakmukh, to which place the boat convoys from Kobo were for a time able to proceed, and thus transport was saved between Pasighat and Janakmukh. When the Dihang river got low, however, the mules, which had by that time arrived, were used in bringing up supplies which had been left by the boats at Pasighat.

* * * * * *

The main argument in favor of Janakmukh was that it divided the two marches from Pillung to Renging in the best possible manner. Neither march caused an undue strain on the transport, whereas the march from Pasighat to Renging, though only about 15 miles, was particularly arduous for the transport working from Renging on the staging-meeting system. Even with the meeting place as much as eight and a half miles above Pasighat the Renging transport had to climb daily 3,000 feet up and 3,000 feet down.

It was after the move of the Depôt to Pasighat that this became necessary, and it proved particularly hard on the Renging mules when the mule road was deep in mud.

Before long it became necessary to place an extra relay of mules at Sirpo until carriers were available to relieve the mules altogether on this part of the road. While, however, Janakmukh was the stage between Pillung and Renging, the transport working upward from Janakmukh could take a good share of the climbing and of the bad going near "Cooly Col." Moreover the march from Pillung to Janakmukh, though longer by five and a half miles than that from Pillung to Pasighat, did not exceed seventeen miles, was nearly all on the flat, and never put a serious strain upon the transport.

The suggestion to place the Advanced Supply Depôt at Rammi Dumbang instead of either at Pasighat or at Janakmukh was unacceptable for it would have necessitated a halt at Pasighat as well as at Rammi Dumbang and so added one whole march to the line of communications. However, with the Advanced Supply Depôt at Pasighat, Rammi Dumbang could have been used, had there been a post there, to hold an extra relief of transport such as was for a time placed at Sirpo.

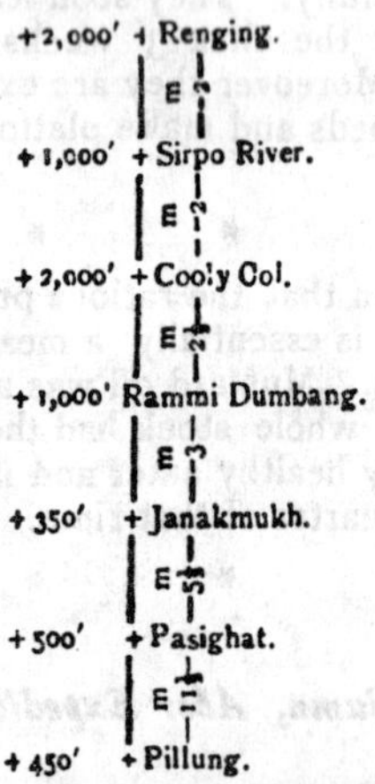

I have added in the margin a list of the places here mentioned showing approximately their distances from one another and their respective altitudes.

The objections to Janakmukh were its contracted space and its separation by an inconvenient distance of five and a half miles from the boat convoy terminus at Pasighat.

The delay caused by this, however, was reduced when the staging-meeting system was introduced.

The distance from Janakmukh to the boat convoy terminus was, perhaps, most felt by the sick proceeding to Kobo. However, it was always practicable to send many of them half way to Pasighat in the three boats that were kept on the Janakmukh reach, and they were not prevented from reaching Kobo from Janakmukh in one day.

* * * * * *

Loads.--The 60 lbs. gross carrier load was a very convenient figure to deal with. When dealing with stationary reserves in bulk, if a due allowance were made for packing material, probable losses in store, extras and a proportion of extra heavy Naga rations, it was found that *60 lbs. gross* fairly represented the weight of *twenty* average rations. The same unit was equally useful in calculating the net carrying power of a given number of carriers, from whose gross carrying power had to be subtracted the number of days' rations for themselves which they were also carrying.

* * * * * *

Extracts from Report of Inspector of Communication and Base Commandant.

* * * * * *

Sufficient space is not always taken for the Base Supply Depôt. This time it was and enabled the Supply Officer to handle his stores with comfort and without confusion.

Clothing.—This arrived in original bales of 2½ maunds each, in some cases, a large quantity of which had to be repacked into carrier loads. This could easily have been done in stations in India in neat pressed bales, instead of having to be done in the jungle—where only very *kutcha* bundles could be made up. One very noticeable bale was the coarse cloth ; these bales weighed 5 maunds each and had to be opened on the flat and taken ashore in sections.

Supplies.—The Staff of the Base, *e.g.*, Commandant and Assistant Director of Supply and Transport and certain Supply and Transport officers were sent on ahead. There being no village or shops near Kobo, it seems as if the supply depôt with stores should have been sent on with them instead of 12 days after to the Base. But although all the menial staff of the Supply and Transport without their implements were also sent on ahead, they had to land practically in jungle. The menial establishment were not fitted out with field service clothing, and were somewhat uncomfortable as most days it rained heavily. In future, if sent in advance, they should be fitted out at Calcutta.

The cost of living for all British officers concerned also was high owing to all stores having to be brought from Dibrugarh.

The lesson seems to be that, in case of future expeditions beyond Dibrugarh, the Supply and Transport staff should be sent up completely equipped, with clothing and implements, bakeries and so on, and rations for British officers.

Were it not for locally purchased stores, which after much correspondence, were allowed to come first, delay and inconvenience would have occurred.

APPENDIX VII(*b*).

List of local supplies purchased in connection with the Abor Expeditionary Force, 1911-12.

Articles.		Quantities.	Average purchase rate.			Per	Names of contractors.	Remarks.
			Rs.	A.	P.			
Rice	... lb.	16,22,230	5	11	3	md. of 82 lbs.	Deep Chand, Chuni Lall, Mohesh Dass, Messrs. Lemon and Company.	
Potatoes	... "	43,112	6	12	0	"	Deep Chand and Messrs. Lemon and Company.	
Onions	... "	99,258	6	10	8	"	Deep Chand and Messrs. Lemon and Company.	
Ghee	... "	21,580	56	12	0	"	Deep Chand, Chuni Lall, Mohesh Dass.	
Gur	... "	40,240	7	0	0	"	Deep Chand, Chuni Lall, Mohesh Dass.	
Garlic	... "	5,046	10	10	8	"	Hurri Bux, Daulat Ram, Deep Chand, Messrs. Lemon and Company.	
Salt	... "	56,694	3	2	4	"	Deep Chand, Chuni Lall, Mohesh Dass.	
Turmeric	... "	4,040	20	0	0	"	Deep Chand, and Messrs. Lemon and Company.	
Tea	... "	17,714	0	8	6	lbs.	Planters Store and Agency Company, Limited, at Kobo.	
Bacon	... "	491½	1	1	0	"	Planters Stores and Agency Company, Limited, at Kobo.	
Butter, tinned	... "	1,121½	0	11	0	½ lb tin	Planters Stores and Agency Company, Limited, at Kobo.	
Milk, condensed... Russell's.	"	1,096½	0	6	3½	tin.	Planters Stores and Agency Company, Limited, at Kobo.	
Milk, condensed Ideal.	"	...	0	8	0	"	Planters Stores and Agency Company, Limited, at Kobo.	
Milk, fresh, cow's	"	1,160	0	4	5	Seer	Hospital Store-keeper at Kobo.	
Milk, fresh, buffaloe's.	"	402	0	2	0	"	Hospital Store-keeper at Kobo.	

Articles.	Quantities.	Average purchase rate.			Per	Names of contractors.	Remarks.
		Rs.	A.	P.			
Kobanies ... lbs.	5,318	30	0	0	Md. of 80 lbs	Planters Stores and Agency Company, Limited, at Kobo.	
Chocolate (Mexican) „	110	1	10	6	lbs.	Planters Stores and Agency Company, Limited, at Kobo.	
Essence of Chicken, Brand's. „	18	1	12	0	tin.	Planters Stores and Agency Company, Limited, at Kobo.	
Pickles, mixed „	21	0	15	0	Bottle of 1½ lbs.	Planters Stores and Agency Company, Limited, at Kobo.	
Oil, mustard „	11,460	25	0	0	Md. of 82 lbs.	Chuni Lall, Mohesh Dass, Hurri Bux, Daulat Ram.	
Oil, kerosine galls.	1,304	1	0	3	Gallon.	Planters Stores and Agency Company, Limited, at Kobo.	
Goats ... No.	3,659	17	8	0	Each	D. C. Barooah and G. R. Barooah.	Average outturn from 18 to 30lbs. per goat.
Sheep ... „	286	15	6	8	„	D. C. Barooah and G. R. Barooah.	
Geese ... „	144	3	0	0	„	Munshi Saffullah, Hazat Ali and Hafizuddin.	
Fowls ... „	407	0	10	0	„	Hafizuddin and Planters Stores and Agency Company, Limited.	
Ducks ... „	1,208	1	2	0	„	Hafizuddin and Planters Stores and Agency Company, Limited.	
Dhan ... lbs.	530,825	2	13	4	Md. of 80 lbs.	Deep Chand, Bansidhar Shaharia.	
Paddy straw „	51,375	0	12	0	lbs.	Villagers of Behrung village.	

APPENDIX VII (c).

Statement showing the percentage of loss on Supplies in connection with the Abor Expeditionary Force, 1911-12.

APPENDIX VII (*c*).

Statement showing the percentage of losses on Supplies in connection with the Abor Expeditionary, Force, 1911-12.

(Calculated up to 15th April 1912.)

Articles.		Quantities received at Kobo.			Quantities despatched to the Advanced Supply Depôt.	Losses at Kobo.	Losses at and beyond Advanced Supply Depôt.	Percentage of losses at Base.	Percentage of losses at and beyond Advanced Supply Depôt.	Total percentage of losses on Expedition.
		Received from India, Calcutta.	Received by local purchase at Dibrugarh or Kobo.	Total.						
Atta	lbs.	774,180	820	775,000	472,280	...	1,627	...	·34	·21
Rice	„	293,645	1,622,230	1,915,875	1,283,604	...	16,691	...	1·3	·87
Flour	„	25,200	246	25,446	15,743	...	489	...	3·04	1·92
Chillies	„	15,675	952	16,627	9,618	...	40	...	·41	·24
Dhall	„	398,795	246	399,441	243,650	222	189	·05	·07	·1
Garlic	„	6,095	5,046	11,144	7,150	1,045	1,799	9·38	25·16	25·52
Ginger	„	17,105	68	17,173	9,645	...	...	...	...	...
Ghi	„	105,534	21,580	127,114	79,264	351	474	·28	·59	·65
Goor	„	82,503	40,240	122,743	70,042	750	404	·61	·57	·94
Hops	„	14½	...	14½	10½	...	0—5	...	3·05	2·15
Malt	„	183	—	183	84	48	...	16·23	...	26·23
Pepper	„	27	11	38½	19½	...	0—12	...	3·84	1·94

Potatoes	... ...	„	...	43,112	43,112	29,180	1,569	5,086	3·64	17·42	15·43
Onions	... ...	„	...	99,258	99,258	32,109	20,621	4,901	20·78	15·26	25·71
Salt ...	... ...	„	13,365	56,694	70,059	46,615	...	125	...	·26	·17
Sugar	... ...	„	9,900	82	9,982	6,606	100	430	·002	6·5	5·3
Tea ...	... ...	„	17,941	17,714	35,655	18,334	...	35	...	·19	·09
Turmeric	... ...	„	6,270	4,040	10,310	7,315	...	57	...	·77	·55
Tobacco	... ...	„	20,610	...	20,610	14,550	...	12	...	·08	·05
Rum, proof	... ...	galls.	5,562	...	5,562	2,758	108	122	·194	4·42	4·13
Biscuits	... ...	lbs.	7,019	...	7,019	3,800	...	311	...	8·18	4·43
Baking powder	... ...	„	97	...	97	49	...	...	...	...	...
Bovril	... ...	Jars	1,541	...	1,541	804	...	...	...	...	...
Bacon	... ...	lbs.	1,929	491	2,420	2,048	...	20	...	·97	·32
Butter	... ...	„	...	1,121	1,121	1,109	...	5	...	·45	·44
Cocoa	... ...	„	847	...	847	661	...	61	...	9·22	7·2
Chocolate	... ...	„	468	110	578	455	...	9	...	1·98	1·55
Condensed milk	... ...	„	5,700	1,196	6,796	4,371	2—4	44	·03	1·006	·67
Cheese	... ...	„	1,846	...	1,846	641	27	18	1·46	2·8	2·43
Jam	... ...	„	2,063	360	2,423	2,085	...	7	...	·33	66·
Kobanies	... ...	„	10,450	5,318	15,768	9,175	55	291	·35	3·17	·12
Prunes	... ...	„	1,262	...	1,262	967	...	...	...	...	...
Potatoe meal	... ...	„	932	...	932	245	54	...	5·79	...	85·7

APPENDIX VII (c).

Statement showing the percentage of losses on Supplies in connection with the Abor Expeditionary Force, 1911-12.

(Calculated up to 15th April 1912.)

Articles.		Quantities received at Kobo.			Quantities despatched to the Advanced Supply Depôt.	Losses at Kobo.	Losses at and beyond advanced Supply Depôt.	Percentage of losses at Base.	Percentage of losses at and beyond Advanced Supply Depôt.	Total percentage of losses on Expedition.
		Received from India, Calcutta.	Received by local purchase at Dibrugarh or Kobo.	Total.						
Preserved meat	lbs.	17,542	...	17,542	11,881	...	41	...	...	2·33
Pickles	„	917	21	938	493	...	7	...	1·41	·74
Opium	Seers	234	...	234	47	...	½	...	1·06	·21
Oatmeal	lbs.	914	30	944	870	...	...	...	...	...
Tobacco, Cavendish ...	„	692	...	692	484	...	...	...	...	...
Limejuice	Galls.	648	...	648	437	...	6	...	1·37	·92
Vinegar	„	28	...	28	25	2½	2½	8·92	·10	17·85
Barley	lbs.	71,360	...	71,360	22,240	...	...	...	...	...
Bran	„	8,984	...	8,984	1,200	...	...	...	...	...
Dhan	„	...	530,828	530,828	216,380	—	...	...	...	...
Gram	„	218,756	1,024	219,780	119,235	...	...	...	...	...
Baled bhusa	„	256,928	...	256,928	83,440	...	...	...	...	...
Baled hay	„	471,120	...	471,120	205,320	...	...	...	...	...
Paddy straw	„	...	51,375	51,375	...	...	...	...	...	...
Goats	No.	66	3,659	3,725	2,402	60	98	1·61	4·08	4·24
Sheep	„	30	286	316	216	9	18	2·84	8·33	8·54

APPENDIX VII (*d*).

EQUIPMENT.

Extracts from Report of Assistant Director, Supply and Transport.

* * * * * *

For the Abor Expedition, it being imperative that we should proceed as lightly as possible, everything was cut down and only essential articles taken. For posts on the lines of communication in such country and under such circumstances the following equipment should suffice:—

Scales, spring balance, 2, with spare needles and screw driver for adjustment, repairs, etc.; scales, triangular, 1 of improved light pattern with weights up to 1 maund only; scales, copper, medium, 2, with small weights; rum measures, copper, 1 set, properly stamped and with measures for ⅜ dram and ⅝ dram; butchers' knives 2, steel 1, (although no butchery may be present yet these are necessary for sheep or goats, etc., supplied for meat rations at the posts); nailpuller, hammer, chisel, nails, scissors, stencils with large letter plates, and a good supply both black and red marking ink and brushes; 2 good axes, 3 tin openers, 2 tin funnels for filling kegs and bottles; packing thread and needles; box of necessary stationery and forms and books of Field Service Regulations (this is frequently forgotten); paulins, 18 feet × 12 feet, one dozen, to be increased as necessary; Dietz junior hurricane lanterns 3, with spare wicks and globe.

Establishments.—2 efficient weighmen (the 2nd takes the place of the peon authorized), 1 sweeper, 1 bhisty, 6 coolies.

For a small Advanced Depôt these equipments might be doubled and also the establishments, to whom should be added a tin-smith with modern, up-to-date tools and material, and a carpenter with ditto, who could also do cooper's work; paulins and coolies as necessary; small bakery and butchery establishments and equipment.

This reduced scale would effect a great saving in transport, and would not diminish efficiency.

* * * * * *

Waterproof bags.—The usual gunny bags of the markets of India are of one and two maund sizes and had to be reduced, while a special description of waterproof bag after numerous experiments was adopted for this expedition, proving eminently satisfactory and the best pattern ever seen in Assam.

Messrs. Birkmyre Brothers and Messrs. Harley Brothers of Calcutta have been the chief manufacturers and, to the use of these bags must be greatly attributed the few losses from damaged stores on the expedition.

Time however is required by the firms to make them up. The waterproof qualities of the bags were stringently tested and by this means an excellent fixed pattern was secured at a reasonable rate.

Formerly the one maund waterproof bag had an open mouth into which, in spite of close lacing, the rain and damp could penetrate. The Abor Expedition waterproof bag has a 6" flap coming down over the mouth; nine brass eyelet holes, a strong fixed lace that cannot fall off, and a superior quality of waterproofing and varnish.

* * * * * *

The empty bags were returned to the Base and were repeatedly used. Large numbers were also returned to Calcutta to come up again with fresh supplies. They were used also for locally purchased stores.

Some 5,000 of these bags were taken over by the Military Police with supplies and as a reserve. They served also a variety of other useful purposes on the expedition such as for roofing grass huts and for shelters; for carrying water in camp; for protecting stores from the damp ground; as watering troughs for mules and for use in the carriage of mails.

They have also been used as a waterproof cape by coolies and followers from time to time in heavy rain.

There is very little doubt that these bags saved the expedition endless losses. It is suggested that, as the tarred outer side of the bags renders marking difficult, some material of the nature of the ordinary waterproof sheet be tried with the rubber coating inside.

Kegs.—Similarly, as regards kegs for rum, limejuice, and vinegar. These have had to be made of special size for cooly transport and contained 4½ gallons each.

These, on the whole, have proved satisfactory but, at the commencement of the expedition, a few were found to have been repaired at Calcutta with inferior wood such as pine, which affected the quality of the contents.

* * * * * *

Special marking of loads.—Further economy was effected in the marking of bags and boxes to show contents, etc.

As a rule our bags on Field Service are marked in full according to the nature of the contents. The destination is also shown on each load or bag. All this elaboration for each and every load is unnecessary, causes delay in despatch and expense in paint and labour. On bags and boxes of reduced size it would be impossible. As loads are despatched in large consignments at the time it is unnecessary to show the destination on each bag. This is shown on the shipping invoice, receipt, or way bill, and the destination is frequently altered on field service and can, in any case, only be a temporary one.

A standard system of marking the loads was adopted and was published in book orders and routine orders for the information of the force generally. The system is shown in Appendix VII (*e*) and worked well, the only difficulty experienced being in getting a good stick-fast white paint for marking the black, polished surface of the waterproof bags. As the initial letters were of large size (4 inches), they could generally be recognised. It would have been better to have stamped the letters on both sides of the bags. All box loads should be branded instead of painted.

Paulins.—18 feet × 12 feet, 12 feet × 12 feet and 9 feet × 9 feet paulins have all been used on the expedition for protecting stores and supplies generally, and as shelters from rain and damp, and proved invaluable. The best kind are 18 feet × 12 feet, of khaki waterproof Dundee canvas, quality 4, and this size should be the only one sent to the field for protecting stores, etc., 9 feet × 9 feet is a useless size and should be done away with.

Medical Panniers for hospitals.—These were made of reduced size at Calcutta and of light "Venesta" wood. They have proved quite satisfactory as cooly-loads and in weight are much superior to the cumbersome mule panniers. I think further use of this Venesta wood, which is remarkably light and strong, would be a great economy from a transport point of view.

APPENDIX VII (*e*).

Special method of marking ration bags and boxes as adopted with the Abor Expeditionary Force. Bags with painted letters 4″ size; boxes with branded letters.

R	Rice.
S	Sugar.
C	Chillies.
G	Gram.
F	Flour.
A	Atta.
P	Potatoes.
T	Tea.
Kob	Kobanies.
V	Vinegar.
O	Onions.
D. M.	Dhall moong.
D. U.	Dhall urud
D. A.	Dhall arhar.
Tur	Turmeric.
Tobak	Tobacco.
M. oil	Mustard oil.
Salt	Salt.

* Should be altered to avoid confusion with G. (gram). Suggested marking would be CH.

Contents of loads (60 lbs. gross weight).

Tea boxes	35 lbs.
Condensed milk, boxes	40½ "
Tobacco leaf	30 "
Chillies	30 "
Pickles	22½ "
Biscuits	40 "
Oatmeal	42 "
Preserved meat	33 "
Jam	41 "
Prunes	56 "
Rum	4½ gallons.
Vinegar	4½ "

Tobacco, Cavendish	44	lbs.
Cocoa	27	„
Raisins	52	„
Bacon	40	„
Cheese	42	„
Chocolate	42	„
Mustard oil	40	„
Ginger	55	„
Ghee (Calcutta)	37	„
Gur	40	„

APPENDIX VII (*f*).

TRANSPORT.

Extracts from Report of Assistant Director, Supply and Transport.

The variety of transport employed on the expedition has made it one of peculiar interest.

River steamers and flats were employed from Calcutta to Kobo. From Kobo to Janakmukh two routes were used. By the Dihang river, in country boats over difficult rapids, to Pasighat, some 35 miles, and sometimes 5½ miles further to Janakmukh when the river was favourable. By elephant and mule transport by road, from Kobo to Pasighat, 20½ miles. Thence, by mules only, to Janakmukh, 5½ miles.

Along this road portion, until the arrival of the mule transport, the Naga Carrier Corps were employed. Elephants, as a rule, only proceeded as far as Pillung, some 13 miles from Kobo, but were frequently sent also in the Ledum direction.

The river transport terminus was generally at Pasighat but, for a time, the boats worked as far as Janakmukh, thus saving road transport and being of particular value in the absence of the mule transport, which only joined the force later.

The most level portion of the route, being between Kobo and Janakmukh and passing through large grass prairies, was worked by the mules.

As the force advanced, and the line became extended, mules were taken as far as Renging, but the road between Janakmukh and Renging being bad, with a continuous rise, mule transport generally stopped at "Cooly Cof," half way, when carriers met the mules from Renging.

Beyond Renging all transport was by carriers.

The total length by road from Kobo to the furthest point reached by the expedition (Singging) may be taken at 135 miles, and the greatest height reached (Moling Hill) some 10,111 feet above sea level.

* * * * * *

Photo.-Engraved & printed at the Offices of the S. I., Calcutta. 1914.

Naga carriers.
(Angami).

[*To face page 133.*

APPENDIX VII (*g*).

Extracts from Reports on Carrier Corps.

The Carrier Corps comprised 5 Naga Corps and 2 Gurkhali Corps, in all some 4,400 men; the latter gradually replaced the Nagas after these had been some 6 months on service. All the Corps as well as other transport units, except the boat transport, were commanded by officers of the Supply and Transport Corps.

Naga Carrier Corps.

No. 1 Corps.—Was composed of Western Angami and Kacha Nagas, and Kukis, *No. 2 Corps* of Semmas and Eastern Angamis, *No. 3 Corps* of Semmas and Lohtas, *No. 4 Corps* of Aos, and *No. 5 Corps* of Tengkhals.

The Nagas make excellent carriers and, as they have no caste prejudices, will eat almost anything. Under all circumstances and conditions of hardship and exposure, they were willing and cheerful, besides being remarkably honest and careful with their loads. They also possess a childlike faith and trust in the *Sahib*. It is difficult to decide which tribe provides the best carriers, the officers in command being loud in praises of all. In No. 1 Corps, the Kukis were the best for loads; the Semmas and Eastern Angamis of No. 2 Corps were both reported as having done excellent work, as also were the Tengkhals of No. 5 Corps; while in Nos. 3 and 4 Corps it was considered there are no finer carriers among the Nagas than the Semma, the Lhota and the Ao. Comparing the Semma and the Lhota, the latter was said to be the most reliable all round man and much more amenable to discipline. The Semma is very independent and much prefers fighting to carrying a load, requiring a much heavier hand over him. The Ao Naga is one of the finest carriers it is possible to find. He is not a great fighter and is very amenable to discipline. He is a small, wiry man, able to carry his 60 lb. load with ease and to endure great hardships and privations. All the Nagas submit to punishment without bearing ill-will so long as the punishment is deserved and is inflicted by the Commanding officer.

Method of Recruitment.—Generally speaking the following was the method adopted:—Each village was ordered by the Deputy Commissioner, Naga Hills, to bring in so many men to the recruiting centre by a certain date, each man bringing his spear and dao and 15 days' rice, which was calculated to last him until his arrival at the base of the expedition. On arrival at the recruiting centre each man was medically examined, and his name, father's name and village entered on the long roll. In no case did a village bring up fewer men than ordered and in many cases sent spare men to allow of rejections for medical unfitness. The number of men per village varied from 5 to 25.

Strength.—The strength of each Corps was approximately :—

British officer	1
Sub-Assistant Surgeon...	1
Clerk	1
Havildars (appointed from the Military Police) ...	2
Gaonburas (headmen)	30
Carriers	600

In one or two cases a Civil officer was attached.

Organisation.—As a rule the Corps were organised in sections, each under a *Gaonbura* or headman, the sections being composed of men from the same village or group of villages who would work best under a man they knew. The Naga pays no attention to the orders of a headman of any other but his own or an adjacent village and one with which his own village is on friendly terms. Another reason for this organisation under their own headmen is that in many cases even one section of a tribe cannot understand another, as the dialect varies considerably in different parts of the country. Thus sections varied somewhat, but were generally from 15 to 25 men in strength. In cases where villages brought up only a few men they were allowed to arrange amongst themselves as to their grouping together to form a complete section.

Rations.—Their scale of rations as fixed in the Abor scheme was as follows :—

Rice	2 lbs.
Dhall	4 ozs.
Salt	$\frac{3}{8}$ ozs.
Chillies	$\frac{1}{6}$ ozs.
Onions	1 oz.
Tobacco leaf	$\frac{1}{2}$ oz.
Mustard oil	1 oz.

It was found that they did not care for the mustard oil, and $\frac{1}{2}$oz. tea was substituted. Later this was changed to $\frac{1}{6}$ oz. tea and 1 oz. gur, which was more economical and better appreciated. The mustard oil was suggested by the Deputy Commissioner, Naga Hills, in lieu of the more expensive ghee, and to take the place of a meat ration, regarding which it was known there would be great difficulty in the supply in the Abor country, except when *mithan* were obtained.

All Nagas are great meat-eaters and are also accustomed to rice-beer of which they consume large quantities. Whenever available *mithan* were issued them as meat, a corresponding reduction being made in their dhal ration at the rate of 1 lb. meat per 4 ounces dhal, and ; latterly as an extra when fresh meat was unobtainable, an issue of tinned-meat was sanctioned. In lieu of 1 oz. of onions, $\frac{1}{2}$ oz. potatotes was subsequently substituted and the change was much appreciated.

On the recommendation of the Medical Officer an issue of rum was given them once a week at the rate of one keg of 4½ gallons per Corps, and this partly made up for the rice-beer to which they are accustomed, the rum being of course diluted largely with water to enable each man to have a share.

Clothing.—The scale of clothing issued per Naga, was two blankets and 1 follower's coat, and was found sufficient. Although Nagas were paid more than Gurkhalis, their clothing as well as their rations cost less.

Pay.—The pay of the personnel was as follows :—

	Rs.	as.	
Interpreters	60	0	per mensem
Clerks	45	0	ditto.
Havildars	35	0	ditto.
Head men	1	0	per diem.
Mates	0	14	ditto.
Carriers	0	12	ditto.

Notes and recommendations for future employment of Nagas.

Pay.—For the payment of men invalided, each Corps should deposit say Rs. 1,000 with the Treasure Chest Officer at the Base. The latter should be empowered to advance Rs. 5 to each man sent back from the Base to the Naga Hills. It is often impossible to send in bills in adjustment of advances, and the scheme proposed would do away with the necessity for such bills, as all advances given by the Treasure Chest Officer could be accounted for in the final settlement.

Rations.—The salt ration of ⅓ oz. per diem is insufficient and should be doubled ; the Naga is a great salt eater.

A ration of tinned-meat should be issued twice a week at the rate of ½ lb per issue, when fresh meat is not obtainable ; the Naga, if deprived of meat, falls off in condition very quickly.

Cooking pots.—Each man should have an aluminium cooking pot capable of holding a seer of rice. The earthenware pots which the majority of Nagas use for cooking their food get broken very quickly. The large cooking pots issued on loan are much too cumbersome and it takes a long time to cook food in them. It is very much better for each man to have his own, in case he is admitted to hospital or sent on detachment.

These aluminium cooking pots should be issued at the recruiting station before the Corps arrives at the Base.

Clothing.—The mates should be given scarlet blankets instead of brown ones. The coats, warm, followers, were much appreciated. The provision of an umbrella in addition to the sanctioned scale was suggested.

Supervising Establishment.—It is desirable that, in future, each Commandant should be given an Assistant; that, as each Corps is frequently split up on detached convoy duties, the supervising establishments should be increased and more carefully selected; that there should be 2 interpreters per Corps, unless the headmen speak Hindustani, which is uncommon, and a clerk from the Supply and Transport Corps, preferably a strong Mahomedan who can march.

Sickness and disease.—Considering the continuous hard work the corps were called upon to perform, the percentage of sick was not great. There were seldom more than 5 per cent in hospital at a time. The biggest percentage of sick was in the month of November when pneumonia, dysentery and fever caused by the continuous bad weather were common.

The Naga should be given doses of quinine twice a week during this time of the year, for he is liable to fever, as he is unaccustomed to the plains in the rainy season. Making the Naga build bamboo machans to lie upon at night, was a good preventative against fever and rheumatism.

Early Starting.—Early starting in the morning should be avoided whenever possible, as the Naga always cooks his food before leaving camp. He also likes a mid-day halt for at least an hour for cooking another meal.

Medical.—The hospital arrangements at Dibrugarh for sick Nagas left much to be desired. There was apparently no interpreter to be had there, and no one to understand the Naga and instruct him how to reach his home on discharge from hospital, and to write up advances of pay, etc., in his Service Book, or to inform the Deputy Commissioner, Naga Hills, of his departure and arrangements made. It would have been better if they had been kept in hospital at Kobo and not sent to Dibrugarh at all. There should have been a special hospital with an interpreter for them at Kobo, and a Medical Officer in charge who could see that on recovery they were either sent back promptly to their corps on the lines of communication or returned in batches to their own country under supervision.

The medical arrangements at Kobo for the regular return of men discharged from the hospital to their corps on the lines of communications appear to have left much to be desired.

Sick Attendants at the Base.—At least two Nagas who can speak Hindustani, should be enlisted specially per corps, as sick attendants. These men should accompany the corps to the Base, and remain there at the Naga Hospital throughout the whole expedition.

Draft.—In the event of an expedition lasting over three months, drafts to replace casualties would be an advantage to keep corps up to their full strength. At the termination of the last expedition we were at least a corps short, owing to men having been sent back to their homes.

Burial Expenses.—The estate of two Nagas of one Corps who died at Dibrugarh was charged Rs. 2 on account of burial expenses, which was wrong considering these men died owing to Field Service.

Service Books.—Service Books appear unnecessary for Carrier Corps, and discs and long rolls are quite sufficient. All advances are supposed to be entered up in the Service Book, but in no case was this done by the Medical authorities when they gave advances to sick men before being sent to Dibrugarh. In consequence this gave Commandants of Corps a lot of unnecessary trouble.

* * * * * *

The chief reason for the Nagas wishing to return to their homes in January was the fear that fields would not be sown. This fear was realized in some cases amongst the Semmas on their return. If in future, when Nagas are required, the Civil Authorities promised to see that their fields were properly looked after by those remaining behind in their villages under penalty of a fine, one of the great difficulties of obtaining recruits would be removed.

* * * * * *

Extract from reports on Gurkhali Carrier Corps.

Two of these were raised at Darjeeling to take the place of the Nagas and for work with the Survey parties beyond Yembung.

* * * * * * * *

No. 1 Carrier Corps was enlisted rather hurriedly, at the end of December 1911, the Assistant Director of Supply and Transport, Lucknow, stating that, at that period, the coolies were emigrating rapidly from the Darjeeling District in search of cold weather employment and that, if orders were not received within a very few days, great difficulty would be experienced in raising the corps.

Some of the men of this corps gave trouble on arriving at Kobo and again at Renging, clamouring for more clothes and more pay, but these were probably Darjeeling *bazar* men. One of the *sirdars* was promptly returned to India as useless and after that the corps settled down and gave no further trouble.

No. 2 Corps was raised in February 1912.

These corps arrived after the road had been made to Yembung; No. 1 Corps did very good work beyond that post, going as far as Geku and Riga. No. 2, arriving at the close of operations, worked on the lines up to Yembung and, on the whole, the men were of better physique than No. 1 Corps.

Both did excellent work, however, and the fresh blood in transport that they brought was a great relief as the Nagas were beginning to suffer from the continuous hard work and exposure of six months and were also becoming home-sick.

Gurkhalis are slower on the march and in climbing hills than the Nagas and wear a great many more clothes, but were generally strong and sturdy fellows who plodded steadily on with their loads, requiring more frequent halts than Nagas but eventually reaching camp. The Nága wears little and goes bare-footed, the Gurkhali a good many clothes including boots. For this reason the latter is better suited for work above the snow-line.

There was some misapprehension regarding the scale of clothing to be allowed to the Gurkhalis, the Assistant Director of Supply and Transport, Lucknow, being of opinion that they should only be given the Naga scale of 2 blankets and a coat. On the Tibet Expedition of 1904, the Gurkhalis and Nepalese were given no less than sixteen articles of this character, including 3 blankets, warm pyjamas, warm coat, woollen drawers, lamb's wool vest, ammunition boots, Gilgit long boots, waterproof sheet, etc. Many of the men, who had been on that expedition were therefore discontented with the scale of clothing issued for the Abor Expedition.

* * * * * *

System of Entertainment.—The Superintendent of Police, Darjeeling, collected twelve local men as *sirdars* who selected their own mates, and were responsible each for bringing in fifty carriers for entertainment.

Before entertainment, the men were examined as to their medical fitness for active service at the Civil Dispensary, Darjeeling. A list of the men passed as medically fit was sent to the Transport Registration Officer who, if he finally approved of the men, entered their names in the Corps Long Roll.

Each man received free rations and firewood from date of entertainment.

* * * * * *

Strength and Organisation.—The full complement of a corps consisted of :—

British officer	1
Havildars (from Gurkha regiments)	2
Clerk	1
Interpreter	1
Sirdars	12
Mates	12
Coolies	600

The corps were divided into twelve sections of 50 men each; each section was in charge of a *sirdar* with a mate as assistant. In No. 1 Corps the *sirdars* and mates were nearly all local Darjeeling men, in No. 2 Corps half the number were soldier pensioners.

Pay.—The rates of pay were as follows:—

					Rs.
Interpreter	...	...	...	...	60 per mensem.
Clerk	...	...	...	...	45 "
Havildars	...	...	...	...	40 per mensem consolidated.*
Sirdars	...	...	...	...	30 per mensem.
Mates	...	...	...	...	15 "
Carriers	...	...	...	...	12 "

Clothing.—On entertainment the following scale of clothing was issued:—

Interpreter and Clerk.—1 pair boots, 2 blankets, 1 coat.

Havildar's.—1 pyjama, 1 jersey, 1 pair putties, 1 waterproof sheet, 1 cap, 2 pairs socks, 1 pair mittens.

Sirdars, mates and carriers.—2 blankets, 1 coat, 1 pair boots.

423 pairs boots were issued to the corps in the field.

Rations.—The corps received the ordinary scale of followers rations as laid down in Field Service Regulations, Appendix III. The free issue was given from date of entertainment.

* * * * * *

Notes and Recommendations for future employment of Gurkhali Corps.

Pay.—It would be advisable before fixing rates of pay at Darjeeling to enquire what rates similar men employed by other departments on the spot are being paid and so avoid discontent and differences amongst the same class of men doing similar work at the base or along the lines of communication.

Rations.—The ordinary scale of followers rations as laid down in Field Service Regulations, Appendix III, is suitable and ample for Gurkhali carriers.

* Havildars with the Gurkhali Corps were paid at this rate as they were drawn from the Regulars, those with the Naga Corps were drawn from the Military Police.

Clothing.—For the north-east frontier the following scale of clothing is recommended. *Carriers,* 2 blankets, 1 pair of boots with nails, 1 jersey or coat, followers. *Sirdars,* in addition to the above should be provided with 1 puggri, 2 pairs of socks, 1 coat, warm, British and 1 haversack; he should wear something to distinguish him from the carrier.

The issue of putties would be well worth consideration. These men seem to wear putties a good deal, and, in wet weather, in the *jungle,* where leeches are plentiful, they would be of considerable service.

Before leaving the recruiting station, private clothing and cooking utensils should be inspected and reduced to a minimum, otherwise the men will be overloaded on the line of march. This weight was more often than not increased by 2 lbs. to 17 lbs. owing to the blankets and coat being wet through. Each man requires two cooking utensils which are invariably made of brass or iron and are, in consequence, weighty.

Time of year for entertainment.—The best time of year for raising a Carrier Corps at Darjeeling appears to be from October to December; men commence coming down to India to find employment after the *pujahs* in October. Between January and March these men have, in the majority of cases, found employment, and towards the end of March they commence returning to their homes.

Time taken in entertainment.—A corps of 600 selected carriers should be easily raised in a fortnight between October and December, provided a sufficient staff is available for clerical work, issue of clothing, etc., and provided also that labour is not in great demand locally at the time of raising, (road making on a large scale was in progress at Darjeeling when No. 1 Gurkhali Carrier Corps was being raised, in consequence of which carriers were difficult to obtain in the time available and little selection could be made). After December, three to four weeks would be required, as recruiting parties would have to go a considerable distance across the frontier to collect their men.

Accommodation during entertainment.—There is no available accommodation for the housing of carriers at Darjeeling while a corps is being raised, and the question of such accommodation is worthy of consideration. The men of No. 1 Gurkhali Carrier Corps lived in the *bazar* which conduced to desertion, and difficulty was experienced in collecting men when required, and in issuing rations.

A fully qualified Medical officer should examine and pass these men for enlistment instead of a Sub-Assistant Surgeon.

Best classes of carrier to entertain.—The best classes of carriers to entertain are the following :—

Magars and Gurungs (Nepal), Sherpas (Sikkim and Nepal), Bhutias (Bhutan), Ghartis (Nepal), Tamangs (Nepal and Sikkim), Mongers (Nepal), Thamis (Nepal), Sunwars (Nepal), Limbus and Rais (Nepal).

The following are generally of bad physique and should not be entertained :—Chetris, Brahmins, Kamis.

The best men are trans-frontier and the entertainment of local Darjeeling men is not to be recommended if it can be avoided. In No. 2 Corps the Bhutias proved the best men while Tibetans and Lepchas were also most satisfactory.

Establishment.—As in the case of the Naga Corps the Commandant should be given an Assistant and have Gurkha non-commissioned officers as *sirdars* and not local Darjeeling men as such. For the supervising establishment, the addition of a third Gurkha Havildar is advisable, owing to the frequent division of the corps into three or more detachments and to allow a margin for sickness.

An interpreter is not necessary and is only an extra expense to Government.

APPENDIX VII (*h*).

Boat Transport.

This proved very successful and greatly relieved all road transport between Kobo and Pasighat, extending for a time as far as Janakmukh.

All heavy and unsuitable loads, either for carriers or mules, were sent by the boats as far as possible, among these being Pioneer and Sapper and Miner equipments and material, telegraph stores and some hospital and advance supplies.

The boats proved extremely useful and convenient also in the transfer of the sick to the Base Hospital at Kobo while their employment proved extremely economical.

Between the 21st October 1911 and the 14th April 1912 the Boat Convoy conveyed some 22,000 maunds of stores, equipments, ammunition, etc.

From a statement furnished by the Commandant this works out at the remarkably low cost of Rs. 2-1-9 per maund.

* * * * * *

Owing to precautions taken, the losses by boat convoy were remarkably few, in spite of the difficulties of transport on such a swift running river as the Dihang and the many dangerous rapids to be crossed.

* * * * * *

Report by the Boat Transport Officer, Abor Expeditionary Force.

Narrative.—Boats and boatmen were collected during September 1911 at Gauhati.

On the 29th September, a flat conveying 44 boats left Gauhati for Kobo. On the 1st October, Lieutenant Webb, Conductor Bray and Sub-Conductor Tyler proceeded in a steamer to Kobo.

Kobo was reached on the 7th October and the boats were unloaded on the following day. It was found that several had been extensively damaged in transit, and five were quite unserviceable. This damage was due to their being packed on top of one another in the flat, and to the pressure on the bottom boats causing the seams to open out. Sending boats loaded on a flat should be avoided if possible both on account of the expense incurred, and the damage done.

Twelve days were spent in repairing the boats and fitting them out with all necessary equipment. Miri boatmen were also entertained locally.

On the 21st October, the boat convoy proceeded on its first trip to Pasighat. The river was very high and great difficulty was experienced in negotiating the rapids. The convoy took 6 days to reach Pasighat, starting each day at 6 A.M and making camp at dark about 6-30 P.M.

The usual distribution of the convoy on the river was as follows:—

Advanced guard boat;
Warrant officer with guide;
Convoy boats;
Warrant officer;
Rear guard boat.

The boats were poled along close to the bank. At any place where the river had to be crossed, it was found most important to station a responsible man to point out to each boat the exact spot from which to effect the crossing, as otherwise the boats were swept down by the force of the current, and failed to reach the correct place on the opposite bank. Another necessary precaution in crossing was to prevent two or more boats starting simultaneously, since there was a danger of their colliding with each other, and so upsetting.

The return trip from Pasighat to Kobo was accomplished in 5 hours.

It was found after the first trip that the large fifty maund boats were too unwieldy and cumbersome for the journey to Pasighat; the labour and risk with which these boats were taken over the rapids, proved too heavy a strain on the endurance of the boatmen; one boatman died from exposure on the first trip. It was therefore decided to abandon the large fifty-maund boats and increase the boat transport to a maximum of 80 thirty-maund boats.

On the second trip the convoy reached Pasighat in 3½ days, and on the third trip in 3 days.

On the third trip the convoy proceeded to Janakmukh, about 5 miles above Pasighat. Two days were however spent in accomplishing this, as the boats had to be dragged up two very steep rapids, through which channels for the passage of the boats were built. Two boats were swamped in these rapids, but the stores were all safely recovered.

On the fourth, fifth and seventh trips the boat convoy arrived at Pasighat in 3 days, and the fourth day was spent in dragging the boats with much labour and difficulty over the Pasighat rapids up to Janakmukh after the channels had been deepened and improved by the Naga coolies.

After the seventh trip on the 6th December, the water became too low in the channels for the boats to reach Janakmukh, and it was decided that the boat convoy should arrive every sixth day at Pasighat, whence the stores were taken by mule transport to Janakmukh. This arrangement allowed for 3 days' journey from Kobo to Pasighat, 1 day's return journey to Kobo, and 2 days' halt at Kobo; the halt of two days at Kobo was employed in repairing the boats and loading up stores for the next trip.

From the 21st October to the 23rd December 1911, the river fell steadily, but from this period onwards it remained at a normal low water-level till the 27th March. From the 27th March the river was liable to sudden rises and equally sudden falls.

As the river fell, new routes were followed; from the 21st October to the 17th November the Bamora *suti* was used; from the 18th November to the 19th December the channel along the left bank of the main river above Namsing village was used, from the 20th December to the 5th April the channel along the right bank of the main river above Namsing village was used; the latter was the permanent route for the river at its normal low-water level.

At the commencement of each trip the boatmen were issued with six days' rations. The daily routine of the boat convoy when on the river was as follows:—the boatmen cooked and fed in the early morning, the convoy then left camp about 7 A.M.; at 11 A.M. a halt of half an hour took place for the Miri boatmen to smoke their opium. It was found that if they were not allowed this halt, the habitual opium eaters were unable to endure for the whole day. The boats were poled along one behind another in the shallow water close to the bank. Camp was reached between 4 and 5 P.M. and the boatmen made lean-to shelters for themselves on the sand with tarpaulins. Food was then cooked and eaten, and the boatmen turned in for the night. The boat convoy on its return trips from Pasighat always brought down sick men, for whom this form of transport was admirably suited.

Goats, sheep, geese and ducks were conveyed to Pasighat on the boats. For goats and sheep a rough pen was erected in the middle of the boat, twenty goats or sheep were placed on board a thirty-maund boat, and when conveyed in this manner never caused any trouble. The best method for conveying ducks was found to be a covered-in erection built in the middle of the boat and divided into an upper and lower compartment by a floor made level with the sides of the boat. An erection of this description built on a thirty-maund boat carried two hundred ducks, which travelled very well in this manner.

On the night of the 15th November there was an alarm at Janakmukh and some firing took place. The boatmen were encamped outside the perimeter close to their boats. Directly the firing commenced the boatmen made a rush for the boats. In case of an alarm arrangements should at once be made to prevent the boats being boarded, and to collect the boatmen in one place till further orders. It is the natural instinct of the boatmen on an alarm to rush for their boats and push out into the stream.

* * * * * *

Description of boats.—The boats employed were mainly of three descriptions :—

(*a*) Thirty-maund boat ; a boat constructed from lengths of wood joined together by iron clamps. The average length was 40′ 2″ and the average girth 6′ 4″. This boat carried thirty maunds of stores if loaded down to the water's edge, but a load of fifteen to twenty maunds of stores could not be exceeded with safety in a river with numerous rapids like the Dihang.

(*b*) Twenty-maund boat; a boat constructed similarly to the thirty-maund boat; the average length was 23′ 6″ and the average girth 5′ 4″. This boat, for work over rapids, carried from ten to fifteen maunds of stores.

(*c*) Ten-maund boat; a boat constructed out of a single tree without any join. The average length was 28′ 2″ and the average girth 3′ 4″. This boat, for work over rapids, carried between five and eight-maund stores.

The thirty-maund and twenty-maund boats were hired from Gauhati and Dibrugarh. A hire of annas 9 per diem was paid for the Dibrugarh boats and Re. 0-5-4 per diem for the Gauhati boats. The ten-maund boats were hired locally from the Miris and a hire of annas 2 per diem was paid. The thirty-maund boats were manned by a crew of five boatmen, the twenty-maund boats by crews of four or three boatmen according to their size and weight and the ten-maund boats by three boatmen.

Equipment of boats.—Each boat was equipped as follows :—

(*a*) Cross-pieces fitted athwart the boat; the object of this was to strengthen the boat and prevent the sides from splaying outwards under strain.

(*b*) Two bamboos lashed together to the cross-pieces running as a free-board along each side of the boat on the outside. The object of this is to steady the boat and save it from swamping when it rolls from side to side in a rapid. It also prevents, to a large extent, the waves in a rapid from splashing into the boat.

(*c*) Bamboo matting laid over cross-pieces raised from four to eight inches above the bottom of the boat. The object of this is to save stores from becoming wet, as they otherwise would, if placed on the bottom of the boat.

(*d*) Each boat was provided with the following stores :—

(1) Towing rope; 3-inch rope varying from fifty to one hundred feet in length fastened to a cross-piece about three feet from the prow of each boat.

(2) Fastening rope; six feet of rope to tie the boat up to the bank.

(3) One large tarpaulin for covering the stores.

(4) 1 large steering oar (*baitha*), 2 paddles (*dhar*), 4 bamboo punting poles (*logi*) and 1 bailing tin.

Each Miri boatman, who was entertained locally, also brought his own oar—a long narrow oar four inches wide at the bottom, and gradually tapering to the top—they use this oar both for poling and paddling. All equipment was made up from material obtained locally; a hard red wood called *bula kath* was used for making the steering oars.

Materials used for repairing leaks in the boats were tow or rope fibre, pitch, bamboo wood, and iron clamp. The leak was caulked with tow or rope fibre steeped in boiling pitch. A flat piece of bamboo, about two inches in width, of the required length was then fixed over the spot and secured by iron clamps; the object of this was to keep the caulking fixed into the leaks.

Establishment.—The boat establishment consisted of—

1 British officer.

2 Warrant officers.

230 Boatmen.

Discipline was maintained by five Pathans, one head Assamese boatman, and one head Miri boatman.

The boatmen comprised Assamese from Gauhati, and Miris and Abors recruited locally. The method of recruitment for the local Miris and Abors was for each village to supply a fixed number of boatmen who were relieved periodically by men from their own village. Thus, after each trip of six days, about sixty Miri boatmen were discharged, and new men entertained in their places. Owing to this method there never was a shortage of boatmen owing to sickness.

Pay and clothing.—Each boatman received 8 annas pay per diem, drew the field service scale of rations for public followers, and received the following articles of clothing —

1 waterproof sheet.

1 coat warm, followers.

1 khaki blouse.

2 blankets.

There were only very occasional cases of boatmen being admitted to hospital for sickness; the usual complaint was dysentery.

Rapids.—Negotiating the rapids formed the chief difficulty in taking the boats from Kobo to Pasighat. To negotiate a long, uniform rapid, each boat was dragged up by its own crew both by means of the towing rope, and by the men wading in water and pushing the boats along. For short, steep portions of a rapid, where the crew of a boat was not sufficient, two boatmen from each large boat, and one boatman from every other boat, formed a line in the water along the steep portion of the rapid and passed all the boats up by hand, no boatman being allowed to rejoin his boat until all had been dragged over the difficult place. For a very steep rapid, such as the Pasighat rapid, a channel for the boats was made; boatmen then lined one side of the channel and passed the boats up by hand. The shape of the channel is very important; the mouth must be narrow, in order that a back-water may be formed down each wall of the channel. If the mouth is wide and funnel shaped, the water, rushing in from either side, causes a series of waves down the middle of the channel which is apt to swamp the boats.

* * * * * *

Remarks.—The boat transport was used without intermission for six months. During this period a very thorough trial was afforded of the capabilities of boats used for transport.

The chief advantage of boat transport is that each boat with the crew is entirely self-contained; in addition to the fixed quantity of stores carried, each boat conveys the rations and baggage of its crew. If boatmen fall sick the carrying capacity of the boats is not affected. The fact that the boats were constantly worked for six months up and down a river full of difficult rapids like the Dihang proves that they are capable of standing a very heavy strain, indeed without breaking down.

The maintenance of the boats in a proper state of repair is very simple, and repairs can always be carried out on the spot without the necessity of skilled labour. The replacement and renewal of all boat equipment such as poles, paddles and oars can be effected from material locally available. The whole management of boat transport is simple and eminently practical.

Boats form ideal transport for the conveyance of sick men and for bulky and heavy articles unsuited for other kinds of transport. Stores, when conveyed in boats, remain undisturbed till arrival at their destination and constant shifting and handling of stores is thus avoided, which diminishes the chance of loss and damage. The disadvantage of boat transport is its slow rate of progress up stream and the fact that it is difficult, in negotiating bad rapids, to prevent stores from becoming wet to a small extent, although this is minimised by having the stores raised off the bottom of the boat and always covered by a tarpaulin.

The economy, or otherwise, of boat transport is governed by the proportion of boatmen employed to the weight of stores conveyed. For a river, without difficult rapids like the Brahmaputra, boats can be loaded very heavily without danger and, if large boats were employed, conveying one hundred maunds of stores with a crew of six boatmen, the proportion would work out to sixteen maunds conveyed for every boatmen employed. But, for a river like the Dihang, with numerous and difficult rapids to negotiate, crews must be increased and the size of boat decreased. The proportion in working the boats on the Dihang river was four maunds of stores conveyed for every boatman employed.

For a country like Assam there is no doubt that boat transport is eminently suitable; the country is covered with forest, and roads are very difficult to make and become almost impassable during the rains.

Boat transport requires organisation and training to become efficient. The boatmen require considerable practice before they can manipulate their boats over rapids with safety; those who are accustomed to one type of boat are often helpless when required to use another type.

* * * * * * *

APPENDIX VII (*k*).

Report on Elephant Transport.

* * * * * * *

Elephants were hired locally from civil departments and others, and were found very useful for cutting jungle and road-making near the Base.

Their daily ration was dhan, 20 lbs., salt 2 ozs., oil 1 oz., and the rate of hire Rs. 5 per diem.

The mahouts were chiefly Assamese, with a few Indians, the latter being by far the best.

The scale of rations for mahouts was as for Indian followers with opium, one *tola* per man weekly, for opium eaters.

Mahouts were paid Rs. 15 and their coolies Rs. 10 per mensem.

They were also given clothing as for Indian followers on the summer scale.

* * * * * * *

When the force had advanced the elephant establishment was reduced and eventually all were discharged.

The men generally were lazy and required much supervision.

The principal employment of the Assam elephant appears to be to clear jungle and pull logs. Rafts of the latter are floated down the Brahmaputra for the various saw mills and, when these rafts stick on sand banks, etc., the elephant is useful for proceeding into mid-stream and pushing or pulling them off. Beyond bringing in grass from the jungle he is not much employed for transport purposes and arrives when hired with little or no gear or equipment.

Gadels and pads had to be made up from any material available such as gunny bags, and tent *saleetahs* and girths were improvised with boat-rope. To assist in retaining loads on their backs, camel loading nets were tried with partial success. The maximum loads these elephants could carry was 8 maunds.

Two elephants were lent by the Deputy Commissioner, Lakhimpur, and one by the Superintendent of Police, Dibrugarh, without charge. Four were hired from the Raja of Chowkham, and six from the civil population of Tinsukia.

The elephant of Assam for transport purposes is distinctly disappointing.

* * * * * *

APPENDIX (*l*).

Report on Mule Transport.

Mule Transport.—The 26th Mule Corps from Lucknow reached Kobo in two detachments, the first arriving on the 28th October 1911 in two steamers the "Damari" and "Chitrali." The second detachment did not arrive until a month later in three steamers.

A full Mule Corps was asked for, but 32 mules had been detached by the division and sent with the Mishmi Expedition. As the corps also lost three mules from being bogged on the bank of the Brahmaputra while *en route* in the steamer to Kobo, the Mule Corps actually joined the force 35 mules short and calculations of transport had to be readjusted accordingly.

* * * * * *

* * * * * *

Mule transport was allotted to the most level and flat portion of the lines of communication—that between Kobo and Janakmukh, with a few mules beyond. This enabled the mules to take full advantage of local fodder resources from the large grass *chapris*, etc., and the utilization of this local fodder supply to the fullest extent has proved the economic value of mule transport in the country.

There appears to be a difference in opinion as regards the relative advantages of Pasighat and Janakmukh as a Supply Depôt in connection with mule transport. Both posts, as frequently happens in the field, had their advantages and drawbacks. Pasighat had more space, but fodder was available in the vicinity of both places; and when the Dihang was high the boat convoy could reach Janakmukh direct with stores from Kobo instead of having to unload at Pasighat—a valuable saving of transport being thus secured.

Atta, rice and dhall bags were chiefly conveyed by the mules to avoid possibility of contents being damaged by river water in the boats.

Extracts from Report on 26th Mule Corps.

* * * * * *

2. *River journey.*—As regards the river journey from Calcutta a few points might be found useful in the case of a future expedition on the north-east frontier, which may necessitate the despatch of mules by river steamer.

The first and most important is the unsuitability of iron decked steamers for animals transport. Five steamers in all were used to convey the corps up the river, *viz.*, the "Chitrali," "Dewari," "Battani," "Madaya" and "Moulmein." Of these, the first three are iron decked, the other two wooden decked, and as the accommodation on the two latter boats equals that of the former, I would suggest that, in future, only wooden decked boats be chartered for this purpose. The next point is that, as a preventive to slipping, the shipping company supplied saw-dust, which is not nearly so effective or cleanly as river sand; the weight of the latter prevents it being washed away whenever an animal stales, whereas the saw-dust was washed away at once. A third, though minor, point was that the bamboos for the stalls were by no means as well finished off as they should have been, as small branches had been roughly cut off and not levelled with the surface of the poles, and several minor wound cases resulted before we had time to square off all the poles.

As regards the river rations issued, I should like to see linseed meal replaced by an equal weight of barley; the animals did not take at all kindly to the linseed meal, and it had to be cut out of their feed. Bhoosa might with advantage take the place of grass, as the small quantity of the latter is consumed very quickly, and also bhoosa bales take up less hold accommodation.

3. *Climate.*—The climate of the country is an important factor, and in this case I think that there is no doubt that it is eminently suitable for mule transport, and I see no reason why bullock-cart transport should not be employed in future expeditions as far as Pasighat, up to which point the Public Works Department have built a *kutcha* road. Rain when it does fall, is heavy, and the roads cut up badly, but the proportion of wet days is small. From the end of October to the end of March we have not suffered from excessive heat at all; in fact the climate has been extremely mild.

* * * * * *

5. *Water.*—Mules at Kobo, Pasighat and Janakmukh were watered from the river on the banks of which these camps are situated. This water, however, is very cold, presumably through the river being snowfed, and the mules have never drunk their fill at any of these posts. At Pillung a stream called the Mora Lalli runs alongside the camp and the water here is excellent, both quantity and quality being as good as could be desired, and the mules have drunk readily. Water at Renging and Rotung is scarce; and arrangements must be made for troughs at both these places if any number of mules are to be stationed there. At Renging the arrangement made was to sew a number of waterproof bags together in the form of a trough and fix them on the trestles; bamboos were then split and the water drawn off from the small hillside stream by means of these and run down into the troughs, the water being kept continually running; by these means forty mules at a time were watered, whereas on our first arrival there, only three could be watered at a time from an impoverished pool formed by damming the stream. This could also be easily done at Rotung. Mules were also watered on the line of march whenever and wherever practicable, but except for the stream at six-mile camp, this supply was precarious, as several streams dried up during the cold weather.

6. *Local supplies.*—There is practically no grain ; the only large consignment I saw was brought in from Balek by order of the Inspector of Communications as a punishment to the village (about 40 maunds). With fodder, however, the case was very different, as throughout the operations the mules have been very largely self-supporting in this respect. Large *chapris* exist near Kobo and Pillung, either of them sufficient in extent to feed ten times the number of animals employed. Pasighat also has a good local forage supply, sufficient for a full mule corps, and Janakmukh can be depended on to feed about three troops for one month (the figure was surpassed on this expedition, but it must not be forgotten that a very large quantity of the fodder at this post was paddy and *marua* straw off Rammi Dumbang *jhums* which in a future expedition might not be again available). Supplies of fodder for Renging, Rotung, and Yembung would have to be imported, as no local fodder is available, except small quantities of bamboo leaves. As regards quality, the grass on the *chapris* is generally speaking eaten greedily by the mules, being short and sweet, but the grass on Rammi Dumbang and around Janakmukh is inferior, except in a few small patches.

* * * * * *

9. *Sickness and Casualties.*—The health of men and animals has been good on the whole. A good deal of dysentery occurred at Janakmukh to start with, but latterly improved. Percentage of sorebacks amongst animals worked out to about 5 per cent. Lameness, except for one outbreak of mud fever, was practically non-existent, and only one girth-gall occurred. During a heavy spell of work through 11 days continuous rain over the Renging—Coolie Col section, an outbreak of mud fever caused the temporary lameness of nearly every mule on the section, these mules were moved out as soon as they could move on three legs, and except for a few virulent cases recovered shortly. No single case of thrush occurred, due, I think, to the liberal use of Stockholm tar as soon as heavy rain occurred. Altogether, twenty-five cases of poisoning amongst the mules were brought to notice ; only three were fatal, the remaining cases yielded to liberal drenches of linseed oil. Symptoms of attack were violent and sudden vomiting and diarrhœa and profuse sweating. No trace of the poison or plant could be found, as mules, in wandering through jungle, pick a leaf here and another there, and it is impossible to state which was the actual plant responsible. Biting flies were very few, only one small fly occurring in any numbers and raising a small blood blister after the bite. These did not attack the animals. Leeches, however, attacked men and animals freely.

20 animals killed.
12 per cent drivers invalided.

12. *System of carrying loads.*—Owing to the fact that all loads had to be made up to suit coolie transport, it was found necessary to increase the pack mule load by 20 lbs. as three 60 lbs. loads had to be carried instead of two 80 lbs. loads. This worked very well and no

trouble was caused, once the men had got into the way of tying the top loads. The latter load should invariably be a bag, and all boxes slung on the sides in the usual manner. The best way of securing this load is to first put on the side loads, then take the third load and adjust it on the top of the saddle, now take two of the slack ends of baggage ropes securing side loads and pass them underneath the two arches of the saddle from the opposite ends and bring them up over the load and tie off; the other two slack ends are then thrown over the top load and also tied off. The chief advantage noted from this form of loading is that the top load locks the side loads and makes the whole much steadier. The only possible solution that I can see of the fact that only one girth-gall occurred during five months' continuous work, is that the third load steadied the whole to such an extent that the sway of the load was greatly decreased, and I am of opinion that this system might be given a further trial as tending to economise transport.

* * * * * *

19 The experiment in the line of cheap dubbing at present in use in transport units, has been a failure; as soon as heavy rain commenced, the large proportion (20 per cent) of turpentine set up blisters in every place where the leather work touched the animals, and though not actually putting the animals out of work, except in one or two very bad cases, it caused them a great deal of unnecessary pain and irritation.

21. *Veterinary Equipment.*—In Assam, it is advisable to take about 5 maunds of Stockholm tar per Mule Corps for plugging feet; also an additional 5 gallons of linseed oil, as this article soon disappears when drenching poisoned animals.

* * * * * *

23. *Repairing materials.*—*Newar* for jhools, and dubbing should both be increased in scales, specially the latter, whenever working in a damp climate such as Assam.

Extracts from Report of Inspector of Communications and Base Commandant.

* * * * * *

TRANSPORT.

Unless it is carefully guarded against, it will often be found that Supply forgets that Transport can be overworked, and in anxiety to get up stores and to be relieved of the responsibility of running short, orders movements that lead to the break down or exhaustion of transport.

As soon as possible the meeting-staging system should be instituted for both carriers and mules. Its advantages are well known, such as all returning to their food and bedding, tents or huts—no extra weight on carriers and mules,—yet despite many efforts, this only got started in the end of December. It became at once a great success.

Start the meeting and returning system of transport as soon as feasible.

Carriers.—Previous to roads being made or in default of roads, better carriers than Nagas are not to be found. In addition to his carrying power, he is armed with a spear and dao, and impresses the wild people as a fighting man (which he is not exactly).

The greatest precautions must be taken—

(1) to make these people avail themselves of the sanitary conveniences provided;

(2) to prevent them straying and head hunting on their own;

(3) to prevent them carrying their *lares and penates* as well as their proper load, which they try to do and which often causes a break-down;

(4) to keep them away from liquor shops. The Naga misses his home-made rice-beer.

2. The next best carriers are Nepalese from Darjeeling. They move slowly but steadily. I think they should all be given a khaki outfit, as they come in all sorts of rags, often filthy, and have no change of clothing. This leads to ill-health and also to their being looked down on by both troops and the local people.

They should have a barber per corps, and be made to wash. They are usually well behaved.

3. *Boat convoy.*—When there is a river along the line of communications, boat convoys are most useful if properly arranged for and the assistance expected is generously given by the Civil authorities. Great difficulty was found in getting the cowardly Assamese to volunteer for this work and unfortunately the demand for boatmen was also made the means for squeezing money out of these people for exemptions by Indian subordinate civil officials. The boats sent up by some of the authorities were only useful for firewood—this was particularly so at Gauhati, and Government was put to much expense for carriage to the Base with no return. Perhaps a Supply and Transport officer or warrant officer should be entrusted with the passing of the boats for service. When the Assamese got over their terror they turned out good boatmen.

Secondly, the Miris of the river settlements came freely and arranged for reliefs and did well, and some Abor settlers in British territory also were quite satisfactory.

4. *Steamers.*—Most of the transports arrived overcrowded. Mumps broke out amongst the Pioneers and caused segregation of a double company and of several carriers.

In case of cholera it would have been awful, and cholera is rather prevalent on the river. Great care should be taken to get municipal water at Gauhati and not to take in river water. This requires special arrangements through the civil authorities.

Printed notes embodying sanitary precautions were given to vessels, after they had been asked for. These should be ready before mobilization is ordered, and be always available. Sentries should be posted on water tanks.

All troops from Calcutta brought 15 days' rations.

5. *Transport clothing for attendants.*—The Government of India do not allow a man to draw his quarterly allowance whilst on field service, and at the same time require him to go into the field fully equipped, with one or two exceptions such as water-proof sheets, out of his half mounting. The result is that the man wears out all his ordinary kit and this is replaced by articles which are not up to the quality which in cantonments is found to be most economical in wear and tear. The men return to cantonments clad in garments which have to be discarded and they have to be issued with new kits from the half mounting accounts.

This means putting practically every man into debt, which is not fair to the personnel. Either Government should provide clothing of the quality laid down for peace by the Quartermaster-General in India or else the men should continue to accumlate their quarterly allowances whilst on service. It is suggested that khaki shorts of a decent material and colour be issued as part of field service renewals of clothing, and that pagries be made of Bowden pagri cloth which is ordinarily issued in transport units, and that the khaki blouses for transport be made of spinners khaki. A man who was thus refitted whilst on service would go back with the same outfit as he started with and the units would be uniformally dressed, instead of each man having separate coloured coats, putties, pagries, pajamas, etc., etc.

* * * * *

APPENDIX VII (*m*).

Statement showing particulars of Supply and Transport menial establishment with the Abor Expeditionary Force, 1911-12.

Detail of establishment.	Number.	Rate of pay per mensem.	REMARKS.
		Rs.	
Weighmen ...	11	6	The universal rates of pay for establishments as laid down in the old Field Service Code require revision, not being applicable to rates prevailing at the present time.
Peons	9	6	
Mate bakers	3	14	
Kneaders ...	6	9	
Head butcher	1	10	
Butchers ...	2	8	
Herdsmen ...	2	6	
Bildars ...	1	6	
Bhistis ...	13	6	
Dhobies ...	9	8	
Sweepers ...	9	6	
Pakhali bhistis ...	5	6	
Hospital store-keepers' assistants, 2nd grade.	6	8	
Coopers	6	20	
Carpenters	2	15	
Blacksmiths	2	15	
Packermen	2	8	
Tinsmiths	5	25	
Hammermen	2	7	

APPENDIX VII (*n*).

Approximate distances between posts on Line of Communication.

Name of stage.	Approximate distance; miles.	Remarks.
BY ROAD.	Miles.	
Kobo	...	
Pasighat	20½	By new road; old road longer.
Janakmukh	5¼	
Renging	7¼	
Kotung	8½	
Yembung	9¼	
Komsing	8½	
Riu	6¼	
Geku	12¼	
Simong	17	
Singging	41	
Total ...	135¾	
Yembung	...	
Yekshing	9	
Dosing	9	
Extreme point reached (Riga) ...	12½	
Total ...	30½	*Note.*—Greatest height reached Moling Hill 10,111 feet.
LEDUM COLUMN.		
Kobo	...	
Oniyuk (Oyang)	10	
Ledum	16	
Misshing	5	
Pasighat	31	
Misshing to Balek	23	
Balek to Rotung	6	
BY RIVER.		
Kobo	...	
Pasighat	29½	
Janakmukh	5	
Total ...	34½	

APPENDIX VIII.

REPORT ON THE WORKING OF ALL ARMS.

(By the General Officer Commanding the Force).

Abor defensive tactics.

The Abors on the whole adopted a defensive attitude. They chose sites for stockades, where topographical difficulties, in their estimation, presented insuperable difficulties. The stockades were usually concealed and situated behind some physical obstacle. They did not credit us with a capacity for leaving the ordinary path and our ability to climb even the steepest hill and cut a way through the thickest jungle came as an unwelcome surprise to them. The flanks of stockades, especially the uphill one, could therefore be turned.

The Abors possessed few guns and their armament consisted of bows with poisoned arrows and swords. The field of fire from stockades, owing to concealment, was usually restricted, but great reliance was placed on rock chutes. The Abors were especially clever in this method of defence and all their stockades were flanked with them. The hillsides also for some distance in front of the stockade were covered with them. The searching out of and destruction of these chutes was a troublesome operation.

Abor offensive tactics.

Before the campaign, the Abors were credited with a capacity for assuming the offensive and for rushing the column with swords. In practice they only did so once, and that at night, when they attacked Captain Coleridge's party on the night of 3-4th December.

They however laid ambuscades from which arrows were discharged at columns on several occasions. These ambuscades were sometimes below the path, as the Abors consider that there is a better chance of escape downhill than uphill.

Once, at Rotung, by night, they fired arrows in to the camp. At Puak they made a half-hearted attempt at a night attack, a sentry fired and wounded one of the enemy, of whom no more was seen.

Guns and maxims.

7-lb. guns and maxims delayed the march of columns and experience has proved them out of place in jungle warfare on the north-east frontier. It is to be regretted that Hale's rifle grenades did not arrive, as it is anticipated that they would be a very useful form of weapon in the country.

Infantry.

The difficulties of transport necessitated the carriage of heavy loads by the men. This rather handicapped them and it is desirable that scouts should be allowed a larger scale of baggage than the ordinary man and thus be more mobile for his important work.

Columns were kept well closed up and usually marched in single file. When accompanied by carriers, use had to be made of whistles as signals from front to rear and *vice versa.* When opposition was anticipated the baggage column was left behind under suitable guard and columns then moved silently and messages were quietly passed up and down the line. Both sides of the path were picquetted by small groups of 2 or 3 men placed by the Advanced Guard some few yards in jungle. It was found better to relieve the Advanced Guard picquets by similar ones from the main body, instead of making the Advanced Guard picquets wait until arrival of the Rear Guard. Hill tops were only picquetted, when there was danger of rocks being rolled down on the column.

Reconnaissance patrols.

During enforced halts the country was quartered up amongst reconnaissance patrols. These were employed as follows:—The company or double company marched to the centre of the area allotted to it for the day and then split up into patrols radiating and working from that common centre.

These patrols surprised and inflicted loss on the enemy on several occasions.

Advantage of Telephones.

Visual signalling, owing to climatic and topographical detail, was of very little practical value The field telephone in jungle warfare proved, however, invaluable, especially in the linking up of flank and main attacks. The difficulties of inter-communication were by this means entirely overcome.

Pacification of country.

The country was rapidly pacified by the employment of patrols in every direction. These moved off the regular tracks and surprised and harried the enemy in every direction. The constant dread of surprises experienced by the Abors soon made them realise that resistance was useless.

To enable this to be done efficiently posts were established at suitable intervals or near villages. These were garrisoned by Gurkhas and Military Police for tactical purposes, whilst in addition companies of Pioneers were based in posts for road-making.

Road-making.

This was done roughly during the advance of the column and as soon as active operations were finished, the Sappers and Miners and Pioneers worked systematically on the road from Yembung down towards Pasighat. The completion of this road took from 15th December to 31st March.

Camps and bivouacs.

The densely wooded nature of all camping sites made any attempt to demarcate or select a perimeter line impossible before clearing the site. The great point to be borne in mind was the necessity of rapid clearance of site combined with protection, tactical, and from climate. The Nagas with their daos were especially skilful in clearing. In order to save subsequent moving of loads and to prevent the delay of baggage columns, it was essential for the General Staff to select a camping ground rapidly, and point out to units the location of their camps as the carriers were coming into the camp. To allow of this a standard plan of camp was prepared and issued to all concerned. The principle of this was a core of units not available for defence, round which the defence units constructed a perimeter to suit the site. On arrival at the camping ground the centre of the camp was marked by the General Officer Commanding's flag and the direction of cross roads was either aligned on trees or flags. The carriers of the central units were always placed first in column of march ; as they arrived, their loads were deposited on or as near to the site of the units camp and the carriers and sepoys were at once set to clearing from the centre outwards. As the ground was cleared it became possible to select the site of the perimeter. This was generally formed of the jungle which was cleared off the site. Large trees were not felled. Rough bivouac shelters were made and thatched with leaves. Plaintain leaves were found most suitable for thatching. To keep the men off the damp ground, *machans* of split logs were made as beds.

The standard plan of camp had to be modified to suit the ground at Sirpo, Renging and Yembung. The sites of these camps were, however, cleared previously to the arrival of the force and in each case a plan of the camp was prepared and issued to all concerned before the vacation of the previous camp. At Puak a subsidiary camp had to be made on the high ground above the main camp.

War dogs.

War dogs presented by the liberality of the wife of one of the officers of the force were employed. Owing to the general defensive tactics adopted by Abors they had few opportunities of proving their value in giving timely information of the approach of the enemy, but on these few occasions they did give warning that the enemy were in the neighbourhood.

APPENDIX IX.

REPORT ON THE WORKING OF THE BASE AND THE LINES OF COMMUNICATION.

By the Inspector of Communications and Base Commandant.

Notes on report.

This was the first occasion on which the principles of organisation and administration, as laid down in Field Service Regulations, had been practically tested in the field and the working is therefore worthy of the closest scrutiny. This report shows that difficulties occurred on the lines of communication owing to:—

(1) The insufficiency of the staff provided.

(2) Overlapping of responsibility between the Headquarters of the force and the Inspector of Communications.

As regards (1) it appears to have been a mistake to have combined the duties of Inspector of Communications and Base Commandant. The Inspector of Communications must be free to move up and down his line and inspect, and to go to Force Headquarters when necessary. On the other hand it is essential that the Base Commandant should always be on the spot to decide questions at the base. In the case of small expeditions, only a comparatively junior officer is necessary, but a permanent Base Commandant appears to be essential. It would appear advisable, also, for the Inspector of Communications to have a staff officer.

With regard to (2) there appears to have been a misconception of the principles laid down in Field Service Regulations by which the Officer Commanding is now relieved of certain responsibilities, and of the distinction between Staff Officers and the heads of Administrative Services and Departments. For instance, orders were sent direct from Force Headquarters to convoys on the Lines of Communication without the knowledge of the Inspector of Communications.

It is satisfactory to note, however, that such difficulties as occurred were due to a failure in applying the principles laid down in Field Service Regulations, and not to any defect in these regulations themselves.

Extracts from a letter from the General Officer Commanding, covering the Report on the Base and Lines of Communication.

In accordance with the provisions of paragraph 2, Section 12, Field Service Regulations, Part II, Chapter III, the tactical responsibility for the security of the line up to and excluding Pasighat was vested in the Inspector of Communications. Beyond this the military

defence of the Line of Communications was entrusted to the Commander of Line of Communications defences. The remarks, therefore, of the Inspector of Communications in Chapter I, as to the clashing of headquarter orders with those of the Inspector of Communications are not understood, as the Inspector of Communications was not in a position to issue such orders. All orders to units on Line of Communications were sent through the Officer Commanding Defences.

It would appear that, ordinarily, it is preferable to have an officer appointed as Officer Commanding, Line of Communications, instead of the two separate branches advocated in Section 11, Chapter III, Field Service Regulations, India, Part II

THE BASE.

General Observations.

In all operations in Assam and Burma, the Base is likely to be on the river, either the Brahmaputra or Irrawaddy. The selection of a Base should depend on its being situated favourably with reference to the line of operations.

It should be accessible at the lowest state of the rivers to the steamboats that brings flats and material, and facilities for landing troops and war materials and provisions should be available.

The Base was at Kobo. As long as the river was fairly full, this was an excellent spot, above flood level, but, when the river gets low, the greatest difficulty is experienced in getting up steamers. The left half of 1-2nd Gurkha Rifles, Nepalese carrier corps and mule corps had to be landed at Pobamukh 4 miles down stream, and marched to Kobo.

When demobilization takes place, troops will have probably to embark at Pobamukh, where a camping ground is ready, unless the rains set in very early.

As regards facilities for landing, a flat had to be kept and paid for by Government at Kobo, otherwise even feede. steamers could not have landed or taken on board their cargos, sick, etc.

Piers are no use. The river bed now shews 50 yards of pebble beach from the full tide bank. Even at Pobamukh a flat is necessary. There are many uses the flat can be put to, for instance, most of the preliminary making up of carrier loads from bulk of provisions, filling and sewing up bags and so on was done on the flat and continued even in the worst weather without deterioration of stock.

2. In any case, beyond Dibrugarh and on the less inhabited north bank of the Brahmaputra river, bases have to be cut out of the jungle.

As soon as the Base is fixed, therefore, Nepalese coolies and a carrier corps or two should precede all except the sappers and miners and pioneers. Nepalese coolies and Nagas are very expert in cutting down jungle, and sappers and miners are required for the building of godowns and bridges, and for laying down water tubes and so on. The pioneers come in to finish the rough work of the coolies. Local troops like the Lakhimpur Military Police are the best supervisors for preliminary work. The initial work at Kobo was carried out by the military police and by the Public Works Department coolies who had come for road-making, and who had to have a Base before proceeding to the road work.

STAFF FOR BASE.

The staff should not be stinted. The Supply and Transport Department made no mistake about this. With two infantry battalions, one pioneer battalion, the greater part of a military police battalion, a company of sappers and miners and five carrier corps of Nagas to disembark, give sites to, arrange the sanitary dispositions, latrines, etc., to send only a senior Colonel and a clerk as a staff for Base was running economy for a dangerous fall.

Fortunately stray officers arrived without their units and accepted the duties of Staff Officer, and Provost Marshal to aid in putting things straight. Later on an Assistant Provost Marshal, Captain Becher arrived, but was taken away by headquarters when they advanced, and the Treasure Chest Officer, Captain Bignall, took over the Staff and Provost Marshal's duties.

In future perhaps these two duties might be combined with that of the Treasure Chest Officer.

I have no recollection of ever seeing before the combined appointment of Base Commandant and Inspector of Communications. No doubt it was economical, but it led to officers having to act as *locum tenens* and also to complications which would have been more accentuated had the advance of the striking force been a rapid one. The line of communications came under two fires, as headquarters had the leisure to send orders to units on line of communications, and they at times clashed with orders of the Inspector of Communications.

From this we may then draw the inference that the duties of Base Commandant, after the advance, might well be either separated from those of an Inspector of Communications, or that the Base should be commanded after the advance by the senior combatant officer present with a staff officer provided.

SANITATION.

When the Base was opened at Kobo, early in September, no medical officer was provided, so I commandeered the medical officer of the Base Hospital about to form at Dibrugarh, who was at leisure. It is well known that September is the most unhealthy month of the year, and yet, except for the Military Police hospital assistant, all the Supply and Transport staff and early arrivals would have had no proper medical attendance.

The Base Commandant should therefore arrive with a properly equipped section of a hospital with a medical officer in charge.

2. Incinerators were most useful in keeping down flies, and the camp wholesome. Sets of bars are sufficient, the corrugated iron accompaniments buckled on the fire, and can be dispensed with.

3. When assisting in the preliminary organization schemes at Shillong in August, great difficulty existed in being able to get sweepers or any sort of sanitary corps enlisted.

Manipur used to have plenty of Nagas who worked as sweepers, so the Political Officer there was addressed and provided 60 excellent fellows who have done splendidly. No one understands their language except one interpreter, and so we never received grumbles either.

In opening a Base, the purchase of old kerosine oil tins must not be forgotten or stinted Each cooking place, officer or subordinate's tents, men's or coolies' quarters, should be liberally supplied to keep down flies, and to keep the ground from being fouled. These tins should be tarred inside. Dirty water need then be never thrown about, and punishment for this act should always ensue.

Spitting on the main roads of camp should be a punishable offence. It soon ceases if the provost staff run men in.

Being advised by Planters that Norton Tube wells were essential in the vicinity of the river, I received sanction to get a dozen and they worked excellently, and were, I am sure, the cause of the excellent health of all units and officers.

The Brahmaputra water has so much sand in it ordinarily, and in flood time is of khaki colour, that it should not be used if possible.

Another thing to remember is the extreme prevalence of goitre, and the advisability, where these tube wells are not available, of boiling the water. (70 cases occurred in the 1-2nd Gurkha Rifles.)

Dhoolies are of no use on this frontier. The Ashanti hammock worked well.

In wet weather men with bare feet get bad sores called *panighas* owing to the poisonous earth. Boots should be allowed for all carriers and road coolies working during the rains.

At all camps of a permanent nature, a drying shed for the men's clothes was found to be a great boon, and assisted in keeping them fit as they moved up on a very light scale, and the region is rainy.

At the Base Hospital great difficulty was encountered owing to the various Naga dialects and each corps should leave behind an

Assamese or Hindustani speaking man, who would come in useful as a sick attendant also.

Base General Hospital.—The feeding arrangements and hospital accommodation for officers and Europeans generally at Dibrugarh left at first much to be desired. All officers sent from here who had no private house to go to, begged to be sent back to Kobo.

Rations, etc., should not be left to hard worked medical officers to supervise issues, there should have been a Supply and Transport subordinate detailed, or a non-commissioned officer (British).

ORDNANCE.

The following should receive attention :—

* * * * * *

Care of stores.—The store tents issued were absolutely useless to keep out rain, pawlins had to be thrown over the stores inside the tents. The outline of the tent is not correct, either the poles are too short or walls too high, this causes sagging of the roof. The poles were placed on empty ammunition boxes to raise the roof up to the required height to remove the sagging but the walls were ill-fitting. If the poles were four inches longer and the roof lengthened about four inches all round, and fitting the walls to the roof in such a manner to give the edge of the roof a distance (or protrusion) over the walls of a few inches, the water would drain off much better. Some ventilation near the top of the tents is badly needed, as a certain amount of damp hot air is always in the roof which rots the tent very quickly.

Ventilators of eyelets are also badly needed near the top of the inner flies of privates' and staff sergeants' tents.

* * * * * *

Packing and supply of stores.—It is absolutely necessary that paragraph 22, Field Service Manual, Ordnance, should be invariably observed, for it is most dangerous to send packages (as was done on this expedition) weighing in some cases as much as 7 maunds.

POSTAL AND TELEGRAPH.

A Base Commandant has to arrange for dâk runners for the post, to provide escorts for telegraph coolies and working parties.

Perhaps the amalgamation of the Telegraph and Postal Departments will obviate one difficulty that has occurred, and that was the difficulty of procuring stamps at posts beyond where post offices existed. Either stamps should be available at these offices, or some system of debiting against corps and staff officers as for rations should come in.

TRADERS.

Traders should always be encouraged. The ordinary Buniah (known in Assam as *Kyahs*) can take care of himself, but protection is needed for locals who bring vegetables, poultry and eggs. They are often mobbed on arrival and get frightened and lose all their articles, as well as their confidence to continue trading. A Miri bazaar was made on the shore, but they preferred dealing from their boats, which they could push out if the soldiers or coolies, etc., rushed them. A military policeman should be told off to protect these sort of people.

The contractor buniah should be encouraged to open a shop at the Base. This was done and was a success at Kobo.

2. Nepalese graziers are to be encouraged with their herds for milk supply. Care should be taken to find out if there is any objection from the Civil Administrative point of view. They should be made to agree to keep their cow and buffalo sheds clean, and to accept fines for watering milk.

3. One of the most useful arrangements made was getting the Planters Stores of Dibrugarh to start a branch at Kobo, which was a boon to the Europeans of the force. Before doing this terms were arranged as regards charges, and 5 per cent on Dibrugarh prices was fixed. A European manager was sent and did excellently.

DEALINGS WITH LOCAL PEOPLE.

A staff officer should have a fair colloquial knowledge of the local dialect. If not, interpreters should be provided.

LINE OF COMMUNICATIONS.

There is not much to add under this heading. The circumstances were peculiar in the Abor Expedition, in that the advance was, owing to the nature of the country, very slow, and headquarters had time to issue orders for garrisons and moves which are, in a rapid advance, entirely issued by the Inspector of Communications.

The provisions of Field Service Regulations, Part II, Chapter III, Section 12, paragraphs 5 and 6, were not adhered to, the Assistant Director of Supply and Transport being, under the instructions issued by the Chief of the General Staff, with headquarters and getting direct orders. Still this point should not be lost sight of in future operations, and an understanding should be arrived at as to what the General Officer Commanding wishes to observe as regards the abovementioned regulations.

All locals approaching a post should leave their arms with the guard, but to save them from being looted a receipt should be given, otherwise arms disappear and there is bad blood. Post Commandants should be encouraged to make friends with local people and obtain supplies through them. Otherwise the arrangements for posts on the line of communications should be much the same as at the Base.

* * * * * * *

Sand from the river bed should be freely used on floors and streets, and mule standings.

Political Instructions.—These should be issued to each Post. The ordinary treatment of the frightened enemy, who is anxious to come in and make friends, by the inexperienced officer is at times calculated to keep the enemy to the jungles for an indefinite period. As likely as not fire will be opened on him when he approaches.

Orders should be available as to giving rations to deputations.

Escorts.—Small escorts for convoys, and the enemy kept off the road by unexpected raiding parties on both flanks, acted very well. Men got useful exercise, made discoveries of hidden grain, drove in *mithan* or pigs, besides every now and then encountering and breaking up Abor gangs. It kept the men interested, and the enemy quiet.

* * * * * * *

APPENDIX X.

GENERAL REPORT ON THE MEDICAL HISTORY OF THE ABOR EXPEDITIONARY FORCE, 1911-12.

* * * * * *

At its maximum strength the force consisted of about 8,500 men of all ranks, including followers.

The medical units of the force consisted at first of sections A, B and C of No. 168 Indian Field Hospital and of a small General Hospital of 50 beds for Indian Troops and Followers at Dibrugarh. On 5th December section D of No. 168 Indian Field Hospital and on 12th January section A of No. 169 Indian Field Hospital arrived at Kobo. Some time after the force advanced from Kobo, a small General Hospital for British officers was arranged for at Dibrugarh.

* * * * * *

In the flat part of the country malaria is common, the inhabitants are infested by intestinal parasites, and sores on the feet, due to the irritation caused by the entrance of the embryos of the ankylostoma through the skin, are frequently met with, while parasitic skin diseases are almost universal.

Among the hills the prevalent disease is goitre: in some parts of the country visited by the force as many as 60 per cent of the adult inhabitants suffered from this affection. Blepharitis and chronic granular conjunctivities with the resulting pannus and entropion were also found to be common, and, doubtless, dirt and the chronic irritation of wood smoke help largely towards their prevalence.

Leprosy occurs occasionally and it is worthy of note that the Abors, in some villages at least, segregate lepers.

* * * * * *

Vegetable and animal products of the country.

The Abors cultivate a considerable number of plants. Rice, of an excellent quality, is their staple food, but they also sow more than one variety of millet, Indian corn and some dhal. They grow yams, sweet potatoes, pumpkins, red and green chillies, sugarcane, ginger (which also grows wild), cucumbers, mustard to a slight extent, *pân*, a coarse variety of tobacco and a certain amount of the opium poppy. Oranges, limes, lemons and citrons are also cultivated, regular orange groves being found at some villages. Oranges and limes of a very good quality are grown in the upper part of the country. The jackfruit tree is met with everywhere and the trees are carefully preserved by the villagers, young plants are protected by a bamboo basket-work and the larger trees are often surrounded by a fence. While their crops of cereals are coming up and ripening, the Abors live largely upon the fruit of the jack tree for about two months in August and

September. Banana trees grow wild, but the Abors also cultivate this tree for the sake of the fruit. Cinnamon is found wild in the jungle and is used by the Abors, as is the pith of the sago palm, which is common all over the country. The bamboo is very common and is highly valued by the Abors because of its usefulness to them in building houses, fencing trees, etc., and, besides bows and arrows, they make many useful household articles from it. They also eat a sort of chutney made from the young shoots of the bamboo. Their clumps of bamboo are, therefore, often carefully fenced in and protected.

They cultivate a certain amount of cotton from which they make their cloth, but this is insufficient for their requirements and a good deal of cloth is imported.

* * * * * *

The wild raspberry and a variety of wild strawberry are common. The screw pine is common and its leaves are used for matting. Rubber trees occur and rubber of inferior quality is sold. Canes are plentiful and are extensively used, some varieties growing to 30 or even 90 feet long and being of good quality. Aconite and croton are used for poisoning arrows.

* * * * * *

The *mithan* (*bos gavealis*) is found in large numbers in a semi-domesticated state all over the country and the Abors eat its flesh, though apparently only on special occasions; curiously enough they (in common, with some other hill tribes) do not use the milk, the reason being that they look on milk as a form of excrement. The milk of the female *mithan* is, however, of excellent quality and has been used occasionally by the troops on this expedition.

In certain villages a few cattle and goats are kept.

Pigs swarm in every village and their flesh is the meat usually eaten by the Abors. The pigs and dogs are the only scavengers in the villages.

Dogs are numerous and somewhat resemble the Tibetan dog, but are of smaller size.

Fowls are plentiful in all the villages and eggs could usually be obtained.

All over the country snakes abound, but the majority are not poisonous. A python, 17 feet long, was killed near Pillung, and a king cobra, 10 feet long, near Rotung. The following species were found near Kobo and were indentified by Dr. Annandale, Indian Museum, Calcutta:—

Trachischium fuscum (Blyth).
Dryophis prasinus (Boie).
Zamenis muscosus (Linn:).
Typhlops diardi (Schleg).
Typhlops Sp.

The streams abound in fish especially near the main rivers. The most common are mahseer, *boka* (blue carp), *goonch* and snow trout. The Abors poison the fish in the smaller streams, but their usual method of catching them is by placing across a swift stream near its mouth an obstruction having gaps, in which conical basket traps are placed, and in these the fish are caught as they descend the stream.

Amongst invertebrates the most interesting find was a species of *peripatus,* first found near Rotung by the Zoologist who accompanied the expedition.

Culex and *anopheles* mosquitoes are not found in any great numbers during the cold weather. The larvæ of *culex,* however, could always be found in the collection of water at the junction of the leaf with the trunk of every banana tree.

Three varieties of biting flies were common beyond Pasighat, *viz* :—

(1) A small fly with a prominent proboscis, a very well marked transverse yellow stripe across the back of the thorax and semi-transparent blue wings. When fresh jungle was being cut, this fly seemed to be ubiquitous. A blood blister forms as a result of its bite, which causes great irritation and occasionally a good deal of local inflammation and œdema.

(2) A larger fly with no yellow band. Its bite results in a blister containing clear serum and a considerable amount of irritation.

(3) The smallest of the three is nevertheless larger than the ordinary Indian sandfly. The result of its bite is like that of (2), but the irritation is not so severe.

All of them are blood-suckers and none of them crosses its wings when at rest.

Leeches abound everywhere and their bites occasionally give rise to sores of considerable size.

Wood ticks are plentiful beyond Janakmukh. They bury their heads in the soft skin and hold on so firmly that their removal is very difficult.

The cinnamon beetle (*aspongopus nigriventries*) is found under stones on the bar... of the Dihang and is eaten with relish by the Abors, who state that, if any considerable quantity is eaten at a time, it produces a sort of intoxication.

Climatic peculiarities.

The chief climatic peculiarity is the heavy rainfall. During the 176 days between 8th October 1911, and 31st March 1912, which includes the driest period of the year, rain fell on 70 days. Mist and clouds are frequent in the hills and there are occasional heavy thunderstorms.

The coldest months are December, January and February; the lowest temperature registered occurred during February.

Principal diseases with their causes.

British troops.—Amongst British officers and men the principal diseases were malaria and "pyrexia of uncertain origin", each of which accounted for about 1-3rd of the total admissions.

The malaria was in most cases apparently due to a recrudescence of a previous infection brought about by exposure to wet and cold and by severe exertion, but one or two cases of fresh infection, or re-infection, occurred.

Among the cases of "pyrexia of uncertain origin" there is little doubt that one or two cases of undetected malarial fever are included. The causes of the other cases are not known. One officer developed a fever which at first was suspected of being enteric, but Widal's reaction was negative.

Indian troops.—Among Indian troops the principal diseases were malaria and dysentery, each of which caused about 25 per cent of the total admissions. There were also a considerable number of cases of "pyrexia of uncertain origin" and a few cases of mumps, of pneumonia, of goitre and of scurvy.

Followers.—Among followers malaria and dysentery caused most admissions, each giving rise to about 25 per cent of the total admissions. A considerable number of cases of "pyrexia of uncertain origin", of anæmia and debility and of mumps also occurred.

The camps of Janakmukh and Sirpo river gave rise to a severe type of malignant tertian malaria. When these two camps had been cleared, however, they proved more healthy but the belt of country between the Sijon and the Sirpo streams must be regarded with suspicion. Dysentery is endemic in the country, and, had it not been so, it must have introduced by the force. The quantity of mica suspended in the water is of itself capable of inducing, or at all events, coupled with service conditions, of determining attacks of irritative colitis and of aggravating true cases of dysentery. In the case of the Naga carriers lack of the meat they are accustomed to eat freely, ignorance at first of the proper manner in which to cook dhal and their own filthy habits in not attempting, except under compulsion, to keep the surroundings even of their cooking places clean, rendered them specially liable to the disease. Even while suffering from dysentery they could not be prevented from eating solid food.

Under the heading of "pyrexia of uncertain origin" are doubtless included some cases of malarial fever and so also were cases of 7, 10 and 14 day fevers. Among followers a number of cases somewhat resembling influenza are included under this heading.

Captain F. H. Stewart, I.M.S., describes under this heading, by the name of "Sirpo River Fever," a disease which he attributes to residence at Sirpo River Camp in the early part of the expedition. This camp was small in area and situated about 50 feet above the Sirpo river in a deep valley with steep hills on the north and south. The camp in the early part of the expedition, when these cases occurred, had only been partially cleared of trees and was surrounded by dense forest jungle, so that it received little sunlight. The rain, which at that time frequently fell, kept the camp constantly damp. The soil is leaf mould and the surrounding jungle is full of rotting vegetation. The characteristic symptoms are—

(1) fever lasting for 14 or more days;

(2) temperature remittent, higher in the evening than in the morning, ranging between 100° and 104°, not apparently showing any definite curve;

(3) pulse relatively slow (92 with a temperature of 104°, 92 with a temperature of 102·6°, 60 with a temperature of 99·4°);

(4) congestion of the conjunctival;

(5) profuse popular rash over the trunk and limbs also extending to the forehead; the spots were slightly raised, their colour was pink tinged with yellow and they did not fade entirely on pressure; in 4 of the 5 cases the rash was visible on the 3rd day, in the 5th case it was visible on the 8th day (on which day the patient came under Captain Stewart's observation), but began to fade on the 10th and had nearly disappeared on the 11th day of the disease;

(6) spleen slightly enlarged and tender;

(7) no diarrhœa or abdominal symptoms;

(8) in one case (the only one in which the test is known to have been tried) Widal's reaction for enteric fever was negative;

(9) temperature not influenced by large doses of quinine.

Captain Stewart observed two cases of this fever among British troops and 3 among Indian troops.

Captain J. S. O'Neil, I.M.S., describes 7 cases of continuous fever which occurred among Indian troops at Sirpo river and Rotung camps in the early part of the expedition. He remarks on the resemblance between these cases and enteric fever, but, had they been enteric fever, it is extremely unlikely that no other cases would have occurred. The chief symptoms were—

(1) fever lasting in some cases about 3 weeks;

(2) temperature varying from 100° to 102°, or higher;

(3) pulse rather slow in relation to the fever, in some instances dicrotic;

(4) tongue furred in the centre, clean at tip, and edges;

(5) a fairly profuse rash, consisting of small pink spots on the chest and abdomen, slightly raised above the surface of the skin;

(6) spleen enlarged;

(7) constipation was the rule, but there were no abdominal symptoms;

(8) headache and pain in the back and limbs.

No complications were observed.

Mumps.—The disease appears to have been introduced by the 32nd Sikh Pioneers, among whom some cases occurred on the voyage up the Brahmaputra. The 1st Gurkhali Carrier Corps, which arrived at Kobo on 6th January also brought the infection, for cases developed in that corps very soon after reaching Kobo. The patients and those who had been in close contact with them were segregated and the outbreak did not assume very large proportions.

Several cases occurred in "contacts" 26 days after they had been segregated.

Pneumonia.—The cases of pneumonia both among Indian troops and followers had undoubtedly, as their predisposing cause, lowered vitality due to fatigue and exposure to wet and cold.

Goitre.—A certain number of cases of goitre occurred, principally among the Gurkha riflemen. Gurkhas are liable to this disease, which occurs in the Nepalese hills, and doubtless some of these cases were small goitres which had been present for some time but had only been noticed for the first time during the expedition. Others were probably due to a recent increase in size of a small goitre of old standing, while some were fresh attacks. A large number were cured and a large number greatly improved by treatment internally by *thymol* and externally by *unguentum hydrargyri iodidi rubri.* Cures are also reported from treatment by liquor *hydrargyri per chloridi* internally and red *iodidi* ointment externally. These results tend to confirm Captain McCarrison's views regarding goitre. Less * goitre was found in Abor villages whose water-supply was derived from land that had not been cultivated than in villages where the water came from land that had been cultivated.

The cases of anæmia and debility among followers were probably due to hard work and exposure to wet and cold and to change of diet, though doubtless malaria and ankylostomiasis accounted for

* FOOTNOTE.—There is less goitre in the villages on the western tributaries of the Dihang; the water in these villages, almost without exception, comes from cultivated land.

some cases. A considerable number of cases of *panighas* (water itch), a pustular eruption on the feet followed by ulceration, which Bentley showed to be due to the entrance through the skin of the embryos of ankylostoma, occurred at and near Kobo during the wet weather at the beginning of the expedition among men who went barefoot. Very few cases of ankylostoma have, however, been reported.

A certain number of cases of scurvy occurred, principally among the Sappers and Miners. This was probably due to the Sappers and Miners living for the most part in separate camps while road-making and to their not getting the full benefit of the issues of fresh vegetables and other antiscorbutics owing to their camps being separate.

The Gurkhas of all classes, and, more especially the Nagas, had the advantage over the natives of the Punjab that they are accustomed to jungles similar to those in the Abor country and were frequently able to add to their rations various fresh vegetables collected on the spot.

The total number of admissions from all causes, including cases of change of disease and including admissions at the General Hospital, Dibrugarh, between 30th September 1911, and 5th April 1912, was—

British officers	21
British troops	18
Indian troops	841
Followers	2,217

The total number of deaths from disease during the same period, including deaths in the General Hospital, Dibrugarh, was—

British officers	1
British troops	0
Indian troops	6
Followers	47

Wounds.

I.—Gunshot	2
II.—Arrow wounds	4

* * * * * *

As regards the poison used by the Abors, it should be held in mind that, whilst the Galong and Minyong on the right bank of the river as far as Kebang use croton almost exclusively as an arrow poison, the Padam, Panggi and mixed Minyong on the left bank use aconite in preference to it.

The best treatment for croton poisoned wounds is that which gives the best drainage along the whole length of the track, and strong antiseptic solutions should be avoided as only tending to increase further the local irritation. Aconite poisoned wounds, on the other hand, are amenable to treatment with potassium permanganate solution.

The total number of men killed in action or who died of wounds received in action between 30th September 1911 and 5th April 1912 was—

British officers	0
British troops	0
Indian troops	2
Followers	3

Water-supply.—No expedition in this country need fear lack of water, unless the actual hill tops are occupied as camps. Every valley has its stream, varying from large and rapid rivers to small rivulets and trickles of water.

The water was usually taken from some stream adjacent to the camp, but at Kobo, where the only river available is the Brahmaputra, the water of which at all times contains a certain amount of sediment, Norton's tube-pumps were used and provided an ample supply of water, which on chemical examination proved to be of excellent quality. The soil here for the top 3 or 4 feet consists of pure leaf mould and below that is a thick layer of fine, clean sand. The Norton's pumps, therefore, provided water that had been filtered by a natural and, as nearly as possible, perfect sand filter. Norton's pumps were also used at Pillung and at Oyang (Oniyuk) for a short time. Since all the streams in the plains are more or less liable to pollution, Norton's tube-pumps ought to be made use of on every possible opportunity in that part of the country. When, however, the hills are reached and at Pasighat, when the Dihang emerges from the hills and where the soil is full of boulders, Norton's pumps can no longer be used and recourse has to be had to streams. The water of the Dihang, which was used at Pasighat and at one or two other camps, always contains a certain quantity of sediment and this has to be allowed to settle before the water is used for drinking or cooking. Where it was possible, the water from the smaller tributary streams, or, best of all, from small streams coming from high up an adjacent hill, was used, because that was usually beautifully clear, only becoming muddy as the result of heavy rain. Usually the supply was plentiful; in only a very few camps was the quantity insufficient for even a force of considerable size. The quality has proved to be excellent and, though streams are open to the objection that they are liable to pollution, this risk was minimised by using the ubiquitous bamboo as a channel for the water. In this way the water was taken from a point above any probable pollution, was raised above the ground and was delivered at convenient spots and in a convenient spout near the camp. When recourse was had to the water of the Dihang and on a few other occasions, at camps where the water-pply seemed specially liable to pollution, the water was boiled.

The only diseases which could be attributed to the water were diarrhœa, of which certain cases at Pasighat may have been due to the micaceous sediment in the Dihang water ; dysentery, of which one predisposing cause was probably the sediment in the water; and of which a certain number of cases at Pasighat were probably due to infection carried by the water from neighbouring Abor villages ; and the goitre which a certain number of men developed.

Rations.

The scale of rations issued was that laid down in Appendix III of Field Service Regulations, India, as far as regards British troops, Indian troops and followers, except Nagas. For the Nagas a special scale was laid down.

Men who were performing specially hard work were given an extra half pound of atta or rice daily. Those to whom this issue was most often given were the Sappers and Miners, the Pioneers, the Signalling Company and the Boat Transport boatmen.

The quality of the rations over all was excellent, though occasionally a bag of rice or of atta or a tin of ghi or of gur proved to be bad.

The only insufficiency was in the supply of fresh meat and this fell most heavily on the men on the line of communications. The men at the head of the advance, as far as Yembung, occasionally got a pig or a *mithan** to help to make up for the defect, but beyond Yembung very little, if any, fresh meat was procurable. The want of meat was most felt by the Nagas, because they are accustomed in their own country to a considerable quantity of meat. This ought to be taken account of, should Nagas be employed on any future expedition.

The Dihang Exploration party at Shimong were for some days on reduced rations, but no ill effect resulted.

The rations for British troops were on the scale laid down in Appendix III of Field Service Regulations, India. The quality was good and the amount sufficient.

Considerable quantities of fish can be obtained from pools in the smaller rivers by using dynamite. This could be used as a means of supplementing the supply of fresh meat.

As was proved by the experience obtained on a small scale at Kobo, all sorts of vegetables grow very readily in this country, so that, on a future occasion, market-gardening on a large scale could be made use of to provide fresh vegetables.

---

* Cooking of these shuld be specially attended to, as infection by *Taenia Solium* and *T. Saginata* occurred.

Spirits and malt liquor.

No malt liquor was issued. The only sort of spirits issued was rum and that was issued occasionally to all ranks of troops and to followers on the recommendation of the Senior Medical Officer present, when the weather was very inclement or when the men to whom it was issued had been undergoing specially arduous labour.

Medical comforts for the sick.

The quality of the medical comforts for the sick was excellent and the quantity was sufficient.

Milk is the only one which calls for remark. Only at Kobo was fresh milk available in any quantity, as the Base Commandant succeeded in arranging for a Gurkhali milk dealer to bring and keep his cattle there. Even at Kobo, especially at first, tinned-milk had to be used and beyond Kobo nothing but tinned-milk was available. Of the various brands used all were good, but on an expedition, such as this, where the difficulties of transport were great and every additional pound of weight was of importance, the greater convenience in carriage of condensed milk far outweighs the advantage in flavour that sterilized milk enjoys.

Clothing.

The troops and followers, except carrier corps, were given at first clothing on the summer scale laid down in Appendix VIII of Field Service Regulations, India, and this was afterwards supplemented by the issue of the winter scale of clothing. The Naga carriers were given two country blankets and one followers warm coat each and the Gurkhali carriers were given the same clothing plus boots. Except the Naga carriers all followers were supplied with boots.

The scale was suitable to the country, but, as at first the scale of transport allowed was only 10lb. of baggage for an Indian officer or sepoy, the clothing actually taken from the Base by the troops consisted of only one waterproof sheet and one blanket and the balance did not reach them till December, 6 to 8 weeks afterwards. In a climate such as that of the Abor country, where rain is frequent, this amount of clothing is insufficient, since it does not allow the men a change of clothing to put on when they arrive in camp soaked through by the rain. There is no doubt that this want of change of clothing during the rainy period acted as a predisposing cause of much of the sickness that occurred in the early part of the expedition. I am very strongly of opinion that it would be less harmful to cut down the scale of rations temporarily than to cut down the amount of transport allowed for clothing in a wet climate like that of the Abor country.

Sanitary condition of camps, latrines and transport lines.

On the whole the sanitation has been very satisfactory. Any defects have occurred, almost without exception, at the starting of new camps and in the cooly transport lines; when the force was assembling at Kobo, the ordinary establishment of sweepers of units was found to be insufficient, but the arrival of the Manipuri Naga sweepers made it possible to keep the whole area of the camp clean even in the wet weather. Again, as the main body of the force moved forward, military exigencies rendered it necessary to include within the perimeter of each camp not only cooking places but also urinals and latrines, a most objectionable system and one which was given up on the very earliest possible opportunity.

Overcrowding.—The camps of the main body during its advance had of necessity to be as circumscribed as possible, partly owing to the necessity for defence and partly because every square foot of the ground had to be cleared of jungle and undergrowth. In the fixed camps on the line of communications, however, there was no overcrowding except in Janakmukh and Renging. The overcrowding in Janakmukh was soon relieved to a great extent by clearing away more jungle, which, however, was very dense, and by extending the camp on to the sand and shingle left uncovered as the water of the Dihang fell, so that latterly the only objectionable point was that the mule lines were rather too near the Field Hospital. Later still, Janakmukh was given up and Pasighat was occupied instead, where there is ample room, so long as the river is low.

Renging, however, remained for a long time distinctly overcrowded. Two camps were occupied here, the second one being below the level of the mist that daily shrouded the first camp, but as the only ground available slopes very steeply, is much cut up by *nullahs* and is covered by dense jungle and few men were available for defence and for clearing the jungle, there was little that could be done to remedy the overcrowding. After the departure of the Naga carrier corps the overcrowding was relieved. No sickness that could be set down to overcrowding occurred.

Housing.—Very few tents were taken beyond Kobo, the only ones being for the use of the sections of Field Hospital and none were taken beyond Renging. Huts were used by every one and latterly, even at Kobo, huts were built and occupied instead of tents. The amount of jungle made the erection of huts an easy matter and, where grass was available, excellent watertight huts were built. Where grass was not available, leaves had to be used for walls and roof and then it was difficult to make, or keep, the hut watertight. Benches were made in all the huts of the hospitals for the sick to sleep on and in most of the other huts similar benches were made use of. The huts gave more space and were airier and, except when a cold wind was blowing, were preferable to tents.

Cooking places.—Except at Kobo, in every camp, the cooking places were at first made inside the perimeter, but, as soon as space became available, they were moved to ground outside the perimeter and roofs were raised over them to keep off the rain.

After the wood, which had been cut in clearing the camping ground, had had time to dry, fuel was abundant and, before that, a little search always revealed dead trees or bushes in the jungle sufficiently dry to burn.

When the cooking places were inside the perimeter, tins were, when available, used to collect the scraps of cooked and uncooked food, the ashes and the waste water, the tins being carried away and the contents buried or burned. When tins were not available pits were dug near the cooking places into which all the refuse was thrown and which were afterwards filled up with earth.

When the cooking places were outside the perimeter, pits were dug near them into which all refuse and waste water were thrown and earth was then thrown in. When the refuse and earth had filled the pit to about a foot below the surface of the ground, that pit was filled up with earth and a new one dug.

At Yembung, where the water was brought in bamboos to the outskirts of the camp and the ground lent itself to the plan, the drains, in which the surplus water ran to the river, were used to carry off all the waste water from the cooking places.

Refuse.—All the refuse collected in sweeping up the camps was buried or burned.

Waste water was collected in tins, removed outside the camps and thrown into pits, earth being then thrown into the pits.

Bathing and washing clothes.—The water of any stream near the camp was utilized for bathing and for washing clothes, care being taken that no fouling of the drinking water for men or animals could occur.

Urinals.—During the day, trenches or pits were used and into these the urine from the night urinals was poured and sometimes, when there was difficulty in carrying out incineration, the urine from the latrines was also thus disposed of. Pits of two kinds were used :—

1. Simple pits about 2 feet square and 2 feet deep, into which men micturated and into which a disinfectant solution or powder was sprinkled and earth was thrown, till the pit was nearly full. This pit was then filled up with earth and a new one dug.
2. Large pits, 6 feet in diameter and 6 feet deep, were dug and filled with large stones. Broad beams, flattened on the upper side, were then stretched across the pit and on these beams the men stood, or squatted, while they micturated on the stones. Night and morning a disinfectant powder or solution was sprinkled over the stones. This kind of pit was found to answer the purpose very well.

In the evening, empty kerosine or ghi tins were placed at convenient places about the camp as night urinals and, early in the morning the tins were removed and their contents poured into the trenches or pits described above.

1. *Latrines.*—Trench latrines, being the easiest to construct, requiring a smaller number of sweepers and not being affected by rain, were the first to be used at every camp. Two kinds of trenches were used—

(*a*) At first a narrow trench was tried, across which the men were meant to straddle, but this had to be given up, because the men would not use it ;in this fashion but kept both feet on one side of the trench.

(*b*) A wider trench was then used, at which the men sat side by side.

Both kinds of trenches were made with a tree trunk along each edge to prevent the friable soil giving way beneath the weight of the man using the trench. The trenches were made 2 or 3 feet deep, a sweeper was on duty from daylight till dark at each trench or set of trenches and shovelled earth at once on to the dejecta and over that a disinfectant was sprinkled. The only form of trench latrine that will avoid fouling the ground and be appreciated by the men and followers, is that wherein a series of short narrow pits are dug so that the men may sit side by side, the pit being narrow enough to be straddled and long enough to catch urine as well as solid dejecta. Men will not sit one behind the other.

2. *Removal system.*—At every camp from Kobo to Yembung as tins became available for receptacles, latrines on the removal system were substituted for trenches and the nightsoil was consumed in an incinerator.

Incinerators.—The fæces from these latrines were disposed of by incineration. Various forms of incinerator were used. At Kobo a large cylinder made of corrugated iron was employed and this was very good. Round iron bars, about ¾ inch in diameter, were used in this and air was admitted by 4 openings at ground level made by cutting away bits of the edge of the corrugated iron. The only defect was that the corrugated iron was inclined to crumple up at the lower end of the cylinder owing to the weight of the load of wood and fæces. This was obviated by two posts being used to support the cylinder, as these cylinders were too heavy and bulky to form convenient loads for coolies or mules, they were not used beyond Janakmukh.

Beyond Kobo, incinerators were for the most part built of stones and earth and, when iron bars were not available, strips of iron from the edges of packing cases were made use of to form a grating to take the place of bars. Putting 2 pieces of this iron diagonally across the grating was found to strengthen it very markedly. I am informed that the unserviceable lid of a galvanized iron tub was even made use of, on at least one occasion, in place of iron bars

The incinerators made of stones and earth had 4 holes at the level of the ground to admit air and in some cases bits of bamboo of large diameter were built into the walls in order to admit more air.

Until the rains ceased, about the middle of October, incineration could not be properly carried out at Kobo, but later, when the weather was drier and all the trees and undergrowth that had been cut-down in clearing the camping ground had dried, incineration worked admirably. Roofs had to be erected over the incinerators to keep off the rain.

Incineration, however, can only be carried on properly when there are ample supplies of (1) pans, (2) labour and (3) fuel. (1) A large number of pans are required at the very start and pans or empty tins should be sent specially since it takes a considerable time before empty oil, ghi or gur tins becomes available. (2) One sweeper has to remain on duty beside each incinerator from daylight to dark and he requires to be relieved to let him get his food, etc.; this is in addition to the sweepers kept busy sweeping up the camp. Collecting and chopping up fuel and collecting leaves, grass and twigs require a lot of labour, for a large quantity is, necessary. (3) In this country mule litter seldom gets a chance to become dry enough to be of use as fuel, so wood has to be used and large sheds are required to store and keep dry sufficient fuel.

Night latrines.—In nearly every camp these consisted of tins which were placed in position at night and removed early in the morning, when their contents were buried or burned. Otherwise trenches were used.

Transport lines.—The lines of the 26th Mule Corps have, in all camps, been kept very clean. It was not possible to burn the litter in the incinerators used for the latrines, so it was removed to a distance from the camp, down stream, spread out on a sloping bank and, when dry enough, was set alight and thus destroyed. When this could not be done the litter was buried in pits or trenches.

The Cooly Transport lines required very careful supervision, as none of the carriers or headmen had even the slightest idea of sanitation. Frequent inspections of the lines had to be made to see that scraps of food, etc., were collected and taken away and in the course of time the carriers were taught that the cleanliness of their lines must be maintained.

Conservancy establishment.

When the force assembled at Kobo the authorised conservancy establishment of units was found to be quite insufficient and 60 Manipuri Nagas were sent for. This establishment proved sufficient, except when the line of communications was extended to Simong, when it was not sufficient to permit of incineration being carried on in all posts.

Since a permanent unit like a mule corps has no conservancy establishment attached to it even in peace time, and such temporary collections of men as carrier corps and Telegraph Department coolies are not provided with sweepers, it is evident that sweepers must be engaged temporarily for active service, since the authorised conservancy establishments of regiments is only sufficient for the requirements of the regiment when it remains united. A convenient scale for estimating the temporary conservancy establishment required for a force on active service would be—

4 extra sweepers for each battalion of Indian infantry,

6 for each mule corps,

1 for every 100 men of small bodies of Indian troops,

and 1 for every 75 men of such temporary aggregations as carrier corps, Telegraph Department or other coolies, etc., who are quite undisciplined and have never been accustomed to obeying any sanitary rules. This would allow for the efficient sanitation of posts on the line of communications and for the use of incineration, a mode of disposing of night soil and refuse, which, it must be remembered, requires a larger conservancy establishment than trenching.

General working of the medical (including ambulance) service in the field.

* * * * * * *

To meet the medical requirements of the force each regular unit had its usual medical establishment, except the 1-8th Gurkhas, who brought an extra ward orderly, and the Lakhimpur Military Police, who brought one medical officer, one assistant surgeon and two civil sub-assistant surgeons but no ward orderlies. Sanction was obtained and one sub-assistant surgeon was placed in sub-medical charge of each of the 5 Naga carrier corps, and there were 3 sections of an Indian Field Ambulance, two of which had only 6 bearers each, while the third had 120. The usual medical equipment of the regular units was altered by replacing the pair of field medical panniers suitable for mule transport by a pair of miniature field medical panniers, and extra boxes, made of venesta wood and containing some extra medicines and dressings and a supply of medical comforts were sent with each unit. Two of the three sections of Indian Field Ambulance were supplied on mobilization with light boxes and baskets, in which the equipment was repacked for cooly transport in uniform 60-lb. loads.

The field medical companions and field surgical havresacks from the sections of Field Ambulance were made use of in the carrier corps and a spare pair of miniature field medical panniers with a field medical companion and a field surgical havresack were issued to the Lakhimpur Military Police, who had only a pair of old field medical panniers suitable for mule transport, and extra miniature field medical panniers were obtained for use with detached parties. All columns were compelled to march in single file, the principle followed in the distribution of the medical personnel on the line of march was to place first-aid parties at regular intervals, each party self-contained, consisting of a medical officer or sub-assistant surgeon, a ward orderly and a proportion of kahars with hammocks, so that, should the long column be attacked at any point, no wounded man need remain more than 20 minutes without surgical assistance.

Special syringes were carried by all qualified medical personnel for the immediate treatment by irrigation of arrow wounds with potassium permanganate solution, this being reputed to be the most effective way of dealing with wounds poisoned by aconite.

"A" section of No. 168, Indian Field Hospital, was detailed as the field ambulance to accompany the main body, "B" section of the same field hospital as the clearing hospital at the head of the line of communications and "C" section as the Stationary Hospital at Kobo, from which patients were transferred to the General Hospital at Dibrugarh by means of small steamers, which at first ran irregularly, but later plied up and down twice a week.

The following statement gives some idea of the work done The fortnightly average is given and he date showo :—

Average daily sick.

	October 1911.	November.		December.			January 1912.		February.		March.		April.	
	22	5	19	3	15	29	12	26	9	23	8	22	5	19
Indian troops...	36·50	67·23	80·21	121·73	119·85	84·34	51·90	31·98	36·92	34·99	42·21	42·86	55·43	33·42
Followers	24·57	90·29	142·76	311·20	302·24	229·86	203·34	178·73	219·36	195·77	250·57	130·92	58·71	42·35
Total ...	61·07	157·52	222·97	432·93	422·09	314·20	255·24	210·71	256·28	230·76	292·78	173·78	114·14	75·77
	3 sections, Indian field hospital and general hospital of 50 beds.			4 sections, Indian field hospital and general hospital of 50 beds.			4 sections, Indian field hospital and general hospital of 100 beds.				4 sections, Indian field hospital and general hospital of 100 beds.			

Ambulance Transport.—The transport of sick and wounded in country such as this presents great difficulties. There are no roads, so wheeled transport and riding mules cannot be used until the military road is made, and the hills are so steep and the paths are so narrow and often so slippery that the use of dandies is impossible and even Ashanti hammocks are often useless. On this expedition the difficulties were overcome by using canvas carriers and cane chairs (made by the Naga carriers from bamboos found in the jungle) to carry the sick on the backs of coolies on the steep and slippery paths, and by using Ashanti hammocks on the less steep paths. Country boats were used for sending sick from Janakmukh, at first, and afterwards from Pasighat to Kobo and, after arrival of the mule corps, mules were used to a slight extent, mostly for the transport of the less severely affected patients from Janakmukh to the boats at Pasighat after the Dihang fell so low that boats could not go beyond Pasighat.

Dandies can only be pushed forward as the military road lengthens.

The Ashanti hammocks, with which the expedition was equipped, are much better. They are lighter and the bearers can see sufficiently well to avoid being tripped up by obstructions on the paths. They are, however, too long for use on steep, slippery and narrow hill-paths, and they sag very much under the weight of the patient, so that a man with a recent fracture cannot be carried in them and on very uneven ground a patient is apt to get bumped against any projection. A broad band of newar, capable of being easily adjusted, passing over the pole and under the pelvis of the patient would prevent bumping. The hooks supplied for keeping the ends of the hammock apart are not strong enough. Some simple means of keeping the ends apart without weakening the pole by making holes in it, yet capable of being readily transferred from one pole to another (so that in a country, where bamboos are plentiful the poles can be easily changed) is wanted. A padded circlet to fit round the pole, with strong ends to tie it firmly on to the pole, might be useful to make an adjustable shoulder on the pole. Another objection to these hammocks is that they have no legs to support the patient clear of the ground when the hammock is set down. A copy of a report on the Ashanti hammock is attached.

The canvas carriers were very useful on the steep hill paths and so were the basket chairs, but special coolies, hill men, are required to carry them. The chairs, when made with a foot-rest, are much the more comfortable method of carrying a patient. The patient sits in the chair with his back towards the back of the cooly who carries him. On the canvas carrier the patient is supported by the carrier as he sits pickaback on a cooly's back. Both with the chair and the canvas carrier the strain on the cooly is very great and frequent changes are necessary, so that six coolies are required for one patient, if he has to be carried for more than a very short distance. A copy of a report on these canvas carriers is attached. When ambulance tongas and riding mules are not available, the less serious cases, who would otherwise ride, have to be carried, and this makes it necessary to have a much larger number of bearers than would be required were they supplemented by animal transport. For this reason 100 extra bearers of the Army Bearer Corps had to be obtained for this expedition. The bearers of the Army Bearer Corps are not accustomed to carry heavy loads on steep hills, and, even when walking without a load, are very clumsy-footed on the hill side, so they compared very unfavourably with the Naga and Gurkhali carriers in these respects. Nagas or Gurkhalis had always to be used to carry patients in chairs or on canvas carriers. But on a moderately level road the Army Bearer Corps men carried the hammocks very well and throughout the expedition have worked willingly and well.

The boats were very useful, being comfortable and (down stream) speedy. They brought sick from Pasighat to Kobo in eight hours, whereas it took two days to cover this distance by road.

On any future expedition in this country I should strongly recommend that basket chairs, canvas carriers, Ashanti hammocks, boats and a certain proportion of stretchers (for patients with fractures of the lower limbs) be supplied, with riding mules, when roads fit for mules have been made.

Elephants are very useful in the more level country, when they are available.

APPENDIX X (*a*).

Report on the Ashanti Hammock.

This hammock is intended to take the place of the standard pattern dooly in country where the dooly is too unwieldy and heavy, and the country in which this force was working is admirably adapted for finding out weak points in transport of sick.

The Ashanti hammock supplied is made of coarse fibre, strengthened along the free edges, and has at either end the strands gathered round a metal ring, which rings are intended to fit on to hooks passed through the pole to which the hammock is slung. When not in use, the hammock is folded and put into a canvas bag, slung over the shoulder of a *kahar*. There are two short sticks, 18" in length, used to keep each end of the hammock open when in use. The weight of the hammock in the bag, with the sticks, is 5 lbs.—6 ozs., the length thereof 10½ feet, but stretches to 11½ feet after use. The length of bamboo required as a pole is at least 14 feet 4 inches and the weight thereof 20½ lbs., the whole thus weighing nearly 26 lbs. Two hooks are also supplied from which to suspend the hammock. This is undoubtedly a great improvement on the standard pattern dooly in many ways:—it is lighter, shorter, and less bulky; when not in use, the pole can be carried over the shoulder of one man and the hammock in its bag over the other shoulder, road space being thus greatly economised and, when in use, requires a team of four men instead of six, two men carrying and two as relays. The rear carrier can also see the ground at his feet and thus is not so liable to stumble. A waterproof sheet flung over the pole acts as an efficient sun and rain shield, and this can be obtained from the patient if necessary. At the corners of sharp zig zags on hill sides, the shortness of the pole alone enables the hammock to be used. There are however a few drawbacks to its use in this severe country. Most of the paths followed are so steep as to make any litter carriage almost impossible. The hooks supplied are hardly strong enough to take the weight of the loaded hammock and are apt to draw. I have abandoned the use of these and tie the ends directly to the pole, thus shortening the stretching hammock, giving more room for the kahar's shoulders on the pole, and lifting the patient further from irregularities of the ground.

Hammocks in fact were only used latterly on roads made by the sappers and pioneers.

They are not good, of course, in fractures of the lower extremities.

APPENDIX X (*b*).

Report on the "Carriers, canvas, man," or canvas seats, used for the transport of sick and wounded on the Abor Expedition, 1911-12.

From what was known of the Abor country at the beginning of the expedition, it was recognized that the carriage of sick and wounded on the narrow, sharp-angled paths on the steep, slippery, hillsides would be a matter of great difficulty and it was seen that patients would often have to be carried *pickaback*.

To make this mode of transport easier for the patient, the Officer Commanding, 1-8th Gurkhas, provided his battalion with seats of leather, for the patient to sit on, with bamboo ropes as head and breast bands by which the cooly could support the weight of the man carried.

More seats of the same pattern were wanted for other units of the force, and the only materials available at the time were stout canvas and strong newar. On making a trial with the seats belonging to the 1-8th Gurkhas, it was found that, if the length of the seat were not sufficient, the ropes pressed painfully against the thighs of the patient. The seat was accordingly lengthened and the improved seats, the "Carriers, canvas, man" of this report, made by the warrant officer in charge of the Ordnance Base Depôt, were two feet six inches long, by one foot wide. They were made of double canvas and had three holes at each end, the edges of the holes being strengthened by an extra layer of canvas on each side.

The newar was used as the breast-band for the men carrying the patient. A piece of newar, 11 feet long, was passed through the four corner holes in the seat, as shown in the diagram, the ends being knotted under the seat and the length of the breastband being adjusted by this knot.

The centre hole at each end was used for the head-band and, for that, the coolies used their own carrying (bamboo) ropes. The head-band is shown in the diagram. These canvas seats were found to be an improvement on the leather ones, as the hard edge of the leather was apt to press painfully against the cooly's back.

These canvas carriers were found to be of great use, being light, strong and adapted to the usual cooly transport. Patients had often to be taken from a hammock and put on a canvas carrier, when a steep hill was reached.

The patient ought to lean well forward on the shoulders of the men carrying him and he aids the cooly by clasping his hands over the cooly's head and supporting part of his weight on them.

The strain on the cooly is very great and he has to be relieved frequently, so that six coolies (or even eight for a heavy patient) are

Photo.-Engraved & printed at the Offices of the Survey of India Calcutta 1914

Method of Carrying Sick and Wounded
by " carrier, canvas, man ".

[To face page 192.

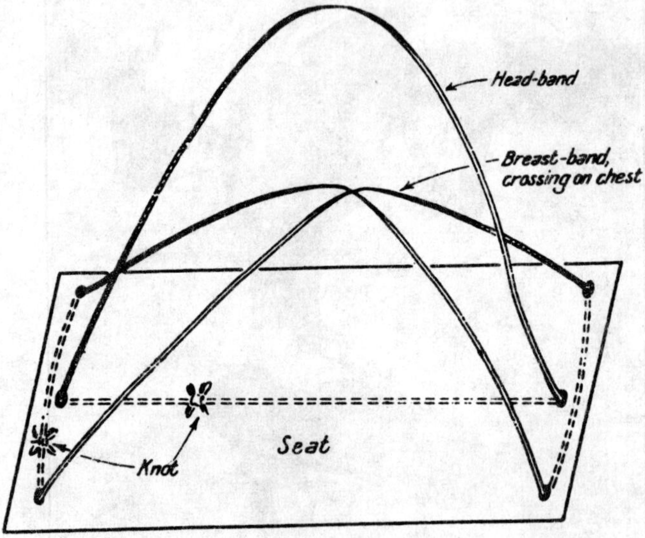

"Carriers, Canvas, Man."

8. D. O. No. 849 January, 1914.

required when the patient has to be carried any distance, since one man cannot carry a patient more than 200 yards on bad hills.

When similar conditions of field service necessitate the use of similar carriers, the following improvements should be introduced :—

1. The holes in the canvas should be oblong instead of round, to let the newar lie flat.

2. Both breast and head-bands should be of newar.

3. Both breast and head-bands should be fitted with a strong buckle at one end to admit of ready adjustment of the length of the band.

Canvas carriers are not suitable for patients with fractures of the limbs.

APPENDIX X (*c*).

Proposals for improving the field medical service in expeditions on the North-East Frontier.

I—Establishment.

(i) *Units.*—In jungle clad country, it is inevitable that much of the work must be done by means of small columns, with each of which there must be some medical personnel and equipment. The normal establishment of a battalion of Indian troops, *viz.,* one medical officer, one sub-assistant surgeon and one ward orderly, is only sufficient for two columns ; and one section of an Indian Field Hospital can only supply one more sub-assistant surgeon and it is unlikely that more than one section of a field hospital will be posted at any one camp in such a country. It would be advisable, therefore, that, for such work, each battalion should be provided with one medical officer, 2 Sub-Assistant Surgeons and 2 ward orderlies.

The additional sub-assistant surgeon could be utilized, when not required for detached columns, for duty in posts on the line of communications intermediate between posts in which sections of field hospitals are stationed. This applies with even more force to battalions on the line of communications, which are broken up into detachment at various posts.

Units such as mule and carrier corps should each be supplied with one sub-assistant surgeon, to accompany them when they are advancing, and to take medical charge of intermediate posts on the line of communications, when the corps is stationary.

(ii) When only Indian troops and Indian field hospitals are employed, each field hospital, or detailed part, should be provided with a cook who is capable of cooking for sick British officers and British troops.

II—Equipment.

(i) *Units.*—For service where only cooly transport is available, the ordinary field medical panniers, suitable for mule transport, should be replaced by miniature field medical panniers, suitable for cooly transport, and additional light boxes for extra drugs and dressings and a small supply of medical comforts, as has been done on this expedition. A book of medical certificates (A. B. 172) should form part of the contents of each pair of ordinary or miniature field medical panniers supplied to units.

If 2 sub-assistant surgeons are sent with a battalion, 2 field medical companions and 2 field surgical havresacks should also be supplied and each mule or carrier corps should be provided with one field medical companion and one field surgical havresack for the use of the sub-assistant surgeon attached to the corps.

For service on the north-east frontier where intestinal parasites are common, each unit and section of Indian Field Hospital should be provided with a supply of santonin and taeniafuges.

Field Medical Panniers.—The field medical panniers for cooly transport should be brought down to 60-lb. weight as suggested for the field hospital packages.

If miniature panniers similar to those used on this expedition are supplied, a 4-oz. brass syringe should be added.

Add a small airtight tin box for dressings, one dozen microscope slides and six glass capsules for specimens of blood.

Stationery.—Increase supply of envelopes and foolscap paper and add some sealing wax.

Blank Forms and Books, increase—

I. A. F. A.		28	to 500	
„	F	969	„	2000
„	F	974	„	2000
„	Z	2,011	„	4 books.

Add—

I. A. F. A.		175—20
„	A.	1,042—20

When no British field hospital is sent with the expedition, a set of kitchen utensils, diet requisites and a supply of pepper, concentrated soups, extract of beef and essence of chicken, as for a British field hospital, should be supplied with each section of Indian field hospital for the use of sick British officers and British troops.

Spare helves for the axes, felling and pick, should be available either in the field hospital or in the ordnance base depôt.

APPENDIX XI.

Report on Engineering Operations by the Assistant Director of Works, Abor Expeditionary Force.

Kobo.

(1) No. 1 Company, 1st King George's Own Sappers and Miners and 32nd Sikh Pioneers arrived at Kobo on 28th September. The following works were carried out at Kobo—

(*i*) Enlarging and clearing site of Base Camp.

(*ii*) Water-supply from Abysinian pumps. These pumps were of the greatest value.

(*iii*) A road was cut for 3 miles towards Pobamukh, which became the steamer terminus when the Dihang fell too low to allow steamers to reach Kobo.

(*iv*) A landing stage was erected for steamers. This was made of cribwork, the logs being 18 feet long by 4 feet girth, and the piles were driven 6 feet into the river bed. This was totally washed away on 12th October when the Dihang rose 17 feet. Such a flood at this season had been unknown, the river reaching summer flood level.

(*v*) Salvage of the river steamer "Scinde", which ran on to the fluke of an anchor and settled down on to the river bed. Sappers and Pioneers, working continuously in relief for 60 hours at 13 pumps, got the water out and the Sappers caulked the holes temporarily. But for the work of these troops, the "Scinde" would probably have become a complete wreck during the flood of 12th October.

(*vi*) On 10th October, ½ Company, Sappers with a detachment of Pioneers marched to Kemi River on the Oyang road and built a light trestle bridge for foot traffic. This was carried away by a 9 feet flood. On 16th October, the half company of Sappers commenced a *jhula* or country bridge which was completed on the 17th. This bridge was made of bamboos interlaced between six one inch steel wire cables; the span being 140 feet. On 17th October a trestle bridge was commenced and finished on the 18th, when the Sappers returned to Kobo.

(*vii*) Various works in camp, roads, drains, incinerators, etc.

Kobo to Pasighat.

(2) As far as Pilung, the road had already been improved by the Public Works Department. Between Pilung and Lokhpur the path was bad, being blocked by many fallen trees so that progress was slow. Between

Lokhpur and Pasighat the path was better, the jungle consisting of smaller trees and less under-growth.

(3) During the halt at Pasighat, from 26th to 28th October, a defensible post was made for the Advanced Base, the road between Lokhpur and Pilung was improved, and the Sappers and Pioneers also worked on the road forward, reaching the top of Red Cliff, 4½ miles from camp, on 28th. At Red Cliff the path entered the hills, the ground hitherto having been flat.

Janakmukh.

(4) During the march, to Janakmukh, Sappers and Pioneers worked on a new alignment of zigzags leading down from Red Cliff to Janakmukh camp on the bank of the Dihang.

(5) During the halt at Janakmukh, the Sappers and 3 companies of Pioneers completed the road from Pasighat, made a post at Janakmukh, and carried the road forward 1¾ miles to the Sijon stream, where the road leaves the Dihang.

* * * * * *

(6) From 3rd to 5th November, the Sappers and 1 company of Pioneers made the road forward from Rammidumbang to Sirpo Camp. Throughout this stage, a new line was taken to "Coolie col" and down to the Sirpo valley. The latter part was a steep descent which had to be negotiated in the short time available by continuous zigzaging.

Sirpo.

(7) As far as Sirpo Camp the gradient had been made at or under 1 in 7 and the path was passable by mules, but required widening before being fit for daily convoys; it was considered that the Pioneer companies on the line of communications could complete this widening gradually.

(8) Beyond the Sirpo river was a very sharp rise of about 1,000 feet, the Abor track going straight up at a slope which in places was as steep as 1 in 2. To save time, it was decided to make a coolie track at 1 in 5. This was finished on 8th November. The road was also continued from camp down to the Sirpo river along a steep cliff down which the Abor track was carried by means of a ladder. A 25 feet bridge was built over the Sirpo.

Rengging.

(9) On 9th November the road was carried on from the Sirpo col to a point above Rengging Camp.

(10) Between Rengging and Rotung the road works round high hills on the left. These are off shoots from Bhapu mountain, and form steep spurs and deep valleys radiating out to the Dihang, which lies hidden in a deep gorge on the right.

The Abor track crossed four *nullahs* taking a more or less straight line regardless of the descent or ascent involved. The names of these *nullahs* and intervening spurs or *cols* are:—

	Approximate heights. Abor track.	New road.
Rengging Col	2,200	2,200
Marshing Nullah	1,500	2,300
Jhum Spur	2,500	2,500
Yernu Nullah	1,900	2,750
Yernu Col	3,000	3,000
Lalek Nullah	1,600	1,700
Razor Edge	2,150	2,150
Igar Bivouac	1,600	2,000
Rotung Col	2,350	2,350
Rotung	1,100	1,100

This necessitated the finding of an entirely new alignment. From each *col*, the next was visible, but the intervening valley was mostly out of view and its sides covered with dense jungle, precluding any accurate estimate of the nature of the hillside. It therefore only remained to determine the approximate gradient which would hit the next *col* and to cut a line forward on it, trusting to chance not to run into a cliff which would involve a retreat and a fresh trial line above or below the cliff. On the steep hillside the jungle generally limited the view to 20 or 30 yards. The actual roadmaking was not difficult, the soil being soft and rock disintegrated: the chief delay being the cutting and removing of the larger trees.

* * * * * *

Igar Velley.

(14) The Igar valley proved to be the most difficult section between Kobo and Kebang, the ground being very steep and often rotten and treacherous: the alignment took three days and the making of the road another five. Time after time the trial trace ran into impossible ground and a fresh line had to be cut.

Rotung Ferry.

(15) On 30th November, the first attempt was made to cross the Dihang at Rotung. For tactical reasons the crossing was to be made at night. The narrowest site available for the crossing was in a stretch of the river just below a rapid and about half a mile above the next rapid. The width in the narrowest part was 180 yards and the current variable up to 6 miles an hour. On the far side was a cliff of rock rising some 30 feet above water level and on the near side the bank was covered with immense rocks rising up at a steep slope.

(16) The materials available for the crossing were:—

Wheatley bags, line, wire, and steel wire cables 5-8ths, 1, and 1½ inches in circumference. The Wheatley bags were filled beforehand:

to save weight, a small gabion, 2 feet high and 1 foot diameter made of split bamboo, was wrapped round with rope of rice straw, and placed in each bag. It was found that this method reduced the dead weight of a bag to 63 lbs. as against 80 lbs. when stuffed with straw only; moreover there is not so much straw to become waterlogged.

(17) A raft of 10 bags was made up with bamboo framework and Lieutenant Cave Browne R.E., and five sappers tried to row across with a line at 5-20 P.M. The current and drag of the line proved too strong and the line had to be cut to enable the raft to reach the far bank above the rapid. An attempt was at once made to run out an *otter*, 5 feet by 2½ feet which had been previously prepared, out the otter would not go further than half way. Work was now being carried on by moonlight. After several attempts and various readjustments, the otter dived and became fast in the river bed, so at midnight further attempts had to be abandoned.

(18) At dawn on 1st December Lieutenant Cave-Browne recrossed with the raft. The failure of the otter appeared to be due to the whirlpools in the river which overturned the otter. During the day, therefore, two larger otters were prepared and an attempt was made to run one across at 5-20 P.M. Again this method failed. The otter, 6 feet by 3 feet, dived and broke away, and another 8 feet by 4 feet kept rising and falling over. At 1 A.M. work was stopped and the party bivouacked on the bank.

(19) Next morning Lieutenant Cave-Browne crossed with the raft at dawn and seven successive attempts to run the otter failed. Various alterations were tried in the lengths of the bridles, etc., and finally, bamboos were lashed along the waterline of the otter to increase its buoyancy and the weight of the keel was increased to give more stability. The raft was attached to the far bank by a 1 inch steel cable and swung out about one-third across the river and at the eighth run of the otter, Lieutenant-Cave-Browne succeeded in catching its tail. The position now was that the raft and the otter were in mid stream 200 yards from the near bank and 150 yards from the far bank. The joining of the two cables was a difficult and hazardous operation in heavy water, and was successfully carried out by Lieutenant Cave-Browne, who then cut the otter adrift. It was now 5 P.M. and there were only 5 men on the raft who were very much fatigued, so the raft was recalled. As it was, the crew could only just succeed in making the near bank.

(20) As more men would be required on the far bank next morning, a rectangular raft of 16 more Wheatley bags, arranged in fours, had been prepared, ready to lengthen the small raft. Work at dawn on 3rd December was again checked by the 350 yards of 1-inch cable having fouled a rock in the river and it had to be cleared by sending the raft out from the near bank along the cable. The large raft of 26 bags was then rowed over with Lieutenant Cave-Browne and 12 Sappers. They at once pulled over a 1½-inch cable attached to the 1 inch, and the cable was tightened up clear of the water. At 5-15 P.M. the large raft was pulled back to the near side by a ⅝ths inch

cable attached to a traveller running on the 1½-inch cable. At 5-30 P.M. the first party of 20 Gurkha scouts was ferried over, the crossing being completed in 19 trips at 10-35 P.M. when the maxim gun detachment of the Assam Valley Light Horse, 2 companies, 1-8th Gurkhas, 1 company, 1-2nd Gurkhas with maxim, ambulance, and reserve ammunition carriers had crossed.

*   *   *   *   *   *

Rotung to Yembung.

(24) On 4th December, after the capture of the Kekar Monying stockade, the Sappers and one company, 1-8th Gurkhas demolished the stockade, cut down 40 stone chutes and repaired the track through Kekar Monying.

*   *   *   *   *

(25) Between the 5th and 11th December a coolie track was made from the Sireng river to Yembung.

*   *   *   *   *   *

Yembung Ferry.

(29) On 29th December, the Sappers established a ferry across the Dihang at Yembung. The first line was taken across by a Berthon boat, which had now been received from the Base. No difficulty was experienced, a good site being available for the crossing, where the river was very deep and current about 3 miles an hour. The crossing of the boat was covered by two maxim guns, and two rounds were fired from the wooden mortars which threw shells containing 3½ lbs. dynamite well into the jungle on the far bank; the explosion of these shells was sufficient to frighten any Abors who might have been concealed in the jungle. As soon as it was seen that the line had been successfully taken over, a raft of 32 Wheatley bags, carrying 16 sappers, was rowed across by five pairs of oars. With the help of the first line, cables of 5-8ths and 1½-inches steel wire were pulled across in succession. As at Rotung, the raft was attached to a traveller, running on the 1½-inch cable and the traveller was pulled across by 5-8ths inch cable from each bank. A capstan was built for winding in the cable. (Subsequently on 12th January a raft of Polyanski bags was tried in place of the Wheatley bags and proved satisfactory.)

(30) On 22nd December, a section of Sappers under Lieutenant Cave-Browne re-established the Rotung ferry, which had been dismantled on 5th December on the return of the right flank attack after the capture of Kekar Monying stockade. A strand of telegraph wire had been left up over the river on 5th December so there was no delay in getting the steel wire cable over the river.

Permanent Mule Road.

(31) On 20th December, the Sapper company commenced an 8 ft. mule road back towards the Base from Yembung. About 15th December a portion of the 32nd Pioneers had been released from escort duties, and 3 companies under Lieutenant Burn-Murdoch had begun work on the permanent mule road from Razor edge to Rotung. Lieutenant Burn-

Murdoch had obtained a good alignment from the col, involving a 30 feet cutting, which eliminated the zigzags made during the first advance.

(32) On 28th December, the Sappers moved back to Puak, where 1 company Pioneers was already working on the mule road. From Yembung to Roṭung an excellent alignment was obtained between 80 and 200 feet above the Dihang, as far as the Sireng, whence the road rises steadily into Rotung, the maximum gradient being 1 in 10. Sappers built bridges over the Puak and Sembong streams of 25 and 20 feet spans.

(33) On 13th January, the Sappers and 1 company Pioneers moved to Side and were joined by another company of Pioneers. The Sappers built a cantilever bridge of 45 feet over the Side, and cut the road through Kekar Monying in solid rock, some 100 yards.

(34) On 30th January, a half company of Sappers moved to the Sireng stream and commenced work on a suspension bridge 84 feet span, dip 1-12.

Sireng Bridge.

All woodwork was sawn out of logs. The timber available was all heavy, being as much as 72 lbs. per cubic foot. The roadway was 4 feet wide between ribands and 6 feet between handrails, to take laden mules and infantry in single file. Braces to the handrails and inverted cables gave great stiffness to the bridge. The left frame was on top of a rock cliff and the right frame on a cribwork pier built on soild rock foundations. Eight 1½-inch steel cables were used on account of the great weight of the roadway due to the high specific gravity of the timber. The completion of the bridge was delayed by the cables not arriving from Calcutta until 23rd February; it was finished on the 27th when the section remaining at Sireng marched to Rotung.

(35) On 30th January a half company of Sappers and 2 companies Pioneers marched to Rotung, whence they finished the road down to the Sireng bridge and commenced building a post at Rotung for the Military Police, to accommodate 200 men. The post was enclosed in a stockade of bullies, 6 to 8 inches diameter, 8 feet high, with barbed wire fence, ditch, and *panjies* outside. The stockade was rectangular, 73 yards by 63 yards, with two bastions at opposite corners.

Rotung Post.

(36) The general type of building was 48 feet long by 25 feet wide (15 feet room with two verandahs each 5 feet wide). One barrack of this size was allowed for each section of 25 men. All buildings were raised 2½ feet off the ground on logs resting on dry stone walls. Floors and walls were made of split bamboo. Roofs were designed for corrugated iron sheets, but pending sanction for necessary expenditure, roofs were temporarily covered with split bamboo and 18 feet by 12 feet tarpaulins supplied by the Supply and Transport Corps. Officers' bungalows and mess were floored with sawn planks. The post was well drained, being sited on ground with a slope of 1 in 10 to the west.

(37) About the 10th February, the Pioneers completed the road from Rotung to Lalek stream, and moving to Rengging, finished the road from Rengging to the Lalek by the end of February, a new alignment giving a practically level road round the Marshing Nullah from Rengging col to Jhum Spur.

(38) The sappers built a suspension brigde across the Sirpo and made the approaches on both banks, whilst the pioneers carried on the road by a new alignment, 2¼ miles total length.

Sirpo Bridge.

(39) The Sirpo bridge had a span of 100 feet, 60 feet above water level, with roadway of the same type as at Sireng bridge. There were 12 cables 1½-inch steel wire, arranged in half parabola, dip 1-10. On both banks the cables were carried straight to the anchorages without any frames. On the right bank the cables ran straight up from the longest sling into the cliff, to a shore transom resting on solid rock, behind which a platform was blasted out 12 feet wide. On this platform an anchorage was made with boring bars. Each set of 6 cables was fastened to a hard wood anchor, 4 feet 8 inches by 6 inches with a 1½-inch boring bar forming its core. This anchor was fastened behind a row of 4 jumpers set in holes 3 feet deep. The heads of these jumpers were tied back to 2 more jumpers, whose heads again were tied back to 1 jumper like a 3, 2, 1, picket holdfast. The whole anchorage was covered with dry stone walling to a height of 4 feet. With braced hand-rails and inverted parabolic wind-ties a good stiff roadway was obtained. The method for adjusting the main cables is worthy of mention. Each 1½-inch cable was fastened permanently to one anchorage, and after a turn had been taken round the other anchorage, was stretched as tightly as possible by block and tackle and temporarily fastened with clips. After all 12 cables had been stretched once, they were again stretched, as the first cables had sagged owing to the anchorages taking up their permanent bearing under the accumulated strain. This left the cables on a catenary with 1½ feet dip. The length of the cable in this catenary and in its final position on bridge, *viz.*, that of a parabola with a straight back guy having been calculated, it became necessary to pay out the difference, which in this case was 14½ inches. Four inches were allowed for stretching under full load, and 10½ inches were paid out, which length was carefully marked on each cable.

The result was most satisfactory, each set of 6 cables lying perfectly even at the required dip of 1-10, thus ensuring an equal distribution of the total load, and it was unnecessary to readjust a single sling, which fully justified the time taken in stretching the cables. The slings were attached to flat iron plates bolted above and below the 6 cables.

* * * * * * * * * * *

Balek Post.

(41) On 25th March, the Sappers marched from Sirpo to Balek to build a post for the Military Police. Lieutenant F. S. Collin, R. E., and 2 companies, Pioneers had already built the stockade. The post was built

for 100 men, the huts being of the same type as at Rotung, but were raised off the ground on piles instead of on stonewalls.

* * * * * * * * * * *

(43) On 22nd February, a party established a ferry over the Dihang below Geku, using a raft of Polyanski bags. Between 28th February and 2nd March, the Dihang exploration and survey party crossed by the ferry to the right bank, and the ferry was dismantled.

Work above Yembung.

(44) Another party left Rotung on 26th February and improved the path up the right bank of the Dihang above Yembung, made eleven foot bridges and one ferry over various streams and assisted survey work by improving tracks and clearing jungle for observation stations. This party rejoined at Balek on 28th March.

Passighat Post.

On 8th April, Sappers and Pioneers moved to Pasighat to build that post. The Pioneers left Pasighat for India on 10th April, and the Sappers were assisted in clearing site, digging the ditch, collecting materials etc., by 2 Companies 1-8th Gurkhas, a detachment of Military Police and 300 Gurkhali Carriers. The post was built for 100 men, rectangular in plan, 50 by 66 yards, with a double-storey block house at two opposite corners. A stockade was not considered necessary, but could be added. A breastwork was made inside the ditch from the trunks of trees felled in clearing the site. As no sanction had yet been received to the proposal, submitted in January, to provide corrugated iron roofs, the roofs were built at a steeper slope to carry thatch. In seven days the clearing of the site was completed, including removal of some immense trees; the framework and split bamboo flooring of all buildings was finished, one hut was thatched, and planks were sawn for flooring the officers' quarters.

(46) The post being so far advanced that it could be finished by the infantry and carriers, the Sappers left Pasighat by half companies on the 16th and 17th April.

APPENDIX XI (*a*).

Notes on Engineer Equipment.

* * * * * *

(2) *Dahs.*—For the Abor expedition a *kukri* or *dah* was issued to each Sapper. A kukri is perfectly useless in the hands of anyone but a Gurkha, who has been trained to its use from youth, moreover the kukries issued by the Ordnance Department were of inferior metal. The dahs also were of a bad pattern and material. Whilst awaiting the advance from the base of Kobo, I saw some Hkamti dahs belonging to an officer of the Lakhimpur Military Police and bought some for the Sapper officers, and carried one myself in place of a sword throughout the expedition. This dah was invaluable for cutting jungle in aligning the road and with it I could compete on equal terms with the Gurkha and his kukri.

* * * * * *

The weight is 1 lb. 6 oz. The grip was rather too small for an Englishman. The blade is made of soft iron with a thin strip of steel on one side only: the other side is sharpened on a stone as required, the steel side remaining flat. The balance is excellent and the blade cut through young saplings with ease. This weapon should be issued to everyone except Gurkhas on another expedition on the north-east frontier.

* * * * * *

(5) *Crossing rivers.*—The whole difficulty is to get the first line across. In the case of a big river like the Dihang, when boats are not available or the current is too heavy to let a boat take a line over, an *otter* appears to be the best method, but an otter will not work satisfactorily unless there is a fairly even current. At Rotung, the Dihang kept boiling up in eddies which upset the otter. On the other hand I got an otter at the first attempt successfully across the Kabul river in the Mohmand expedition, 1908, width 200 yards, maximum current 6 miles an hour, but there were no eddies. I think experiments should be made to devise a rocket to carry a ¾ inch line 250 yards. I understand that marine life saving rockets carry a much heavier rope about 150 yards, so that there should be no great difficulty in obtaining our requirement. I believe that a marine rocket apparatus is very heavy: a light equipment is required that can at all events be carried on two mules. These rockets could be kept in an arsenal, a few being issued yearly to Sapper and Miner Corps for practice. When an expedition goes into a country where large rivers will be met, these rockets would be specially issued. The saving of one day in crossing a river might mean the saving of one day in the duration of the expedition, the financial gain of which would well repay the cost of the proposed equipment.

* * * * * *

(7) ***Venesta Equipment Boxes.***—12 experimental boxes were made up in the 1st King George's Own Sappers and Miners workshops, smaller than the ordinary mule equipment box, to carry tools, etc., in 60-lb. loads suitable for coolies. For over 5 months the Sapper Company was entirely dependent on coolie transport, and these boxes were of the greatest value and stood the test well. A small reserve of these boxes might be maintained for similar expeditions.

APPENDIX XI (*b*).

List of stores expended from Engineer Field Park.

Axes, helves, 34½ inches	No.	84
Axes, helves, 16 inches	„	30
Mules, helves, 34½ inches	„	200
Sandbags	„	231
Mamooties, helves	„	36
Shovels, helves	„	55
Bars, jumping, 1½ inches.	(in anchorages)	15
Galv. iron wire, No. 14	cwt.	25
Barbed wire	„	32·16
Dogs, 15 inches	„	19
Dogs, 12 inches	„	44
Pencils, carpenter's	„	24
Saws, handles	„	8
Cordage, Manilla, 3-inch	fathoms.	150
Cordage, Manilla, 2-inch	„	62
Cordage, Manilla, 1½-inch	„	150
Canvas, sail	yards	25
Canvas, Willesden	„	41
Lines, hambro	skeins	10
Twine, country	lbs.	20
Log line, 1½-inch	skeins	20
Log line, white, 4 lbs.	„	10
Spunyarn	lbs.	20
Solder...	„	1
Copper sheet	„	4
Tin sheet, 20"×14"	sheets	6
Steel, round, ½ inch	lbs.	32
Steel, round, ⅜ inch	„	12
Steel, round, ¼ inch	„	10
Steel, round, ¾ inch	„	40
Steel, flat 2"×⅜"	„	31
Steel, flat 1½×¼"	„	29
Steel, flat 1½"×1½"	„	18
Steel, flat 2½"×½"	lbs.	2

Bolts, ¾"× 9" inch	No.	2
Bolts, 3/8"×6" inch		2
Wire nails, 2½-inch	lbs.	40
Wire nails, 3-inch		188
Wire nails, 4-inch		388
Wire nails, 5-inch		230
Wire nails, 6 inch		244
Spikes, 5-inch		84
Spikes, 7-inch		700
Spikes, 9-inch		734
Screws, 1½-inch	gross	1
Screws, 2½-inch		1
Screws, 3½-inch		1
Screws, 5-inch		1
Composition, waterproof	lbs.	2
Oil, Rangoon	gallons	5
Oil, Mustard	„	1
Turpentine	pints	2
Dynamite	lbs.	800
Guncotton, primers		50
Guncotton, slabs		510
Gunpowder		150
Cordite		50
Detonators, octuple	No.	800
Detonators, sextuple		700
Fuze, safety	fathoms	500
Matches, vesuvian	boxes	36
Leather, buffalo, light	lbs.	30
Ropes, steel wire, ⅝- inch	fathoms	2,400
Ropes, steel wire, 1 inch		700
Ropes, steel wire, 1⅛ inch		1,100
Clips for wire cable, ½-inch	No.	4
Clips for wire cable, ⅞ inch	No.	11
Clips for wire cable, ⅝-inch		10
Wheatley bags	No.	60
Polyanski bags	No.	125
Pitch	lbs.	40
Sal ammoniac	lbs.	

APPENDIX XII.

Report on Signalling and Telephonic Arrangements.

By the Chief Signalling officer, Abor Expeditionary Force.

I. *Signalling.*

The chief difficulties to be encountered are (*a*) the bad weather (*b*) the jungle—

(*a*) *Weather.*—Up to the first week in January 1912 the weather was on the whole good and favourable to signalling, the atmosphere being very clear, but since then there was comparatively little sunshine, but much rain, mist and haze, which prevented helio work and often lamp as well.

(*b*) *Jungle.*—Extensive cutting of jungle was always necessary to obtain communication. Where the country has been at one time under cultivation, the jungle can be cleared with kukries or daos, but virgin forest can only be cleared by a large number of men with saws and axes, and these were never available for signal stations.

Altitude of stations.—For the above reason stations were kept at as low an altitude as possible, as the higher peaks and ridges are invariaby covered with virgin forest.

Another reason for keeping stations at a low altitude is that the higher hills are frequently enveloped in clouds or mist when there is bright sunshine lower down.

*But for this latter reason Bapu Namkam and Arte Hill now they have been cleared for survey work would in the future form fine signal stations, especially for any advance up the right bank of the Dihong.

Maps.—A third difficulty peculiar to this expedition, was the lack of a map of the country north of Kebang, in which most of the signalling operations took place. It was never possible, with the aid of the map available, to determine on the possibility of communication between any two points. This could only be decided by visiting both points and cutting the jungle. It will be seen, therefore, that signalling operations on this expedition were conducted under considerable difficulties.

With the aid of a map, and given fine weather and facilities for clearing the thickest forest, lines of stations could easily be laid out and worked in any direction, but this may be said to apply to any hill country.

---

* It will probably be found that these clearings will be completely over grown in 2 years' time.

Tactical signalling and moving stations.—Owing to the jungle, tactical signalling is quite out of the question, and almost as much may be said of signalling with any moving station, such as a column on the march, which rarely has time to clear jungle for signalling purposes.

Lamps.—Communication depended greatly on lamps, and it is most important that lamps should be carried, and a force operating in this country should be equipped with CC. lamps as well as BB.

Summary.—It cannot be said that signalling is a reliable form of communication in this country, even for fixed stations, as the weather may prevent signalling for several days together, while the jungle renders tactical signalling quite impracticable.

II. *Telephones.*

Tactical uses.—Telephones are indispensable for tactical communication, and a force operating in this country should be well equipped with telephonic apparatus, and especially with cable.

Amount of cable.—The 8 miles allowed to a brigade section of a signal company is quite inadequate. Wide turning movements will often be made. As much as 23,000 yards of cable were laid to maintain communication at the attack on the Kekar Monnying stockade.

Great use was made of telephonic communication and, except on two occasions when a line which had been standing for a long time in wet weather failed temporarily and on the few occasions when the line was cut either by Abors or working parties, etc., telephonic communication was never interrupted.

General uses.—Undoubtedly the most reliable method of keeping communication in this country is by telephone, and it should take the place of visual signalling as far as possible.

For other than tactical purposes a light field cable is not sufficiently well insulated, and a heavy cable at 80 lbs. per mile, or a copper wire at 51 lbs. per mile should be used, the former being the better, as an insulated wire is preferable in jungle country.

Transport.—The objection to laying long lines of cable is the large amount of transport required, transport being a matter of considerable difficulty in this country. The weather during February and March was so bad that telephones had to be used to replace visual signalling, as far as possible, but there was not sufficient cable with either the Chief Transport Officer, or signalling officer, to run telephonic communication to all the stations existing.

* * * * * *

APPENDIX XIII.

DESPATCH DESCRIBING THE OPERATIONS AGAINST THE ABORS.

BY

MAJOR-GENERAL H. BOWER, C.B.,

Commanding the Force.

INDEX.

—	Paras.
Report on operations—	
(*a*) Active operations	1—18
(*b*) Political, Survey and Exploration	19—31
Summary	32—38
Mentions	39—54
Casualties	55—59
Map, Abor Handbook	

PHASE (A):

Active Operations.

Formation of Base.

1. Colonel D. Macintyre, Base Commandant and Inspector of Communications, with a staff of Supply and Transport and Medical Officers arrived at Kobo on the forenoon 26th September and assumed command of the Base.

Kobo had been selected as a Base, as the Steamer Companies had assured me that large steamers would be able to reach it even when the Brahmaputra was at its lowest. A clearing of the jungle had been made here by the Civil Authorities, but on the arrival of the troops an immense amount of work was necessary to clear the camp and make it healthy.

A guard of Lakhimpur Military Police was provided for the Base.

Great attention was paid to sanitation and a pure water supply was obtained through the use of Norton Tube wells.

Arrival of Troops.

2. The following troops arrived at Kobo on dates specified and were taken on the strength of the force :—

No. 1 Company (K. G. O.) Sappers and Miners ...	28th September 1911.
32nd Sikh Pioneers	28th September 1911.
Lakhimpur Military Police	28th September 1911.
"A" Section, 168 Indian Field Ambulance	28th September 1911.
No. 5 Carrier Corps	4th October 1911.
1/8th Gurkha Rifles	6th October 1911.
1/2nd Gurkha Rifles less 4 Companies ...	8th October 1911.
No. 31 Company, Signal Unit	8th October 1911.
Survey Party	8th October 1911.
'B' and 'C' Sections, Indian Stationary Hospitals ...	8th October 1911.
Assam Valley Light Horse Maxim Gun Detachment ...	10th October 1911.
No. 4 Carrier Corps	10th October 1911.
Nos. 1, 2 and 3 Carrier Corps	11th October 1911.

3. I arrived at Kobo on the 6th October and assumed command of the Abor Expeditionary Force from that date. The weather was hot and sultry. On the 8th October heavy rain started and continued until the evening of the 14th. The camp was soon a quagmire. The Brahmaputra rose 18 feet and fear was experienced for some time that the camp would be flooded. In the interval attempts had been made to explore and discover a route towards Ledum, but all tracks were flooded and temporary bridges over the Kemi were washed away.

Preliminary organisation.

The Carrier Corps were Nagas, they were without any ideas of drill and discipline, and advantage was taken of this halt to attach Naga Corps to each regiment for instruction.

4. The Ledum Column was placed under the command of Colonel J. Fisher, 1-2nd Gurkha Rifles, and marched on 20th October for Ledum with instructions to establish a post in vicinity of Ledum, open signalling communication with Kobo, and to operate against such villages as were within reach of the post, subject to the condition that the force was always to sleep in Ledum stockade. The object of the column was to protect the left flank of the main column advancing up the Dihang.

Ledum Column advance to Misshing.
1/2nd Gurkha Rifles. ½ Batn.
32nd Pioneers, 13 Rank and File.
Lakhimpur Military Police, 300 Rank and File.

Rations for 28 days were sent with the force but only one carrier corps could be spared to carry the loads, this necessitated a slow advance and a restriction of the troops to a 10-lb. scale of baggage.

The road for this column had been improved as far as Oyang.

After this the road had to be reconnoitred and cut through thick jungle, the men sometimes working waist deep in water. The advance was therefore slow and the head of the column did not arrive at Ledum until 23rd. Ledum was found to be deserted and to be situated on low hills, from which signalling communication with Kobo was impossible.

The 24th and 25th were occupied in pushing up supplies and on 26th October a reconnaissance was pushed on to Misshing.

This reconnaissance surprised and killed a few of the enemy and selected a site for a post.

The 27th, 28th and 29th were employed in moving up troops and rations to Mishing.

5. The organisation of the main column and line of communication troops was completed on the 21st October. Owing to transport difficulties troops had to be restricted to a 10-lb. scale of baggage. On this day

Main Column advance to Pasighat.

the boat convoy under Lieutenant Webb left for Pasighat and 2 companies 1-8th Gurkha Rifles escorted carriers with rations as far as 6-mile camp. The carriers returned to Kobo the same day. On the 22nd and 23rd October, the troops for Pasighat left in two columns and, by the 26th of October, were concentrated at Pasighat, distant 24 miles from Kobo.

The road for 14 miles, as far as Pilung, had been made, but after that only an Abor path was available. The condition of this path after the late heavy rain was very bad. It was boggy and several unbridged streams had to be crossed, jungle had to be cut, and gigantic fallen trees offered frequent obstacles. A march of 8 miles took some 9 hours to accomplish.

The clearing of camps and of the road gave the columns arduous labour. On arrival at Pasighat a clearing was made on the bank of the river and a fortified post was made.

9. The 27th and 28th October were employed in road-making both back towards Kobo and onwards to Janakmukh. In this latter direction an entirely new road had to be cut through the jungle and made. For the first 3 miles no special difficulty was experienced, as the country was still level, but after that the foot-hills were entered. Therefore in addition to the difficulties of cutting through thick jungle was added that of grading the path. By the 28th October sufficient road was completed to enable me to advance. My plan was to do so with the main column, making the road roughly as I advanced and leaving improvements to be made by the Pioneers, who were to form line of communication troops, until the arrival of the remaining half battalion of 1-2nd Gurkha Rifles would set Pioneers free from convoy work for their more legitimate occupation of road-making.

Road-making.

7. On the 28th, therefore, the Main Column, consisting of No. 1 Company, King George's Own Sappers and Miners, 1-8th Gurkha Rifles, Maxim Gun Detachment, Assam Valley Light Horse, No. 31 Company, Royal Engineers Signal Unit, 'A' Section, 168 Indian Field Ambulance, with the addition of 2 companies Pioneers for road-making and 1 Carrier Corps, advanced and camped at the mouth of the Sipi stream. The camp was called Janakmukh. Great difficulty was experienced in the last mile in the descent off the high ground. Camp was formed on a small piece of level ground on the bank of the Dihang River. After Janakmukh there was again no trace of a path, as the usual cold weather Abor path was under water. I therefore had again to halt and reconnoitre for the best alignment for a track for the advance.

Advance to Janakmukh.

In addition to road-making, these halts were utilized to carry up supplies.

8. From the 31st October to 5th November, the Ledum column displayed great activity in reconnaissance and small parties under British officers scoured the country in every direction, and surprised the enemy on several occasions. On the 5th November a party of 100 rifles 1-2nd Gurkha Rifles under Major Lindsay captured an Abor stockade near Dosing. This stockade was 150 yards long and 12 feet high, and was invisible at a distance of 10 yards owing to the thickness of the jungle. Several officers and men were knocked down by rocks let loose from stone chutes. Our casualties were one rifleman, 1-2nd Gurkha Rifles, severely and one slightly contused from rocks. The enemy left 1 killed in the stockade and though several others were seen to fall, the dense jungle prevented pursuit and enabled them to escape. After the capture of the stockade Major Lindsay pushed on to Dosing village which was found deserted. The enemy again attacked his picquets, but were driven off with the loss of 1 man killed. After destroying the village defences, Major Lindsay returned to Mishing which he reached at 10 P.M. after being 16 hours under arms.

Operations of Ledum Column.

These reconnaissance parties encountered great topographical difficulties. Steep ascents and descents up and down precipitous hill sides covered with thick jungle.

9. On the 2nd November, the main column, with addition of 1 company Pioneers, having completed the onward road for two miles, pushed on to Rammi Dumbang, and line of communication troops moved on to Janakmukh. The 1st mile of the road was on the bank of the Dihang and had to be cut out of the hill side. It was commanded by hills 1,000 feet high, which had to be searched for stone chutes. After a mile the path left the banks of the Dihang and climbed up through thick forest to the jhums at Rammi Dumbang. No contact had as yet been obtained with the enemy, though on several occasions the tracks of hostile scouts were observed. 2nd, 3rd, 5th were spent in road-making, pushing up supplies and reconnaissances for forward route. This was now found to climb up over the Rammi Dumbang hill and then descend steeply to the Sirpo river. This river runs through a deep narrow gorge and we were fortunate in finding a small terrace suitable for a camp. This was cleared by a reconnoitring party, in the hopes that it would dry somewhat before it was necessary to camp there. Unfortunately, owing to the jungle and to the narrowness of the gorge, little sunlight could reach the camp and it subsequently proved unhealthy, and a very high percentage of the 32nd Pioneers were incapacitated by a new type of virulent fever.

Advance of main Column to Rammi Dumbang.

10. From the 6th to 20th November, the Ledum column were very active in reconnaissance in every direction. I had, on the 6th November, withdrawn the order prohibiting the column sleeping out of the Post

Operations of Ledum Column.

(but in order to comply with my instructions issued a proviso that nothing was to be done to make the enemy in my front nervous). The weather broke on the 10th November and these reconnaissance parties suffered severely from exposure to the inclement weather which lasted until 15th November. The enemy was encountered on several occasions and loss was inflicted. Our casualties were one follower killed.

Main Column advance to Renging.

11. On the 6th November the main column moved camp to Sirpo River and line of communication troops to Rammi Dumbang. During reconnaissances a glimpse had been obtained of a village to the west of the road. This was visited on the 7th November by 2 companies under Major Wilson. Some resistance was encountered in which a Naga scout was wounded. The defences of the village were destroyed. All other troops were employed in road-making, which was now becoming more and more difficult. The Abor paths found were so steep and slippery as to be quite useless for long convoys of loaded carriers. The Sirpo river was bridged and sufficient track towards Renging made to allow of an advance there on the 9th November. Line of communication troops pushed on to Sirpo river.

Road-making, which was sufficiently difficult before, now became exceedingly difficult and arduous. The Abor path was found to alternately ascend and descend a series of steep precipitous ridges thrown out northwards from Bapu towards the Dihang. These ridges spread out like a fan with hill 6,290 as a centre and edges on the Sireng and Sirpo rivers. Two features of these ridges are remarkable—(1) the dense jungle, clothing almost precipitous hillsides, (2) extreme knife-edge narrowness of the top of the ridge. For these reasons it was found quite impossible to make a graded track to follow the Abor path between Renging and Rotung and it was determined to cut a path all on one level round the main hill. This entailed arduous reconnaissance for alignment, followed by still more arduous jungle cutting and spade work. This was rendered more trying owing to the inclemency of the weather, for on the 10th the weather broke and there was incessant rain and mist up to the 15th November. The troops suffered from being continuously wet at work on the road or in their shelters. For it must be remembered that owing to difficulties of carriage men had had to be restricted to 10 lbs. kit. The camp at Renging was some 2,000 feet high and was, therefore, very cold after the sultry heat of the march between Kobo and Pasighat. Although, during this enforced halt, reconnaissances were pushed in every direction, the enemy managed on the 13th November to ambuscade some telegraph coolies between Sirpo river and Rammi Dumbang. These coolies had left camp without permission. One was killed and one, severely wounded, afterwards died. On the 17th November some arrows were fired at a returning reconnaissance and Captain J. R. Hutchisson, Assam Valley Light Horse, was severely wounded.

My slow advance was, therefore, having the desired effect of emboldening the enemy.

12. On the 19th November sufficient forward road had been completed to permit an advance. Line of communication troops advanced to Renging. Opposition was expected as friendly Abors had reported the presence of a strong stockade between Renging and Rotung. The column advanced with only 170 carriers and was prepared to bivouac out. The remainder of the baggage column under escort of ½ company, Sappers and Miners, 2 companies, 1-8th Gurkha Rifles and 1 company, 32nd Pioneers was left at Renging. Line of communication troops moved up to Renging.

The affair on the Igar Stream.

The main column marched at 6-15 A.M. The advance proceeded smoothly as far as the track had been completed. After this the Abor path across the Lelek valley had to be followed. This was exceedingly slippery from the late heavy rains and the progress of the gunporters of 7-lb. gun and maxims was very slow and much delayed the column. After crossing the Lelek river a steep hill had to be carefully reconnoitred. No signs of a stockade were seen. The advanced guard reached the Igar stream at 2-30 P.M., and as the condition of the path from the top of the *kotal* between the Lelek and Igar streams was very bad and the forward path was quite unknown and certain to be stockaded, it was determined to take advantage of a small piece of flat ground on the edge of the Igar stream to make a bivouac. Until the bivouac was cleared it was impossible to see what the country was like. As the camp cleared, it was seen that it was situated in a very narrow gorge and was commanded by a precipitous wooded hill on the opposite bank of the stream. No sign of the enemy had as yet been seen or heard. At 3 P.M., taking half a company as escort, I pushed on along the track to reconnoitre the forward path for the morrow.

Almost immediately a stockade was reported by the scouts. The enemy kept so quiet that it was believed that the stockade was not held. Our scouts were soon undeceived, as suddenly a gun was fired and several rock chutes were let off. Several men were knocked over by rocks and one man, a Gurkha refugee from the late Mr. Williamson's massacre, was wounded by a gun shot. Rocks were continuously let loose from chutes. In the meantime the alarm had been given in the camp. At first owing to the echoes and the impossibility of seeing, it was thought that an attack was being made on the camp.

When, however, it was ascertained that an attack was being made on the reconnoitring party, reinforcements of 1½ companies, 1-8th Gurkha Rifles, were sent out. At this time the baggage column had not yet reached camp and the rear guard was busy clearing the kotal between the Lelek and Igar streams of rock chutes. With these reinforcements a turning movement gallantly led by their

officers { Lieutenants Buckland and Kennedy,
Subadar Jaichand Thakur, 1-8th Gurkha Rifles,

stormed and captured the stockade. Four of the enemy's dead were found in the stockade that evening and 6 more subsequently; some were wounded and escaped; I cannot tell the number, but am informed by Abors that one of the wounded died on arrival at Rotung. After the fight a piquet of 30 men was left holding the captured position and the remaining troops returned to their bivouacs.

Advance to Rotung.

13. On the 20th November, the main column advanced to Rotung without opposition. The enemy on retiring through Rotung the previous evening had burnt the village.

The baggage column and ration convoy, which on the same day moved from Renging, experienced great difficulty from the road, so much so that, though the head of the convoy reached the top of the *kotal* between the Lelek and Igar streams by 2 P.M., the remainder of the convoy of some 500 carriers did not reach the Igar stream bivouac some ¾ mile further on till 3 A.M., next morning. The paths on the Igar stream side of the *kotal* descended straight down a steep shaly slope. So steep and shaly was this slope, that the path was worn away by the traffic, and the rear carriers practically had to glisade down a precipice.

Ledum Column.

14. The column now began to suffer severely from fever as a result of the exposure undergone and the exertions entailed by their constant activity. 50 per cent of the British officers were invalided and one, Captain A. M. Hutchins, subsequently died. 15 per cent of the men were invalided.

The neighbourhood of Misshing was now clear of the enemy and on the 28th I sent orders for the break up of the Ledum column. The 2 companies, 1-2nd Gurkha Rifles were to march to Rotung *viá* Kelek and 150 of Lakhimpur Military Police were to march to Balek, whilst 150 Lakhimpur Military Police under Captain Sir G. Duff Dunbar were to remain at Misshing. The reduction of this post much facilitated transport questions.

Main Column at Rotung.

15. I was now again faced with road-making difficulties. The Pioneers were almost entirely employed on convoy work and could not be released for their more legitimate work of road-making until the arrival of the remaining 4 companies, 1-2nd Gurkha Rifles. These companies arrived at Kobo on 13th November and were pushed up to relieve Pioneers. The making of road between Rotung and Renging necessitated many reconnaissances and entailed much hard work and was only sufficiently completed to justify my advancing again on the 30th November. In the meantime reconnaissance parties were busy in every direction. One of these parties under Major J. A. Wilson on the 21st November successfully surprised two parties of the enemy, of whom seven were killed.

16. Other reconnaissances located a stockade on the road towards Kebang, at a place called Kekar Monying and observed that it was held by a strong force of the enemy.

Affair of Kekar Monying.

The left flank of this position rested on the Dihang. The stockade was, contrary to usual custom, quite visible. On our side of it was the obstacle of Kekar Monying.

Kekar Monying is a high, precipitous, rock face ending of a steep ridge. It is densely clothed in jungle. The ridges above are steep and also densely covered with jungle. The Abors evidently expected us to be unable to move over this country and were confident of defeating our columns thrown into disorder by rock chutes from Kekar Monying and from their stockade.

From personal reconnaissance, I was confident that if our troops could cross the Dihang, they would be able to enfilade both rock chutes and stockade from the high ground on the left bank. This was fortunately *jhumed* in several places. I determined, therefore, to turn both flanks of the position, whilst the main body gave the enemy the impression that we were nervous of attacking. This would keep the enemy in their position until the left flank attack could come down on their right rear and cut off their retreat. Surprise was a necessary item of success. Unsuccessful attempts were made to effect a crossing under the cover of darkness on the nights of the 30th November and 1st December, although the Sappers and Miners worked to their utmost.

At midnight 1st—2nd December, the officer commanding, Sappers and Miners, reported that the river was so difficult and treacherous that he could not get the necessary line across in the dark. He was therefore given permission to do so by day light. He commenced work at dawn and after strenuous exertions succeeded at 4 P.M. in getting a line across the river.

Too much credit cannot be given to Captain Pattenson and Lieutenant Cave-Browne for the success of their labours. The Sappers and Miners were unable to complete the rafting arrangements to permit of a crossing that night and my advance was again postponed. On this day the two companies, 1-2nd Gurkha Rifles arrived from Misshing.

On the 3rd December, I made a last reconnaissance of the enemy's position, the Sappers and Miners completed their rafting arrangements and final orders were issued for the attack. As the 1-2nd Gurkha Rifles companies had arrived, I determined to add them to the force for the day and was enabled to strengthen both right and left attacks. The right attack under Captain Coleridge consisting of three companies, 1-8th Gurkha Rifles, 60 rifles and maxim, 1-2nd Gurkha Rifles, and Assam Valley Light Horse maxim gun detachment, left camp at 4 P. M. for the crossing and by 10-35 P. M. was across the Dihang. On their march thence to the positions they were to occupy, the column was attacked by the Abors at 2-30 A. M. The attack was successfully beaten off, but two riflemen of the 1-2nd Gurkha Rifles were killed, then Abors leaving two dead behind them. The column bivouacked and in the morning, under cover of mist, took up their positions without disturbing the enemy behind their stockade. This column had been very well handled by Captain Coleridge.

The left flank attack of 3 companies, 1-8th Gurkha Rifles, under Captain Giffard, which had to climb over the range protecting the hostile right flank, left camp at 5-30 A. M.

The main attack left camp at 5-45 A. M. and arrived at Sirengmukh, about 1,500 yards distant from the hostile stockade, at 7 A.M. The right and left attacks were connected with the main attack by telephone under arrangements made by Lieutenant Knight. In order to obviate the possibility of attacks firing into one another, a sketch map was drawn up and lettered so that commanders of attacks could inform one another of their position and I was able to turn the fire of any attack on to any desired locality.

The left flank attack encountered great difficulty in climbing the heights, but by 11 A. M. the officer commanding reported that he was behind the hostile stockade, but still on the hills. In the meantime the right flank attack was remaining quietly in position, as I had given orders that they were not to open fire, until either ordered to do so, or the main attack fired, unless a good opportunity offered itself. By this time the enemy was seen to be moving about behind their stockade and it was thought that they were retiring. A shot, accidentally fired, was taken as a signal by the right flank attack that fire was to be opened. An accurate and hot fire was opened on the stockade and rock chutes. This was too much for the enemy who bolted, leaving only six actually seen dead behind, in the stockade and on the hills. But the Abors afterwards admitted to 30 killed, and said that the fire was so intense that they realised further resistance was useless. No further organised resistance was encountered. Directly after the action the right flank attack advanced and captured Sissin and, after destroying its defences, bivouacked preparatory to returning to recross the Dihang at Rotung. Three companies, 1-8th Gurkha Rifles under Lieutenant-Colonel Murray, D.S.O., 1-8th Gurkha Rifles, pursued the enemy to Babuk and pushed reconnaissances to within four miles of Kebang.

The remainder of the main column destroyed the hostile stockade and rock chutes, of which some 100 altogether were destroyed, and advanced to bivouac at the mouth of the Sidé river, whilst the rear guard of two companies, 1-2nd Gurkha Rifles, went back to fetch up baggage.

Advance on Kebang.

17. As a result of the discharge of rock chutes the path was impassable for loaded carriers and a halt was made on the 5th whilst the path was made. The pursuit to Babuk returned to camp at 4 P.M. On the 6th an advance was made to Puak, and Captain Coleridge's party

rejoined. The force halted to road-make on 7th and 8th. On the night of 7th, at 11-30 P.M., a party of the enemy attempted to surprise the camp, but the vigilance of the sentry thwarted their purpose and when fire was opened, the enemy bolted leaving traces of blood on the ground. On the 9th an advance was made in two columns on Kebang. Right column under my command, main column (less 5 companies and ½ company, Sappers and Miners). Left column under Colonel Murray D.S.O., 3 companies, 1-8th Gurkha Rifles, and ½ company, Sappers and Miners. No opposition was encountered.

Kebang village was found to be situated on a high ridge without an adequate close water-supply. It was in a filthy condition. After destroying its defences, the column withdrew and bivouacked for the night. On the 10th an advance was made up the Dihang and a camp formed at the mouth of the Yembung River in a situation convenient for an advance either up the right or left banks of Dihang against Komsing or for further operations against Kebang and Yemsing.

End of operations.

18. Between the 13th and 15th, a column of 5 companies, 1-8th Gurkha Rifles, under Colonel Murray, visited Yemsing and inflicted a known loss of 4 killed and 7 wounded on the Abors.

In the meantime on the line of communications, parties of the 1-2nd Gurkha Rifles from each post were busy in every direction. The Abors were surprised on several occasions. I attribute the subjugation of the Abors and the comparative safety of the lines of communications largely to the system adopted of small parties continually scouring the country in every direction and giving the enemy no rest.

The 32nd Sikh Pioneers were busy road-making.

The operation stage was now over, as no more organized resistance was encountered. Small columns from Yembung were busy in the vicinity of Kebang, locating the Abors food supplies.

PHASE (B.)

Political, Survey and Exploration.

19. I now considered that the Abors chiefly concerned in the massacre of the late Mr. Williamson had received punishment. Mr. Bentinck, my Assistant Political Officer from a study of the evidence, was convinced that although the massacres took place below Pang-i and in Komsing, the latter village was not implicated in the massacre, but were accessories only after the fact. The Abors were evidently of the opinion that my columns were to fight any Abors seen, so I determined to try and get into touch with them. With this object in view my Assistant Political Officer despatched the *gams** of the friendly Pasi villages to summon the gams of Pang-in, Komsing and Riu. These gams returned by the left bank on the 17th after visiting Komsing and Riu and stated that these villages were anxious to make friends and that the gams were coming in bringing presents. They also stated that the gams of Pang-i were anxious to make

* Headmen.

friends. As I was not yet convinced that the latter village was not directly responsible for the massacre of Dr. Gregorson's party I refused to parley with them. On the 18th the gams of Riu and Komsing arrived in camp and later in the day the gam of Pang-i. On the 19th the Pang-in gams arrived. The gams of Riu and Pang-in were informed of our friendly intentions and the gams of Komsing and Pang-i were given terms on satisfaction of which we would be friendly. All expressed great delight. The gams of Pang-i were ordered to fetch in the gams of Kebang.

20. Having established friendly relations with a few villages up the river and having also in the meantime got into friendly relations with the Panggi villages of Pongging who were quite innocent of any offence against us, and Jaru through Rotung, I organized two exploration and survey parties.

Exploration.

1. Under orders of Colonel Macintyre to explore and visit the Panggi villages in the Yamne valley; (2) under my Assistant Political Officer to explore the Dihang.

The Panggi villages had invited a visit, but for Dihang exploration, I was as yet only in touch with 3 villages and, as it was necessary to gain the confidence of the people, I gave instructions that conflict was to be avoided if possible.

On the 27th December both columns started.

No. 1 Column had 10 days' supplies and No. 2 had 24 days' supplies.

No. 1 Column visited Pongging, Jaru, Sibbum and crossing the watershed between the Yamne and the Dihang, visited Shumsing and Geku, and returned on the 7th January to Rotung.

Exploration.

21. No. 2 Column advanced up the right bank and visited Pang-in.

After visiting Yekshing Mr. Bentinck crossed the Dihang and visited Komsing, Riu and Geku.

On the 7th January, I sent out a support of 100 rifles, under Colonel Murray, with instructions to form signalling communication between Mr. Bentinck and my headquarters.

On the 11th, the weather broke and rain commenced and lasted until 16th, after which fine cloudless days were exceptional. No signalling communication was possible On the 12th, in order to carry out Government of India instructions, I sent out 60 rifles to escort rations to Komsing for Colonel Murray, and also sent out instructions to Colonel Murray that I was sending him more rifles and rations on the following day, to enable him to organize a line of communication as far as Geku and a support to the exploration party.

On the 14th, Mr. Bentinck had, however, crossed the Dihang by rafts and had visited Riga, the most important Minyong village. As it was easier and shorter to form a line of communication on the left bank, Mr. Bentinck had to recross the Dihang again on 17th January. Captain Coleridge assumed military command, as Colonel Murray, to my great regret, was invalided.

Political.

22. In the meantime, on the 31st December, the gams of Kebang had come in and were given terms on 1st January. They promised to comply and also to bring in the gams of Yemsing, Babuk and Kalek. Active operations against Kebang were suspended on 25th December, and on 11th January, I gave orders to all posts on line of communications to suspend active operations against the Abors.

Exploration.

23. Mr. Bentinck marched to Komkar 18th, to Simong 19th. The latter village appeared friendly.

On 20th January, Colonel Macintyre and survey party left Janakmukh to visit Damro and report on the frontier to the north.

To facilitate supply matters for the Dihang exploration, as soon as carriers were obtained from the line of communications, the advanced supply column marched on 22nd for Komsing and Geku.

On 23rd January, a survey party under Captain Molesworth was despatched to visit the villages of Dosing and Parong and reconnoitre Shimang and Siyom Rivers. On this same date, Mr. Bentinck's party left Simong for further exploration up the Dihang Valley.

On 26th, 50 rifles were despatched from here to reinforce the line of communications for Dihang exploration and to form a garrison at Geku.

On 28th, Colonel Macintyre reached Damro.

Exploration.

24. Persistent reports from friendly villages were received that Simong was contemplating an attack on Mr. Bentinck's party and that Geku would join in with Simong.

I therefore despatched, on the 1st February, a further 50 rifles for Geku, where they would form a support to Captain Coleridge at Simong. The attitude of this village was for a short time very threatening, but a display of force was sufficient to bring it to reason.

Heavy rain had again started on the 29th, and no signal and survey work was possible until 7th February. Mr. Bentinck reached Singging on 31st. The weather was abominable. It was quite impossible to see 30 yards on account of fog. Further, the survey officer represented that it was impossible for him to do any useful survey work by merely traversing up the river and that observations from certain hills were essential for him to fix satisfactorily a snowy range. Signalling communication was quite impossible, and as there were only three small Abor villages further on left bank unvisited, Mr. Bentinck turned back on 3rd February.

25. On the 3rd February, Captain Molesworth's party returned, after completing useful work. During this time Captain Dunbar from Misshing was busy visiting 6 Galong villages, amongst others Kambang and 13 Minyong villages. On 7th February, I received news from Simong that Mr. Bentinck had turned back from Singging. On 8th February, Mr. Bentinck reached Simong. On the same day, the Chief of the General Staff wired to ask whether it was not feasible to push exploration up to furthermost Abor villages and visit on the spot the place where the frontier should cross the Dihang Valley. I wired to Mr. Bentinck for a report. His answer was to the effect that it was impossible to decide where this frontier would cross the Dihang Valley until certain snowy ranges were located, and that the survey could only locate these ranges from observations from certain hills. Further that the Naga carriers were worn out and that the season was too far advanced for further exploration up Dihang Valley.

As on 27th January, I had already received instructions to return the Naga Corps to their homes; further exploration up the Dihang Valley was impossible without carriers. I represented these matters on 10th February. Since it was quite possible that a further advance would be ordered, I was enabled to adhere to my original programme of sending out Survey parties in every direction, but Captain Trenchard was able to carry on his observations.

On 10th February, Colonel Macintyre returned from Damro, after visiting the villages of Dukku, Silli, Sibbuk, Bina, Sitkor, Damro and Milang. The survey work had been much restricted by the inclemency of the weather.

26. To return to Captain Trenchard. The work of clearing the hill at Simong gave work to 150 Nagas for 10 days of 6 hours, and on account of the weather it was the 14th February before he completed his observations. He then proceeded to Geku. The clearing of the hill here had already commenced.

Survey difficulties.

Captain Trenchard arrived on Geku Hill on 20th February and, favoured with fine weather, was fortunately enabled to complete his snow range observations.

In meantime other hills near here had been cleared and observations taken by survey officers.

27. On 25th February, the Assistant Political Officer held an important meeting of gams at Komkar. The gams of Simong, Komkar, Damro, the Geku group of Panggi villages and Minyong villages of Komsing and Riu were present. This was the most representative meeting of gams that had ever been held in the country. The objects of Government were fully explained.

Meeting of Gams.

28. On the same date, having received instructions that the Government of India accepted my assurance as to the infeasibility of further exploration up the Dihang valley, I gave orders for the withdrawal of the

Organisation further survey parties.

line of communications from the left bank of the Dihang and for the crossing of a survey party to observe from Arte hill. It was the 2nd March, however, before Captain Trenchard left Geku, as his back observations had been interfered with by the clouds and rain which persisted between 23rd February and 2nd March. This entailed a delay in organizing a column to proceed to hill 10,090 at the head of the Shimang Valley, as no carriers were available until the left bank line of communication came in.

On the 26th February, Captain Molesworth, with 50 rifles, left for Dosing to organize posts for a line of communications for a survey party for hill 10,090.

Evacuation of Misshing.

29. On 29th February, Misshing was evacuated, and the garrison of 150 Military Police under Captain Dunbar marched *viâ* Kelek to Rotung, arriving on the 2nd March.

Survey operations.

30. On the 4th March, Captain Giffard, with a survey party, left for Dosing so as to enable Captain Molesworth to leave on 6th. On this latter date all troops from the left bank returned here.

Captain Molesworth's party reached the top of hill 10,090, on 15th March. Unfortunately a thick haze prevented any observations from this hill, much useful survey and exploration work was, however, done by this party which returned to Dosing on 21st March.

In the meantime Captain Trenchard had been on Arte hill, but it was the 23rd before he obtained any observations. Mr. Bentinck and Captain Hore left Arte hill on 8th March and made a useful tour across the Shimang Valley to the Siyom River and Bori country, returning to Riga on 19th. Survey work was hampered by the dense haze prevailing. Both parties returned to Yembung by the 28th March, by which date troops commenced to withdraw to Kobo.

Departure of Nagas and 1-2nd Gurkha Rifles.

31. Three Naga carrier corps left Kobo on 7th March, and 2 on 11th March, to ruturn to their homes. The 1-2nd Gurkha Rifles left Kobo for India on 14th March.

Probability of Abor coalition (summary).

32. Previous to the advance of the force, informatiom pointed to the great probability that we would not only be opposed by the Minyong, but that several other tribes would coalesce with those responsible for the massacre in opposing our advance, and from information obtained afterwards it appeared that very many villages assisted in the preparation of stockades and stone chutes. It was soon apparent, however, that the tribes who promised their support to the Minyong had done so under the belief that the punitive force would be on the small and insufficient scale that has been such a marked feature of former expeditions against the Abors. As soon as our strength became manifest the coalition fell to pieces and the guilty villages were left to fight out their own quarrel with us alone. This materially reduced the active opposition.

33. On the other hand the physical difficulties of the country presented even a greater obstacle to a rapid advance than had been anticipated. The Abor paths were quite unfit for use by laden carriers, and as an example of the difficulties encountered I may mention that a small exploration party leaving camp soon after daylight only completed a march of 1½ miles by 4 P.M. Many other cases showing the difficulty of rapid movement could be quoted, and the necessity for searching out and destroying stone chutes, of which an incredible number had been prepared, also involved delay.

Physical difficulties (summary).

34. As the result of the operations, the culpable villages have been punished, six men who took part in the massacre of Mr. Williamson's party have been captured, tried, five found guilty and sentenced. The rifles taken have been restored, and our capability to punish evildoers, which hitherto has not been credited, has been brought home to the tribesmen. Practically the whole Abor country has been visited and excellent relations established. The domination exercised by the Kebang-Rotung group of villages has been broken, the villages in the interior can now trade with India which they express a great desire to do. The part of the north Lakhimpur districts lying to the north of the Brahmaputra can be recolonised, there being now nothing to fear from Abor raids.

Result (summary).

35. A good road, fit for mules, has been constructed from Kobo to Yembung, and Abor paths improved as far as Simong and Riga, and between Misshing and Kalek.

Mule road (summary).

36. The absence of maps, native information being often misleading, was a difficulty. In spite of the fact that the weather could hardly have been less favourable than it was for surveying, the following results were obtained:—

Survey (summary).

(*a*) An accurate series of triangulation, emanating from the Assam Longitudinal series of the Great Trigonometrical Survey, has been carried over the outlying ranges to the latitude of Kebang, terminating in the base Sadup h. s. Namkam h. s. This will prove of the greatest assistance to future surveyors or explorers.

(*b*) From this series, and an extension of reconnaissance triangulation to the latitude of Simong, several large, snowy peaks have been fixed on what appears to be the main Himalayan divide, including one very fine peak over 25,000 ft. high. Many more snow peaks have also been fixed on the watershed between the Dihang and Subansiri rivers, which seems to be a very prominent spur of the main divide. It has only been possible to obtain a mere approximation of the topography of these snowy ranges, but the geodetic results are in themselves of great value.

(c) About 3,500 square miles have been more or less rigorously mapped on scale 4 miles = 1 inch, including the whole of the Yamne and the Shimang Valleys, a portion of the Siyom River, and the whole of the Dihang Valley as far north as Singging. Although I venture to think it is now possible for very small parties to travel about the country, it was found necessary in the first instance that exploring parties showed strength. In addition to reasons of safety a considerable number of men were required to clear hill tops.

Conduct of troops (summary).

37. Campaigning in a country, where the difficulties of transport are so great, necessarily involved considerable hardships on the men and great extremes were experienced, from tropical heat to bivouacking in snow. In one place this was lying 9 feet deep. The continuous bad weather experienced during part of the operations was a greater hardship than it would be in a campaign on which tents could be carried. The work was hard, unremitting, and continued watchfulness was required against an enemy ever ready to take advantage of an opportunity. Difficulties of exploration were accentuated by the impossibility of columns living on the country. The Abors, grow only sufficient rice for their own consumption and are most unwilling to part with it. Unhusked rice was obtained occasionally and considerable labour was required to husk it.

I cannot speak too highly of the conduct of all ranks under trying circumstances and trust that the operations will meet with the approval of His Excellency the Commander-in-Chief.

38. My recommendations, a map, and casualty return, are attached.

I have the honour to bring to favourable notice the names of the following Officers, Non-Commissioned Officers and men.

Staff.

39 Major C. A. R. Hutchinson, 41st Dogras, General Staff Officer, 2nd Grade. I am greatly indebted to this officer for much valuable assistance. He has shown himself a hardworking and capable staff officer.

Captain L. S. H. Smithers, 17th Infantry (The Loyal Regiment) was acting Brigade-Major, Assam Brigade, at the time preparations were being made and a great deal of General Staff Work devolved on him. During the expedition he has often been of considerable assistance in other capacities than that of orderly officer. He is well fitted for staff employment.

Captain W. B. Hore, 120th Rajputana Infantry, Intelligence Officer, has an exceptionally good knowledge of the Abor-Miri language and was of the greatest assistance.

Captain H. S. Becher carried out the duties of Provost Marshal efficiently.

I am much indebted to Mr. A Bentinck, I.C.S., Assistant Political Officer, for useful advice and assistance. He has an extensive knowledge of the tribes on this frontier, and conducted, under difficult circumstances, several exploration parties, showing tact in his dealings with the villages. His services are well worthy of commendation.

Line of Communications.

40. Colonel D. C. Macintyre, Indian Army, Base Commandant and Inspector, Line of Communications, has performed his duties to my complete satisfaction. He conducted missions to the Panggi and Padam countries, being in both political and military charge. Largely owing to his tact in dealing with savage people these missions were most successful and resulted in the establishment of excellent relations and a large increase to our geographical knowledge.

Corps and Departments.

41. *Assam Valley Light Horse dismounted detachment.*—The members of this detachment showed a most soldierlike spirit in volunteering, in many cases at great personal inconvenience and pecuniary loss, to accompany the expedition. They underwent considerable hardship in a most cheerful spirit and played an important part in the taking of the Kekar Monying position. Captain C. L. Lovell commanded the detachment in an efficient manner.

42. *No. 1 Company (K. G. O.) Sappers and Miners.*—The work done by this company is above all praise, and it is to the skill and energy displayed by all ranks that the success of the expedition is largely due. During six months of arduous work this energy has never flagged.

Major E. C. Tylden-Pattenson is an officer of exceptional ability and his advancement would be to the good of the service.

Lieutenant W. Cave-Brown did much good work particularly in the hazardous enterprise of getting a steel cable for rafting across the Dihang.

The good work done by the following was noticeable.

No. 3155 Acting Sergeant-Major J. F. Eltham.

Jemadar Sultan.

No. 12 Havildar Diwan Ali.

43. *1st Battalion, 2nd (K. E. O.) Gurkha Rifles.*—This corps well maintained its reputation for efficiency both on the Ledum Column and guarding the Line of Communications. An excellent spirit pervades the regiment.

Colonel J. Fisher commanded the Ledum Column and acted for some time as Officer Commanding Defences, Line of Communications. He performed both duties to my satisfaction.

Major A. B. Lindsay is a very capable officer with great enterprise. He acted as staff officer with the Ledum Column and accompanied the Panggi and Padam missions as intelligence officer and brought back very useful reports. He has ail the qualities that go to make a good staff officer and his advancement would be to the good of the service.

The good work done by the following was noticeable.

Lieutenant H. F. F. Marsh.

Subadar Major Dalman Ale, I.O.M.

Subadar Tekbahadur Gurung.

No. 2912 Havildar Siri Lal Thapa.

No. 3280 Rifleman Budhiman Gurung.

No. 4144 Rifleman Deosur Thapa, has been the subject of a separate communication.

44. *32nd Sikh Pioneers.*—This corps has done much useful work on the Line of Communications.

Lieutenant-Colonel H. Peterson, D.S.O., is an officer of sound judgment and has commanded his regiment and carried out the duties of Officer Commanding Defences, Line of Communications, to my satisfaction.

The good work done by the following was ıoticeable:—

Major E. H. S. Cullen, M. V. O.

Captain the Honourable M. de Courcy.

Subadar Sundar Singh.

No. 2959 Havildar Budhe Singh.

45. *1st Battalion, 8th Gurkha Rifles.*—On this corps devolved most of the fighting and the very hard work involved in escorting exploration parties. I cannot speak too highly of the manner in which it carried out its differe t duties. A better corps for jungle warfare it would be hard to find.

Lieutenant-Colonel F. Murray, D.S.O., commanded to my complete satisfaction and carried out various important detached duties in a most capable manner. His services are well worthy of recognition. He was invalided as a result of the hardships involved in campaigning in such a difficult country.

Major J. A. Wilson commanded when Lieutenant-Colonel Murray was invalided and carried out his duties to my satisfaction. He has shown energy and enterprise throughout and has commanded detached bodies on several occasions.

Captain J. F. S. D. Coleridge is a most reliable officer of sound judgment and has done excellently in military charge of exploration parties.

Captain A. L. Molesworth has done well ni command of exploration parties.

Lieutenant M. A. C. Kennedy is a good officer, and distinguished himself at the taking of the Igar stockade.

The good work done by the following was noticeable :—

Subadar-Major Nawalsing Rana, Bahadur, I.O.M.

Jemadar Makansing Gurung.

Jemadar Narbahadur Gurung.

No. 2446 Havildar Bhairab Sahi.

No. 3729 Lance-Naik Chitrabir Rana.

No. 3202 Rifleman Kalia Pun.

46. *Signal unit from No. 31 (Divisional Signal) Company.*—Had great difficulties to contend with in the nature of the country and the long periods during which visual signalling was impossible. In spite of these difficulties its work was of the greatest assistance to me. Lieutenant J. H. Knight is a most enthusiastic signaller and I could always feel that, if it was at all possible, he would maintain communication with any detached parties.

The good work done by the following was noticeable :—

No. 1560 Lance-Naik Dharm Singh.

No. 1716 Lance-Naik Dost Mahammad.

47. *Supply and Transport Corps.* The questions of Supply and Transport to a great extent govern operations, and in a trackless country there is a great deal to contend with. I attribute the state of efficiency maintained by the force largely to the excellent personnel of the Supply and Transport Corps.

Major E. G. Vaughan, Assistant Director, Supply and Transport, is an officer who always keeps in view the comfort and efficiency of the troops, while being careful of the financial interests of the State.

Major H. H. M. Brooke did good service at the Base.

Captain W. B. Dunlop has done good work with the Advanced Supply Columns.

The five Naga Carrier Corps well justified their enlistment, better men for the duties they were called upon to perform it would be difficult to find, they were taxed to the utmost of their physical powers, but were always cheery, there never was any trouble with them and on several occasions, they showed themselves quite willing to engage the Abors.

These satisfactory results I largely attribute to the tact and firmness with which they were treated by the Corps Commandants. Where all did well it may appear invidious to select any for special mention, but perhaps I may be permitted to mention Captain G. W. Bond and Captain C. W. Hext, whose work came more immediately under my notice.

Lieutenant A. B. H. Webb, 5th Gurkha Rifles, under great difficulties did excellent work in charge of the boat transport between Kobo and Pasighat.

The good work done by the following was noticeable:—

Captain C. E. Edward-Collins, Commandant, 26th Mule Corps.

Hony. Lieutenant J. Foy.

Conductor W. C. Hayman.

Conductor H. Wright.

Conductor J. Ballen, 26th Mule Corps.

48. *Indian Medical Service.*—To the efficient carrying out of sanitary and other medical duties, the comparatively good health and absence of epedimic disease is largely due.

Major J. Davidson, Assistant Director, Medical Service, has done well in that capacity.

Captain C. W. F. Melville is a very good officer and well worthy of advancement. He acted as Staff Surgeon and also accompanied exploration parties.

The good work done by the following was noticeable:—

Captain J. S. O'Neill.

No. 978 First Class Sub-Assistant Surgeon Mahadeo Parshad.

Second Class Senior Sub-Assistant Surgeon Niranjan Das.

49. *Lakhimpur Military Police.*—On this corps, ever since the massacre of Mr. Williamson's party, has devolved the duty of keeping the North Lakhimpur District free from Abor raids. The difficulties and hardships involved in carrying out this duty during the rainy season can only be realised by those having knowledge of the country and climate. The battalion also did good work in the operations near Misshing.

Captain Sir George Duff-Sutherland-Dunbar, 31st Punjabis, has commanded to my satisfaction, and his services have also been brought to notice by Colonel Fisher Commanding the Ledum Column.

The untimely death of Captain A. M. Hutchins as the direct result of continuous hardships during a long period is much to be regretted. He was a capable and gallant officer.

Surgeon Captain J. M. Falkiner, Assam Valley Light Horse, served as a Volunteer Medical Officer with the Ledum Column and

Lakhimpur Military Police. He has served throughout without remuneration and I consider his services worthy of commendation.

The good work done by the following was noticeable :—

Captain J. Masters.

Subadar Major Dorward.

Jemadar Jangbir Lama.

No. 1120 Havildar Dalbahadur Thapa.

50. The Survey party under Captain O. H. B. Trenchard, R. E., did good work.

The good work done by the following was noticeable :—

Lieutenant G. F. T. Oakes.

Surveyor Sher Jang.

Surveyor Hamid Gul.

51. The Ordnance Base Depôt under Conductor F. I. Williams was most useful and met all requirements.

52. The Telegraph Department under Mr. G. E. O. de Smidt did very useful work. The good work done by the following was noticeable :—

Sub-Conductor W. Davies.

No. 6266 Private W. Rouse, 2nd Connaught Rangers.

53. The postal arrangements were satisfactory.

54. *Corps of Military Staff clerks.*—No. 9584 Sergeant A. Park.

RETURN OF CASUALTIES IN ACTION, ABOR EXPEDITIONARY FORCE FROM 6TH OCTOBER 1911 TO 11TH JANUARY 1912.

Summary.

Officers.—*Nil* killed, *nil* died of wounds, 1 wounded, *nil* missing.

Indian Officers, British and Indian Rank and File—

Non-Commissioned officers and men, 2 killed, *nil* died of wounds, 2 wounded, *nil* missing.

Followers.—2 killed, 1 died of wounds, 3 wounded, *nil* missing.

NOMINAL RETURN OF OFFICERS WOUNDED.

Rank.	Name.	Description of wound—dangerous, severe or slight.	Nature of wound.
Captain...	J. R. Hutchison, Adjutant, Assam Valley Light Horse.	Severe	Arrow wound, right high.

NOMINAL RETURN OF NON-COMMISSIONED OFFICERS AND MEN KILLED, DIED OF WOUNDS, WOUNDED AND MISSING.

I.—*Killed.*

Regimental number.	Rank.	Name.	Nature of wound.
2153 ...	Rifleman ...	Dewan Sing Gurung, 1-2nd Gurkha Rifles.	Gunshot wound (region not given).
3504 ...	Rifleman ..	Balibadra Roka, 1-2nd Gurkha Rifles.	Gunshot wound (region not given).

II.—*Died of wounds—Nil.*

III.—*Wounded.*

Regimental number.	Rank.	Name.	Description of wound—dangerous, severe or slight.	Nature of wound.
3365 ...	Rifleman	Dhanbir Thapa, 1-2nd Gurkha Rifles.	Slight ...	Contusion (region not given) caused by falling stones.
3120 ...	Rifleman	Dalbir Gurung, 1-2nd Gurkha Rifles.	Slight ...	Contusion (region not given) caused by falling stones.

IV.—*Missing—Nil.*

NOMINAL RETURN OF FOLLOWERS, KILLED, DIED OF WOUNDS WOUNDED AND MISSING.

I.—*Killed.*

Rank.	Name.	Nature of wound.
Carrier	Tilchand Bhuman, Telegraph De-Department.	Arrow wound, chest.
Bearer	Bhagwandin, 8th Company, Army Bearer Corps.	Gunshot wound, head and chest.

II.—*Died of wounds.*

Rank.	Name.	Nature of wound.
Carrier	Lalbahadur Gurung, Telegraph Department.	Arrow wound, abdomen.

III.—*Wounded.*

Rank.	Name.	Description of wound—dangerous, severe or slight.	Nature of wound.
Naga Scout ...	Pakaive ..	Severe ...	Gunshot wound, left upper arm.
Guide ...	Dal Bahadur Gurung	Severe ...	Gunshot wound, left shoulder.
Dhobi ...	Bhukal, 1-8th Gurkha Rifles.	Severe ...	Arrow wound, right thigh.

Return showing numbers of deaths from disease amongst troops and followers with the Abor Expeditionary Force.

Corps.	British Officers.	Indian Officers.	Non-Commissioned Officers and men.	Public followers.	Remarks.
No. 1 Company, Sappers and Miners.	...	1	...	...	
1-2nd Gurkha Rifles ...	...	...	3	...	
1-8th Gurkha Rifles ...	...	...	...	1	
Lakhimpur Military Police.	1	...	2	...	Captain A. M. Hutchins.
1st Carrier Corps ...	...	...	...	11	
2nd ditto ...	...	...	...	9	
3rd ditto ...	...	...	...	4	
4th ditto ...	...	...	...	3	
5th ditto ...	...	...	...	8	
1st Gurkhali, C. C. ...	...	...	...	2	
2nd Gurkhali, C. C. ...	...	...	...	1	
66th Punjabis (attached to B Section, 168 Indian Stationary Hospital).	...	...	...	1	
Telegraph Department coolies.	...	...	...	5	
Political Department (Abor).	...	...	...	1	
Abor Prisoner ...	...	...	...	1	
Total ...	1	1	5	47	

Statement showing numbers of sick, British and Indian troops, of Abor Expeditionary Force, invalided to depôts and stations in India.

Rank and name.	Corps.	Remarks.
Lieutenant-Colonel F. Murray ...	1-8th Gurkha Rifles.	
Captain R. L. Gamlen ...	Indian Medical Service.	
Lieutenant S. Sarkar	Indian Medical Service.	
Mr. J. E. Scott	Indian Civil Service.	

British warrant and non-Commissioned officers.

Corps or department.	Number.	Remarks.
Assam Valley Light Horse	1	
Supply and Transport Corps	3	
26th Mule Corps	1	
Telegraph Department	2	
Total ...	7	

Indian troops.

Corps.		Number.	Remarks
No. 1 Company, Sappers and Miners	...	9	
1-2nd Gurkha Rifles	... ...	56	
32nd Sikh Pioneers ...	... ...	76	
1-8th Gurkha Rifles ...	... ...	16	
88th Carnatic Infantry	... ..	1	
Lakhimpur Military Police	... ...	62	
Sub-Assistant Surgeons	... ...	4	One Civil Department.
Total	...	224	

Statement showing number of sick followers invalided to their depôts and stations in India.

Corps.		Number.	Remarks.
No. 1 Company, Sappers and Miners	...	1	
1-2nd Gurkha Rifles ...	...	1	
32nd Sikh Pioneers	...	7	
1-8th Gurkha Rifles	...	6	
26th Mule Corps	...	26	
Supply and Transport Corps ...	...	7	
No. 7 Company, Army Bearer Corps	...	1	
No. 8 Company, Army Bearer Corps	...	20	
No. 9 Company, Army Bearer Corps	...	14	
Postal Department	...	1	
Telegraph Department ...	...	21	
Nagas—			
No. 1 Carrier Corps ...	...	116	
No. 2 Carrier Corps ...	...	6	
No. 3 Carrier Corps ...	...	53	
No. 4 Carrier Corps ...	...	36	
No. 5 Carrier Corps ...	...	83	
Gurkhalis—			
No. 1 Corps	...	33	
No. 2 Corps	...	12	
Private servants, Indian ...	...	3	
Total	...	447	

H. BOWER, *Major-General,*

Commanding, Abor Expeditionary Force.

BB

C65GSE—900—20 2-14—CCBP Simla